D1561913

BEWARE
THE TALKING CURE
Psychotherapy May Be Hazardous
To Your Mental Health

BY TERENCE W. CAMPBELL, PH.D.

Upton
B O O K S

Upton

B O O K S

A division of

Social Issues Resources Series, Inc.
P.O. Box 2348
Boca Raton, FL 33427
Copyright ©1994 by SIRS, Inc.

Library of Congress Cataloging-in-Publication Data

Campbell, Terence W.
  Beware the talking cure: psychotherapy may be hazardous to
your mental health / by Terence W. Campbell.
      p.   cm.
  Includes bibliographical references and index.
  ISBN 0-89777-147-8 : $14.95
  1. Psychotherapy—Evalution. 2. Psychotherapy—Complica-
tions. 3. Psychotherapy—Failure. 4. Psychiatric errors. I. Title.
RC480.5.C25 1994
616.89'14—dc20   94-12852
                                                                CIP

Cover design by Michelle McCulloch

FOR MY PARENTS

This book is entirely their fault. They taught me to question everything, and accept nothing as a matter of blind faith. For that, and for so much more, I will always be grateful.

TABLE OF CONTENTS

PREFACE
AND
ACKNOWLEDGEMENTS

In 1964, a major review of psychotherapy research was introduced by the statement, "Chaos prevails." As a graduate student at the University of Maryland in the late 1960s, I read that review and was forced to admit that its introductory statement was accurate. The available research evidence did not verify the effectiveness of psychotherapy.

I remained confident, however, that more sophisticated methods would substantiate what many regarded as the elusive—but significant—effects of psychotherapy. My own doctoral dissertation addressed this issue. It demonstrated that different kinds of people preferred different kinds of therapists. While a particular therapist might appeal to person A, that did not necessarily mean he would appeal to person B.

Nevertheless, the accumulating data of the 1970s and 1980s betrayed my earlier confidence. It provided little reassurance for psychotherapists who sought scientific verification of their endeavors. As in 1964, chaos still prevailed, reminding one of the French observation: "The more things change, the more they stay the same." Surprisingly enough, the growing number of therapists managed to ignore this chaotic crisis.

The professional organizations that represent psychotherapists preoccupied themselves in hotly contested turf battles. While debating which therapists could provide what services, they overlooked questions about the effectiveness of psychotherapy. Unfortunately, my own professional organization was no exception.

The American Psychological Association progressively evolved

i

into a special interest group committed to pursuing the welfare of private practitioners. Simultaneously, organized psychology was abandoning its origins as a behavioral *science*. This situation influenced many academic psychologists to depart the American Psychological Association. As a result, academicians and professionals grew more estranged from each other.

Because of the growing academic-professional split within psychology, psychotherapists confidently continued to do what they had always done. The voices available to intelligently challenge them were rapidly dwindling. Academic values of objective inquiry and scientific legitimacy were lost in psychology's rush to the health-care marketplace.

Some psychologists protested the increasing commercialization of psychology. Sandra Scarr, a distinguished psychologist with an outstanding record of research productivity, resigned from the Board of Directors of the American Psychological Association in 1989. Her letter of resignation chastised the Association for promoting its interests as a guild and neglecting its scientific responsibilities. This development was personally significant; Dr. Scarr had taught me respect for data and the value of intellectual honesty during her faculty tenure at the University of Maryland.

Beginning in the mid-1970s, and continuing on through the 1980s, a few therapists began to question the appropriateness of traditional procedures. Their doubts led them into new methods for which the preliminary evidence was impressive. The therapists who made these changes, however, were a small minority.

The decade from the mid-1970s to the mid-1980s was especially frustrating for me. Very few of my colleagues recognized the crisis in which psychotherapy found itself. Overconfident complacency was alive and well within the ranks of psychotherapists. Any discussion of why our field desperately needed profound changes usually prompted defensive denials.

In 1985, I was approached by an attorney who asked about my willingness to testify in a matter that raised serious issues of psychotherapy malpractice. The tragic mismanagement of a case had resulted in a client's suicide. To say the least, the lawyer's request created substantial conflict for me. A close friend and respected colleague resolved my dilemma when he said, "Something has to be done; too many people are getting killed!"

My participation as a plaintiff's witness in this case won me few friends and no accolades from most of my colleagues. Nevertheless, that case served as the impetus for this book (see Chapter One). I was convinced the time had come to expose a well-concealed, professional secret—too often, psychotherapy severely damages people.

This volume is organized around case studies taken from the professional literature. This is significant because it underscores the fact that these examples are non-fiction. They were not invented to portray psychotherapy in a negative light. Instead, they reflect the actual experiences of real clients in psychotherapeutic treatment.

Many of the therapists whose work is evaluated in this volume are well-respected individuals who enjoy national reputations. Their reports appeared in journals selective enough that they publish only 25-35 percent of the articles submitted to them. Before these articles could be published, a panel of editors decided they qualified as a significant contribution to the professional literature. Thus, the reader should understand that the examples cited in this volume are not confined to a few, selected eccentrics.

Except for quoting some well-known theorists by name, this book's text does not identify the therapists whose work it reviews. Personal criticism directed at any therapist cited in this book would be inappropriate. The counterproductive therapy procedures outlined in the following chapters are frequently used by many therapists. Thus, psychotherapy's problems correspond not to *who* engages in some practice, but originate in *what* is being done.

Many of the ideas for this book developed as a result of training experiences with Charles Fishman, Jay Haley, Cloe' Madanes, and Jamshed Morenas. Each of these individuals helped me develop professionally and expand my conceptualizations of the psychotherapeutic process.

The encouragement, feedback, and helpful suggestions of Edwin Arnfield and Gregory Bereznoff in reading preliminary versions of this manuscript are also gratefully acknowledged. Special thanks is reserved for Nancy Liebler, who encouraged this work at a time when little encouragement was forthcoming; and for Therese Wolf, whose perceptive comments and proofreading talent aided the manuscript immeasurably. The enthusiasm of my publisher-editor, Eleanor Goldstein, and her confidence in the importance of this book is also deeply appreciated.

Last but far from least, my wife's unwavering confidence in the eventual success of this undertaking motivated me when my own motivation sometimes diminished. Though I frequently wondered whether this project would ever see the light of a publication day, Sharon Kay never doubted that outcome. Her optimism and support were invaluable to the success of this endeavor.

PART ONE
BEWARE THE TALKING CURE

1

Life is real! Life is earnest! and the grave is not its goal...

—Henry Wadsworth Longfellow

A Psychotherapy Tragedy

Robert Andrews is dead. As he lies on a gurney in the emergency room of a suburban hospital, his chest rises and falls. But this apparent sign of life is illusory, created only by the mechanical intervention of a respirator. Despite the valiant efforts of hospital personnel to save him, he is gone.

At the age of 25, this Phi Beta Kappa graduate of a major university has died by his own hand. He committed suicide via self-asphyxiation. His parents face what is probably the greatest of all tragedies for any parent—the tragedy of burying your own child.

From the age of 19, Robert was in psychotherapeutic treatment as an outpatient. He was also hospitalized in a psychiatric facility on three different occasions. All of this treatment accomplished little more than the futile pumping of Robert's respirator. Despite his years spent in therapy, this investment ultimately betrayed his psychological welfare.

The tragedy of this situation raises questions that cry for answers: What went wrong? Why did a young man with so much potential meet such a tragic end? Could Robert's treatment have been more effective? Beyond their relevance to this particular case, these questions also lead to considerations that may

1

shake one's confidence in psychotherapy.

Robert had been engaged in a long history of conflicts with his divorced parents. They sometimes disagreed on what they expected from him, but it would be inappropriate to blame them for his death. Despite their episodes of conflict with Robert, both of his parents were committed to his welfare. On one occasion when Robert was particularly depressed, his father slept on the floor outside of Robert's bedroom. He wanted to be immediately available if his son's psychological welfare necessitated it.

THERAPIST BIASES CAN BE DANGEROUS

In his therapist's opinion, however, Robert was a beleaguered victim who endured the neurotic whims of callous parents. Despite the therapist's minimal contact with Robert's parents, he persisted in his one-sided assessment of them. Preoccupied with the supposed deficits of these parents—while disregarding their strengths—the therapist responded more to his theoretical convictions than to Robert's welfare.

The therapist also assumed that Robert responded to his parents with intense anger and resentment. His animosity supposedly compelled him to aggress against them with unrelenting but self-defeating defiance. The therapist believed that Robert should insightfully understand his anger, and comprehend it in depth and detail. In theory, this understanding should have alleviated Robert's self-defeating defiance. For this therapist, understanding anger necessitates bringing it to one's attention; comprehending anger in depth and detail requires repeated reminders of it.

In fact, however, repetitious reminders of one's anger fail to resolve it. Rather than reduce anger, such reminders escalate its frequency and intensity. Therapists often use their influence to create a client's anger via suggestibility; and Robert's therapist was no exception. He kindled the smoldering coals of Robert's anger and then fanned its ensuing flames.

A competent therapist would have dealt with the cyclical interactions between Robert and his parents. Above all else, Robert was the link that kept his family together despite his parents' divorce. Neither of his parents had remarried; and if they began to drift apart, Robert's depressions dramatically underscored the need for them to reunite. Consequently, Robert's symptoms were both powerful and ultimately benevolent in their impact on his parents.

Robert unilaterally assumed his role as a cohesive force in his family; neither parent asked him to do so. Instead, he exhibited motives often characteristic of children of divorce—he sought to keep his family intact. Committed to his family's welfare, feelings of loyalty and affection influenced Robert more than anger and resentment. Because of his theoretical biases, however, the therapist ignored the bonds of caring that linked Robert and his parents.

When he was seriously depressed, Robert's parents worked together to encourage him. Their mutual concern for their son's welfare motivated them to cooperate with each other. Once sufficiently reassured that his parents were closely aligned with each other, Robert responded positively to their concern and support. In particular, he recovered from these depressive episodes, began to organize his life more appropriately, and moved away from his parents to live more independently.

Robert could maintain his progress until he again sensed that his parents were drifting apart. Though his parents were divorced as husband and wife, Robert's symptoms pulled them together as father and mother. Their parental closeness satisfied Robert's needs for family continuity—until they began to drift apart again. When worried about his parents' relationship, Robert would suffer another depressive episode renewing this entire cycle once more.

THERAPIST NEGLECT

The therapist neglected to address the cyclical dynamics that transpired *between* Robert and his parents. He preoccupied himself with the thoughts and feelings *within* Robert. Committed to reducing Robert's supposed dependency on his parents, the therapist applauded any alienation between Robert and his family as a favorable development.

Alienation from his family, however, did not qualify as an appropriate resolution for Robert's problems. Alienation only intensifies depression and increases the probability of suicide. Because his therapist disregarded the hazards of alienation, continuing to remind his client of how angry he supposedly felt toward his parents, Robert would distance himself from his family for a period of time.

Sooner or later, however, the therapist's divisive influence would diminish, and Robert's sense of despair would increase because of his alienation from his parents. Eventually his condition would deteriorate to where he was seriously depressed.

It was in the course of one such depressive episode that Robert took his own life. A competent, responsible therapist would have treated Robert with his family. His depression originated from a *three-person* problem that defied resolution via *individual* psychotherapy. This therapist, however, acted as if he could resolve that problem by himself. Determined to emancipate Robert from his parents' influence, the therapist excluded them from his therapy.

Because Robert worried about his parents' welfare, he needed their permission—not the therapist's—to cease his sacrifices on their behalf. Any therapist who told Robert not to worry about his family's welfare was intrusively interfering in family business. Only a presumptuous therapist would take it upon himself to arbitrarily decide what was best for Robert and his family.

An effective therapist could have extricated the parents from the cyclical interactions with their son. Once they were aware of these cycles, the parents could have told Robert not to sacrifice himself on their behalf. This entire family also could have been helped to reassure each other about their future relationships. As a result, Robert no longer would have needed his depression to pull his parents together.

PSYCHOTHERAPY AND MALPRACTICE

Following his death, Robert's parents brought suit against the psychiatrist and psychologist responsible for his treatment. After many months of subpoenas and depositions, the case was settled out of court. Mr. and Mrs. Andrews, Robert's parents, accepted a settlement in excess of $300,000.

Presently, psychotherapists are rarely sued. Psychologists can obtain one million dollars of malpractice insurance for only $675 per year. In contrast, physicians commonly pay from $5,000 to $15,000 dollars, or more, for the same coverage. Even when courts return malpractice verdicts against psychotherapists, the damages have been small compared to the six figure awards common in medical malpractice.

In the Robert Andrews case, however, the attorneys representing the psychiatrist and psychologist eagerly settled out of court. They felt less than optimistic about defending their clients before a jury. Given the facts of this case, the attorneys cringed at the damages a jury might have assessed. Mr. and Mrs. Andrews accepted the out of court settlement to avoid the emotional ordeal of a trial.

Remarkable as it may seem, Robert's therapist violated no prevailing standard of care. His treatment of Robert corresponded to customary procedures employed by therapists of his orientation. To the extent that courts suspend considerations of customary practice for defining a standard of care, psychotherapists could face a malpractice crisis.[1] But this potential plight of the psychotherapy professions seems trivial compared to the damage they cause.

The case of Robert Andrews is significant not only because it illustrates how ineffective psychotherapy can be, but also because it underscores therapy's potentially hazardous outcomes. At this point in time, it is neither remarkable nor original to say that psychotherapy is often ineffective. Its reputation for wasting time, money, and energy is infamous.

This book goes farther and emphasizes that psychotherapy is often counterproductive. Worse than being benignly useless, it can do serious harm. Moreover, not only can therapy damage clients, it can also damage the members of a client's family.

Psychotherapy is hazardous not because of who does it, but because of the futility of the techniques themselves. Legions of psychotherapists regularly rely on techniques that severely damage their clients. In fact, the same techniques that betrayed Robert Andrews are used by many therapists. These therapists *think* that their techniques effectively help distressed people; but they confuse reality with illusions. As a result, too many people find themselves more seriously disturbed after psychotherapy than they were before it—and at its worst, the consequences can be fatal.

2

If the facts do not agree with the theory, so much the worse for the facts

—GEORG WILHELM HEGEL

IS PSYCHOTHERAPY EFFECTIVE?

In 1987, approximately fifteen million people in the United States made 120 million visits to psychotherapists.[1] This is more than double the number of visits made to physicians specializing in internal medicine.[2]

Obviously, psychotherapy has come out of the closet. Over the past thirty years, the American public gradually abandoned the prejudices psychotherapy once provoked. Previously, clients commonly concealed the fact that they were in therapy. Relatively few people undertook such treatment, and those who did disclosed the fact in whispered confidences. In the 1950s, it is estimated that only one person in eight involved themselves in psychotherapy.[3]

That number is now one American in three.[4] Today, psychotherapy experiences are readily discussed by present and former clients alike. Some people even flaunt their therapy as a kind of an avant garde status symbol.

Psychotherapy is a growing enterprise. Therapists enjoy a reputation as experts effectively aiding the troubled people who use their services. The public seeks their opinions about a variety of issues relevant to social

7

trends and the human condition. This demand for therapeutic advice has created a never-ending supply of self-help books. Additionally, most talk-radio stations seem to require a resident "shrink," dispensing advice over the airways, in order to consider their programming complete.

Psychotherapy's media acceptance, and the frequency with which people seek this treatment, underscores its respectability. The "talking cure" often receives credit for resolving a broad spectrum of emotional problems. Though psychotherapists certainly welcome their popularity, good standing in public opinion does not guarantee the effectiveness of their work. In fact, psychotherapy's favorable reputation is undeserved; there is a remarkable lack of research evidence to support it.

PSYCHOTHERAPY: DOES IT OR DOESN'T IT WORK?

The 20th century has seen enormous progress in the quality of health care. Dramatic gains in clinical practice have evolved from laboratory research. Research evidence is essential to verify the effectiveness of health care practices. For example, until laboratory research established its effectiveness, the polio vaccine was unavailable for clinical practice.

Ideally, research should steer the direction of practice for all health-care professions. When practice responds to research, the health and welfare of the public are more effectively protected. If practitioners ignore research, they reduce themselves to the status of charlatans and faith-healers—and even more alarmingly, they jeopardize the well-being of their clientele.

H. J. Eysenck, the British psychologist, originated the movement to scientifically examine the effectiveness of psychotherapy. In 1952, he published an article comparing the recovery rates of neurotics in psychotherapy with the recovery rates of untreated neurotics. Eysenck concluded that psychotherapy was ineffective for facilitating recovery from neurotic disorders. The clients in treatment did not recover with greater frequency, nor any more rapidly, than the untreated group.[5]

Eysenck was essentially asking, "Does psychotherapy work?" and his answer was an emphatic "no." Eysenck emphasized that most neurotic disturbances are time-limited. Rather than persist forever, time-limited disturbances spontaneously correct themselves after a period of time. If a neurotic merely awaits the passage of time, his* condition may improve; and this improvement can occur without psychotherapy.

Eysenck's criticisms prompted increased research activity examining psychotherapeutic effectiveness. A 1963 study reported that psychotherapy results in both harmful and effective outcomes.[6] Though psychotherapy improved the psychological welfare of some clients, it caused deterioration in others. Other investigators subsequently substantiated the results of this 1963 study.[7]

Now, after more than thirty years of additional research, the accumulated evidence leads to one conclusion: Psychotherapy helps some people and it damages others. These opposite kinds of outcomes—positive for some and negative for others—cancel each other in studies using large numbers of clients. This cancellation effect creates the illusion that psychotherapy is merely useless—it appears to neither help nor harm. In fact, Eysenck's 1952 article mistakenly originated this illusion.

Psychotherapy is the term that developed from Freud's treatment for psychologically distressed people. The "talking cure" attempts to alter thoughts, feelings, and/or behaviors in order to alleviate psychological distress. This book uses the phrase "traditional psychotherapy" to designate the three major therapy orientations used today: analytic, client-centered or humanistic, and behavioral. More often than not, traditional therapy confines itself to individual treatment. It does not involve the participation of other people who are important to the client.

Throughout this book, the term "client" will be used in preference to "patient." The term "patient" too often connotes the traditional physician-patient relationship that reduced patients to helpless dependency. "Patient" suggests passivity and a corresponding authority for the therapist that is inappropriate.

WHAT CLIENTS SAY

Despite the lack of evidence to verify the consistent effectiveness of psychotherapy, clients often feel positive about their treatment. They may protest any conclusion that traditional

*Here and elsewhere the male pronoun will be used for expediency. Nevertheless, the author wishes to emphasize his awareness that clients and therapists, like all people, are found in two genders.

therapy is a hit or miss proposition. These clients emphatically insist that their therapy experiences helped them immensely. How can we account for their attitude?

Former clients can exhibit substantial bias in evaluating their therapy experiences; it is difficult for them to assess their therapy objectively. They often feel comforted by their relationship with a pleasant, personable therapist. These reassuring experiences predispose clients to evaluate their therapy positively. In fact, however, they are evaluating their therapist—not their treatment.

Clients also invest substantial time, money, and energy in psychotherapy. The possibility that this investment has led to mediocre results is distressing—and difficult to acknowledge. Because of the constraints that limit any client's objectivity, personal testimonials about the effectiveness of psychotherapy demand skepticism. This kind of anecdotal evidence should not—and does not—enjoy much prominence in the professional literature evaluating psychotherapy's effectiveness.

Jay Haley, an especially perceptive critic of traditional therapy, suggests another possibility. He explains that when therapy fails clients—or worse yet even damages them—they become progressively disenchanted with treatment and consider it a futile ordeal. He believes the ordeals of therapy are partially responsible for its undeserved reputation of effectiveness.[8]

Haley emphasizes that if a client wants to terminate the ordeals of therapy, he finds various ways of his own to overcome his problems. Clients who succeed by virtue of their own resources declare themselves cured, the therapist can presumptuously credit himself for therapy's success, and the client exits therapy. If a traditional therapist feels that the client departed treatment prematurely, he could insist that treatment was "limited to supportive goals;" and, as a result, conclude that it was effective.

The therapist might also rationalize that he was limited to supportive goals because of the client's inability to commit to a "working alliance." For many psychotherapists, a "working alliance" prevails when a client is properly indoctrinated about his responsibilities in therapy. Rather than hold their therapist responsible for therapy outcome, properly indoctrinated clients impose that burden on themselves.

WHAT THERAPISTS SAY

Traditional therapists go to significant lengths to claim that their work is effective. Confronted with evidence to the contrary, they wage a vigorous campaign of damage control. Some cite data from the Kaiser-Permanente health insurance plan, which indicate that psychotherapy can be impressively cost effective.[9]

Instead of consuming medical services they did not need, this plan diverted psychologically distressed clients into psychotherapeutic treatment. Unnecessary utilization of medical services is one of the factors contributing to the exorbitant cost of health care. This study reported that psychotherapy reduced medical costs on an average of $2.59 for every dollar spent on therapy. These data, however, are not a sufficient defense for traditional psychotherapy.

The therapeutic orientation of the Kaiser-Permanente organization is generally not traditional. It is a short-term therapy that specifically defines and rapidly resolves a client's problems. In fact, this study emphasized that the savings on medical costs were most effectively realized *within one to four therapy sessions*. Prevailing techniques of traditional therapy rarely work that rapidly.

Some members of the traditional psychotherapy community call for more research. They remain steadfast in their belief that some specific therapy techniques are effective. They argue that available research methods are not yet sophisticated enough to verify the effectiveness of traditional therapy techniques.

For more than forty years, however, researchers have sought to demonstrate psychotherapy's effectiveness; and they invested substantial resources into their attempts. They exhibited an enduring commitment to their work while professing faith that— if not entirely blind—is seriously myopic. Though their determination is commendable, their objectivity is not.

Richard Chapman, a well-respected experimental psychologist, demonstrated that scientists interpret evidence objectively when they favor no particular theory.[10] But when scientists endorse one theory over another, they often overlook evidence that disproves their theoretical preference. Disregarding contrary evidence allows them to cling to their theoretical convictions.

Those who would perpetuate existing research efforts, trying to document the supposed effectiveness of traditional therapy techniques, are committing what might be called "Chapman's error." They ignore the existing research evidence because it fails to support their theoretical assumptions. Unfortunately, "Chapman's error" flourishes within the ranks of traditional therapists.*

Psychotherapists often commit themselves to the kind of therapy they prefer to do, and overlook whether their work effectively assists their clients. For one critic, such practices expose how most therapists ignore research evidence. This critic insists, "Neglecting the emerging research results is as good a proof as any that therapists are not impressed by science."[11] When psychotherapists ignore the importance of research, they also disregard the devastating conclusion to which the evidence leads.

WHAT THE EVIDENCE SAYS

Throughout the 1970s, research efforts sought to demonstrate the effectiveness of specific psychotherapy techniques. Researchers examined what therapists *actually* do to alleviate their clients' psychological distress.

The specific techniques used by the major schools of psychotherapy vary substantially. Analytic therapists seek to enhance a client's understanding of his problems. Humanistic therapists share and reflect the intensity of a client's feelings. Behavior therapists instruct a client on how to stop some particular thought pattern.

Given the differences between various psychotherapy techniques, researchers assumed that some specific techniques would more effectively alleviate some types of emotional distress. Logically appealing as this assumption may be, practically no evidence has come forth to support it.

With the possible exception of some behavioral techniques, used for some specific fears, there is no evidence to verify the effectiveness of any specific psychotherapy technique.[12] Studies comparing different therapy orientations usually reported that they were all about equally effective.

*Despite the wisdom of Aldous Huxley—"Facts do not cease to exist because they are ignored"—traditional therapists seem deeply committed to disregarding this observation.

Nevertheless, different therapy orientations use very different therapy techniques. The dissimilarities between these techniques logically prohibit any conclusion that they are equally effective. Therapy techniques that are so different should not produce basically the same results. If they *appeared* equally effective, this could only be explained by some common factor they shared.

The one and only factor that all therapy orientations share is the client-therapist relationship. Consequently, researchers are forced to conclude that this relationship is the critical factor in therapy outcome. They must also admit that this relationship is more important than any specific techniques that therapists employ.[13,14]

The necessary data are available, and the evidence is clear and convincing: Most traditional psychotherapy techniques fail to alleviate psychological distress. Instead, the client-therapist *relationship* accounts for the apparent effectiveness of psychotherapy. This is a sobering conclusion, to say the least. Traditional psychotherapists are left in a position where they can claim that psychotherapy is effective; but they cannot claim that their techniques are effective.

Additionally, the vast majority of outcome studies appearing to demonstrate the supposed effectiveness of traditional psychotherapy were done in academic settings. Treatment in academic settings is more closely monitored, guided by well-defined procedures, and reviewed by supervisors; consequently, it is less likely to harm clients. Compared to the research-based therapy of academia, the clinic-based therapy that most clients undergo typically disregards the quality-control attempts of research settings. In other words, there is a world of difference between the research-based therapy available to a small minority of clients, and the clinic-based therapy available to the overwhelming majority.[15]

Psychotherapists might still deserve the favorable reputation they enjoy. Perhaps they possess unique skills for establishing therapeutic relationships with their clients. Surely, their education and training afford them special wisdom in how to relate to people.

3

Psychotherapists do not know what they are doing and cannot train others to do it, whatever it is.

CITED BY ARNOLD LAZARUS

TRAINING IN PSYCHOTHERAPY

Consider the following hypothetical situation. A resident surgeon (a surgeon still in training) performs surgery on his own; he is not directly supervised in the operating room. Though assisted by other medical personnel, he is the only surgeon present.

In order to obtain supervision, the resident leaves the operating room and verbally summarizes his surgical work to a senior, experienced surgeon. After hearing the resident's report, the senior surgeon outlines how he could improve his surgical technique. The resident surgeon then returns to the operating room where he does his best to follow his supervisor's instructions.

Suppose that you have developed acute appendicitis and need an appendectomy. How pleased would you be about a surgeon trained in this manner operating on you?

Obviously, the previous example is ludicrous. The training procedures of medicine in general, and surgery in particular, have long been organized around live, moment-to-moment supervision. The experienced surgeon stands next to the neophyte resident in the operating room and tells the latter, "Cut here, retract there, probe this, and feel that."

Unfortunately, the training and supervision of traditional psychotherapists is rarely organized around live, moment-to-moment supervision. This is true regardless of what degree the therapist has earned—including the medical degree of psychiatrists, the doctoral degree of most psychologists, and the subdoctoral degrees of social workers and various counselors. Most training programs encourage trainees to conceal their endeavors behind closed doors.

Therapy trainees are typically alone in a consultation room with a client; no supervisor is present or even observing unobtrusively. In most traditional supervision, there is no recorded record (audio or video) of the interactions between trainee and client. After a therapy session ends, a supervisor relies on a trainee's verbal report about what transpired in the session. Thus, supervisors commonly "supervise" trainees without ever seeing the clients they are treating.

To say the least, what could be called supervision "in absentia" rarely meets the needs of trainees. These circumstances prompted a psychiatrist to vehemently criticize his own training. He recalled:

> When I trained, no one knew what the hell I was doing with patients. I talked about cases with my supervisor, but I could have been an utter sociopath [an exploitative individual with no conscience] and made everything up. There still isn't good supervision in psychiatry, but there is no excuse for it now with video cameras and one-way mirrors. There should and can be closer supervision.[1]

SUPERVISORY CONFUSION

When supervision in absentia prevails, errors in communication between supervisor and trainee can escalate rapidly. As a result of their inexperience, trainees find it difficult to comprehend the problems of their clients. Because they do not observe trainees, supervisors find it difficult to correct their errors. Thus, trainees struggle with what they do not understand; and supervisors labor with what they cannot see.

These kinds of training procedures invite supervisors and trainees to confuse each other. For example, a supervisor asks a trainee, "What did the client say about her husband?" The trainee responds, "I *think* she said he avoids her and refuses to communicate." Supervisor and trainee then proceed to speculate wildly about a relationship they have never seen—the client's relationship with her husband.

The reluctance of traditional supervisors to use live supervision forces them to contend with many unknowns. They must consider all the possible discrepancies between what a trainee actually did in therapy, and what he thinks he did, or says he did, or says he thinks he did! Too often, this kind of supervisory uncertainty deteriorates into the "blind leading the blind." Consequently, trainees cannot develop the objectivity about themselves necessary to increase their competence as therapists.

Even as therapists acquire more experience, the accuracy with which they recall how they respond to clients does not improve. Research has demonstrated that distortions and biases often undermine the memories of experienced therapists. In one study, the therapists overestimated how actively they responded to their clients, while in fact they did much less for them than they thought.[2]

Because experienced therapists overlook important details in treatment, they often supervise in the same manner they conduct therapy: They merely talk about whatever issues spontaneously capture their interest. Nevertheless, speculatively discussing the issues of a therapy case is a futile method of supervision. Well-defined courses of therapeutic action, specifically outlining what a trainee should do, rarely evolve from such dialogues.

There are some situations, however, when traditional supervisors attempt to provide specific directions for their trainees. Nevertheless, they cannot know if the trainees actually follow their instructions in the manner they intended. They are also unable to intervene, via a telephone for example, to direct sessions on a moment-to-moment basis.

Without appropriate supervision, a trainee is left unprepared if a therapy session should move in an unexpected direction. Deprived of live supervision, an unprepared trainee can only ad-lib to the best of his ability; but ad-libbing therapists, especially when they are trainees, fail to meet the needs of their clients.

Because of inadequate supervisory feedback, subjectivity dominates the thinking of trainees. This forces them to rely excessively on their own intuitive impressions which, again, do

not effectively serve the welfare of their clients. Effective therapists respond to what they *know*, not to what they *think* or *feel*.

SUPERVISORY ABSURDITY

Too often, absurdity prevails as standard procedure in the
training of psychotherapists. For example, a practicing therapist recalled an occasion in his own training when he felt lost;
a sullen, severely depressed client had thoroughly confused
him. When he asked a supervisor how he could respond more
effectively to this client, he was told: "'You don't have to *do*
anything—just be'."[3] The trainee considered this advice profound in its wisdom; others would consider it profoundly incompetent.

To say the least, this supervisor provided less than a well
defined course of action for the trainee. The direction to "just
be" was vague, ill-defined, and practically meaningless. Ultimately, one must question the effects of such a directive on a
client's welfare. If he knew that his therapist's supervision was
limited to such superficialities, how confident would any client
feel about his therapy?

When supervisors feel bewildered by the questions of their
trainees, they often resort to platitudes advising them to "just
be." Supervisors who indulge in such absurdity conceal their
incompetence behind a facade of pseudo-existentialism; and
simultaneously, they neglect the needs of clients. On another
occasion, for example, a supervisor encouraged the same trainee
to ". . . 'forget' what he had heard about the ineffectiveness of
therapy."[4] Consequently, any therapist who has been taught to
"just be" is a therapist who likely disregards considerations of
his therapeutic effectiveness.

Not only are traditional supervisors too distant from the
therapy work of their trainees, the trainees rarely see the
therapeutic endeavors of their supervisors. While describing
his experiences as a student in clinical psychology, a recent
doctoral graduate lamented:

> Although professors would discuss their own cases, or
> suggest strategies, it was rare to have a professor model
> therapy. Although there were a few opportunities to be
> a co-therapist with a professor in group therapy, watch-

ing a professor perform in individual interviews occurred rarely.[5]

Indeed, a shroud of secrecy hovers over traditional psychotherapy practices. When therapists and supervisors act as if they should conceal their work, the effectiveness of training programs is seriously compromised. Too often, the psychotherapy training of graduate students is limited to what they read in textbooks and discuss in seminars.

Is Training Effective?

Sometimes, role-playing procedures supplement the training of graduate students. Students simulate therapy interviews by exchanging roles of client and therapist with each other. If this method of training is effective, the therapy skills of graduate students should increase over the course of their graduate school career. Specifically, one would expect advanced graduate students to demonstrate greater competence in therapy interviews compared to inexperienced graduate students.

This very comparison was done at the clinical psychology training program of the University of California at Los Angeles. Advanced graduate students demonstrated no more competence in therapy interviews than less experienced graduate students. In summarizing its evidence, this study concluded, ". . . clinical training per se had no effects on interview performance."[6] This same "non-effect" has also been reported for psychiatric residents[7] and counselors.[8]

Too many psychotherapy training programs disregard whether trainees respond to their clients effectively. Instead, trainees are evaluated according to how they respond to the indoctrination of their supervisors. Trainees who want positive evaluations take care to comply with their supervisor's expectations. Because they rarely if ever observe their trainees interacting with clients, supervisors are more sensitive to how those trainees relate to them. They regularly leap to the conclusion that a deferential trainee, who appreciates their wisdom, is also a competent trainee.

Unfortunately, the bad news does not end here.

A 1979 study compared the effectiveness of trained, professional therapists to a group of college professors.[9] The college professors received no formal therapy training, nor did they possess any previous experience as psychotherapists. The professors were selected for this study simply because they enjoyed a reputation as helpful people who listened well.

In this study, the clients were male college students exhibiting psychological distress of one kind or another. They were randomly assigned to therapy with a professional therapist or a "professor therapist." The results of the study indicated that neither group of "therapists" was significantly more effective than the other. The college students responded as well to the "professor therapists" as they did to the professionals.

The results of the 1979 study allow one to conclude: (1) Traditional therapists do not possess unique interpersonal skills for establishing therapeutic relationships; and (2) The specific techniques of traditional therapists are no more effective than the interpersonal skills of well-educated laypeople.

This study raises the disturbing possibility that traditional psychotherapy is simply the purchase of pleasant companionship—little more than the supportive understanding of a close, trusted friend. Thus, many therapists merely operate "rent-a-friend" agencies; and unlike "professor therapists," professional therapists often promote long-term leases.

4

Psychotherapy is an undefined technique applied to unspecified problems with unpredictable outcomes.

—Victor Raimy

Relationships: For Better . . .

Research published in 1967 specified how the client-therapist relationship influences psychotherapy outcomes.[1] To the extent that clients regard their therapist as an understanding individual, who exhibits genuine sincerity while creating an emotionally warm atmosphere, the effectiveness of psychotherapy increases. Briefly reflecting on this research underscores its common-sense merit.

Clients in therapy inevitably find themselves in a vulnerable position. Disclosing closely guarded secrets and painful self-doubts guarantees their feelings of insecurity. One client explained, "I feel like I'm exposing my backside from a countertop in Macy's every time I see my shrink." Clients feel less vulnerable, however, if they trust their therapist as a warm and genuinely understanding person.

The Placebo Effect

A warm and understanding atmosphere is not a specific therapy technique. The effect of the client-therapist relationship has more in common with a placebo. A placebo may be defined as "an agent of healing or change

21

whose inherent properties do not scientifically account for such healing."[2] A placebo creates the appearance of a cure, but it does not genuinely heal.

In medicine, "placebo cures" are the result of patient expectancy. Physicians sometimes give patients a sugar pill and promise that it possesses great therapeutic value. Unaware that they are taking a mere placebo, many patients report dramatic recovery. When placebos appear to heal a physical ailment, they do so only because the patient expects that the placebo will be effective.

Because of placebo phenomena, traditional psychotherapy enjoys an *appearance* of effectiveness. Indeed, the various psychotherapy techniques have been described as mere "rituals" that create a suitable atmosphere for placebo effects.[3] In other words, traditional therapy techniques reassure clients with an illusion. They think themselves involved in an endeavor relevant to the resolution of their distress. This illusion leads to an expectation that they will improve.

Clients develop their expectations for improvement because of their relationship with a kind, benevolent therapist. They expect that a pleasant, personable therapist is also competent enough to resolve their problems.* Ultimately, these expectations lead clients to conclude that their therapy has been effective.

Expecting improvement, clients look for signs of progress from their therapy. By virtue of being well-motivated in their search, clients find evidence that they interpret as indicative of progress. Clients are willing to exaggerate any scintilla of evidence as indicating improvement. Their willingness to do so demonstrates the power of suggestibility and the influence of their therapists.

Not surprisingly, traditional therapists readily endorse the conclusions of clients who think that therapy has helped them. They do so regardless of how subjective and unreliable the evidence is for these conclusions. Like clients, therapists can find evidence of progress merely because they expect it. Thus, just as a placebo pill "cures" physical ills, traditional psychotherapy "cures" psychological distress.

---

*If a "likeability factor" can create an appearance of competence in a political campaign, surely it should confer the same appearance upon a therapist.

DEPENDENCY BECOMES ADDICTION

Too often, individual psychotherapy encourages clients to practically worship their therapist. For example, listen as the following client describes her therapist's significance in her life.

> It's embarrassing. I know I don't have a legitimate reason for staying but I don't want to give it up. My therapist has become my best friend. I would be very lonely without her, there would be a void in my life. I don't know what I would do without her and I'm going to hang on as long as she'll let me.[4]

When any therapist acquires the status of a client's "best friend," an outcome of tragic proportions has ensued. Most likely, this client lacked a warm and genuinely understanding relationship with a spouse, parent, child, or other significant people in her life. Conflict or estrangement in such relationships probably accounted for the therapist's status as her "best friend."

This client needed to expand her network of real-life supportive relationships, but those needs were severely compromised by the therapist's excessive significance in her life. Her inordinate dependency on her therapist undermined her psychological welfare.

Attracted by the prospect of comforting friendship, many clients are inducted or seduced into a "working alliance" with a therapist. Once inducted, clients demonstrate incredible persistence about their therapy despite its meager results. Clients and therapists may decide there is only one solution for the mediocre progress of treatment—more therapy. This situation leads clients into a "therapy addiction." In fact, therapy might deserve classification as a controlled substance because of its addictiveness.

Once a client is addicted to therapy, another remarkable decision can transpire between client and therapist. They may decide that the only remedy for the client's "addiction" is more of the same substance to which he is already addicted. Sessions may lengthen, or the number of sessions per week may increase. Consequently, the therapeutic relationship between client and therapist remains well-protected.

Therapists maintain their clients' commitment by reassuring them that continued therapy returns significant benefits. As a result, many clients assume that psychotherapy requires their long-term patience. When such assumptions are reported to a therapist, they can inspire praise for a client's supposed perceptiveness.*

Once trapped in long-term therapy, clients feel compelled to justify its length. Convinced that their kindly therapist would not betray them, they reject the notion that long-term treatment is unnecessary. Rather than question the value of therapy, clients inventory themselves to identify what serious difficulties are prolonging their treatment.

Not surprisingly, traditional therapists enthusiastically endorse these inventories; and they cheerfully applaud clients for whatever they find. Moreover, clients whose discoveries correspond to their therapist's theoretical preferences can receive standing ovations.

When no problems severe enough to warrant long-term therapy really exist—and often they do not—clients may respond to the influence of their therapist and invent them. Without realizing it, clients resort to their imaginations to identify the nature of their apparently unrelenting problems. [5]

Because the problems that clients invent are limited only by their imaginations, those problems can seem particularly complex and difficult. Thus, invented problems further encourage long-term therapy while continuously undermining a client's self-confidence; over time, a client's deteriorating self-confidence can become a very real problem.

BLAMING THE CLIENT

Sincere, well-meaning therapists who appear to accept clients enjoy considerable loyalty from their clientele. Despite the ineffectiveness of their treatment, clients rarely become angry with their therapist. It is difficult to be angry with anyone who seems so warm and genuinely understanding.

In order to protect the relationship with their professional friend, clients actively involve themselves in therapy. Never-

---

*Platitudes advising that "Rome was not built in a day" are often invoked for such praise. Therapists who resort to these banalities naively ignore their irrelevance. Instead, they act as if psychotherapy should consume the time and resources of an urban development project.

theless, this "commitment" can succumb to frustration and resignation because their problems remain unresolved. As a result, many clients feel discouraged by their course of treatment.

At this point, therapy can deteriorate into an ordeal. Clients are investing time, money, and energy in an effort that seems increasingly unproductive. Their therapist may maneuver them into accepting responsibility for this mediocre progress. Some therapists extort such an acknowledgment from clients; and these are clients who are paying for their services.

Psychotherapists are unique in the expectations they impose on clients. Other professionals rarely require clients to assume major responsibility for the quality of services they receive. For example, how many physicians would tell a patient, "Your surgery's success depends on whether you *really* want it to work"?

COMPENSATORY RELATIONSHIPS

Long-term psychotherapy survives because clients depend on it as a *compensatory relationship*. As a compensatory relationship, psychotherapy assumes the status of a pleasant luncheon engagement: The affable exchanges between friends are more important than the substance of their meeting.

The reassurance provided by a comforting relationship with a therapist can compensate for the absence of meaningful change in the client's real life. Relationships with spouse, parents, children, and others remain unchanged; but the client enjoys a short-term sense of well-being as a result of talking with his "friend."

When psychotherapy deteriorates into a compensatory relationship, the likelihood of therapeutic progress is reduced to a remote possibility. Clients, and even more often therapists, can enjoy the illusion that they are engaged in a meaningful endeavor. Meanwhile, nothing is happening. Clients talk about the distressing circumstances of their lives, while therapists respond insightfully and/or sympathetically. Nothing else changes; nothing else is accomplished.

5

But as profound as psychology is, it's a knife that cuts both ways

—**F.M. Dostoevski**

Relationships: ... For Worse

I f the client-therapist relationship is so crucial to psychotherapy outcomes, what happens when that relationship flounders? In that case, psychotherapy can degenerate into a negative and damaging experience. Therapy rapidly becomes an ordeal when a client endures a cold, distant, and indifferent therapist. Subjected to this kind of a therapist, a client's psychological welfare can deteriorate markedly.

Because so many therapists treat their clients poorly, two respected researchers estimate that only twenty percent of therapists are competent.[1] This means that many clients leave therapy burdened with feelings of betrayal. The experience described by the following young woman illustrates this kind of situation.

> Her [the therapist's] superior attitude really damaged me. I was just twenty years old, and I didn't have confidence in myself as a woman. She somehow had a way of making me feel my own inadequacies. One time she said, "You know, you're not a baby any more," which was just the thing I was struggling with. I

27

was embarrassed and humiliated that I couldn't handle what was going on. And having her say that confirmed this for me and didn't give me any hope that I could be any different. I'm still angry at her.[2]

This therapist may have felt frustrated by a client she could not help. Nevertheless, she ignored her own incompetence and arrogantly blamed the client for the ineffectiveness of this therapy. She also disregarded how contemptuous therapists undermine the welfare of their clientele. A therapist's ridicule escalates any client's feelings of self-doubt and self-blame.

This client would have benefited from compassionate reminders of how she overcame difficult circumstances in the past. No matter how simple learning to walk, attending school, and going on a date now appear, there was a time when they seemed formidable challenges. The client conquered those hurdles; and she has the same resources available to conquer contemporary hurdles.

With this approach, a therapist would have directed the client's attention toward her strengths. Clients who focus on their strengths resolve their problems more rapidly than clients who feel humiliated by their deficits. Thus, when psychotherapy harms clients, the client-therapist relationship is a critical factor in its counterproductive outcome.

BLAMING THE CLIENT

Clients who respond less enthusiastically to therapy than their therapist expects can endure contemptuous abuse. Commitment to a "working alliance" is often only the beginning. Clients are also supposed to make therapy *the* priority in their lives. For example, consider the following case of a client who found it necessary to reduce the frequency of his sessions.

> **Therapist:** It's obvious you're uncomfortable with your wish to drop to once a week.
> **Client:** Oh sure, I don't like doing it. It's just that I have no choice. Can't afford to spend so much time coming here.
> **Therapist:** You have no choice?
> **Client:** Not really. Just so much work piled up, and the boss doesn't like my being away so much. Anyway, I

want to talk to you about this fight that Janis and I got into again last night.

Therapist: Again you're moving away from what's happening to your commitment to your therapy and to your life.

Client: Oh, come on. It's not that way. I'd be here every day if I could afford it and if . . .

Therapist: Dave, you're very determined to treat this as a minor matter and one that you don't want to really look at. I don't buy it. I think there's something more going on.

Client: I meant to tell you about the schedule change sooner, but we just got started on something else, and I never got around to it.

Therapist: You sound as though you're caught in something wrong and need to make excuses.

Client: Oh, no. Anyway, that's not what I want to talk about now.

Therapist: Wow! You really are going to push this whole thing away if you can, aren't you?

Client: No, no. (Light tone) It's ok if you want to say something more about it.

Therapist: Dave, it sounds as though it's my therapy, not yours, or my life, not yours.[3]

If this client was really fighting a "commitment" to therapy, he could have cancelled all of his future appointments. In fact, the client did not do this; he wanted to use his session as constructively as possible. He cited a problem (his fight with Janis) for which he sought the therapist's assistance.

The therapist, however, insisted on the priority of his own agenda, and he proceeded to direct the client to it. As he did so, one can only wonder what this therapist expected: Was the client to quit his job, take out a second mortgage on his house, or simply disregard his responsibilities at work? In one regard, however, this therapist clearly conveyed his expectations. The client understood that he should make the therapist's agenda more important than his own.

Therapists who exhibit this kind of presumptuousness neglect the needs of their clients. Instead, they respond to their own needs for power and adulation.[4] They expect their clients to endorse them as some combination of sage and saint. Convinced that they and psychotherapy are singularly important, many therapists impose themselves and their values on their clients.

BAIT-AND-SWITCH IN PSYCHOTHERAPY

The previously cited therapist switched the client from his concerns to the therapist's agenda. This tactic allows traditional therapists to distract their clients from the irrelevance of most individual therapy. One critic of traditional therapy describes this procedure as "the bait-and-switch tactic." This metaphor refers to the retail sales practice of "baiting" customers with advertisements of an item at a low price, and then "switching" them to another item at a higher price.

In traditional therapy, a client's hope for problem resolution is the bait. A client presents a therapist with a problem for which he expects a straightforward solution. The therapist explains, however, that such a solution (the bait) is unavailable. The client is told that his problems are more complex than he realized; and he is switched to a treatment method very different from what he expected. Traditional therapists who indulge in these switches . . .

> . . . view patients as one would view naive children: they do not understand what they are doing and need to be shown the right path. If the patient naively believes that resolving a particular presenting problem will make his or her life better, that belief should be tolerated—almost as one tolerates a child's need to believe in Santa Claus. One tolerates that belief but does not take it seriously.[5]

When clients are viewed this way, a therapist's assessment of a client's problem bears faint resemblance to the problem the client thought he had. Instead, clients are indoctrinated into believing that the resolution of their problems necessitates they think like their therapist. Once suitably indoctrinated, clients talk about all kinds of issues. These are issues that heretofore they never imagined as relevant to their psychological distress. As a result, what clients talk about is determined more by their therapist's theoretical preference than by the clients' problems.

The previously quoted critic cited the case of a man referred for psychotherapy because of hypertension. Despite the client's presenting problem, his therapist questioned him extensively about his sex life. Before his initial consultation with a therapist, this man likely thought he needed to resolve stress-related problems of tension and anxiety. The therapist, however, engaged in a wholesale redefinition of the client's problem. Once client assessments of their own problems are disregarded in this manner, the client . . .

> . . . gets the therapist's particular brand of psychotherapy addressing the problem areas that the therapist finds significant. The form of treatment, then, is determined by the therapist's habitual approach and not by the nature of the problem that the patient brings in.[6]

There are some therapists perceptive enough to deplore how bait-and-switch tactics betray the welfare of clients. Two such critics emphasized:

> "Our view is that *the ultimate goal of therapy always should be the resolution of the presenting problem.* There are persuasive ethical, political, and scientific reasons for this stance. Any treatment offered for a psychiatric problem, such as depression, school phobia, or anorexia, should be judged by the primary criterion of symptom improvement. Any marital or family therapist . . . [or any other type of therapist] . . . who is unwilling to adopt such a primary criterion should state this explicitly to his or her clients rather than imply that the treatment is intended to alleviate the symptom."[7]

Unfortunately, however, wisdom such as this too often remains a voice in the wilderness of traditional psychotherapy.

Bait-and-switch tactics remain alive and well in therapy because they create an illusion of therapist competence. When therapists resort to such tactics, they disregard their obligation to design procedures that genuinely help clients. Instead, they define client problems so that their preferred techniques *appear* helpful; and this "switching" allows them to do the kind of therapy they want to do. Unfortunately, such tactics also make the Latin proverb *caveat emptor*—let the buyer beware, especially appropriate for traditional psychotherapy.

6

BEYOND THE TALKING CURE

Despite major differences between various therapy orientations, their techniques share an important similarity. They all require clients to "talk about" issues that supposedly relieve their psychological distress.

The theoretical orientations of traditional therapists primarily lead them to differences in what they "talk about." Analytic therapists want clients to "talk about" dreams and fantasies. Client centered-humanistic therapists want clients to "talk about" feelings and emotions. Behavior therapists want clients to "talk about" specific actions and corresponding patterns of thought.

Committed as therapists are to "talking about" various issues, there is no evidence to indicate that these dialogues help their clients. Regardless of the therapist's theoretical orientation, the preferred topics for discussion correspond to experiences that transpire within clients. Too often, traditional therapists act as if clients are "self-contained" individuals insulated from any social and environmental influences.[1]

In fact, however, relationships with spouse, children, parents, friends, etc. frequently in-

33

fluence a client's psychological welfare. These relationships result in important experiences that are shared *between* people. As a result, merely discussing the experiences *within* clients fails to alleviate psychological distress.

Though "talking about" methods rarely assist clients, they effectively fill the time and space of fifty-minute therapy sessions. These methods create the illusion for clients and therapists that something important is occurring. This illusion conceals the crisis in which traditional psychotherapy finds itself.

PSYCHOTHERAPY IN CRISIS

Traditional psychotherapy faces a crisis of enormous proportions. Research indicates that psychotherapists rarely make their treatment decisions in a logical, systematic manner. In one study, therapists selected treatment goals and therapy methods on the basis of their intuitive appeal.[2] Treatment planning disregarded any relevant research in more than ninety percent of the cases evaluated; instead, the therapists responded to considerations of what sounded good. This study demonstrates how unrelated theory, research, and procedure are in the practice of traditional psychotherapy.

In fact, related evidence demonstrates that psychotherapists typically disregard research in their treatment endeavors. For example, a particularly sobering study reported that less than 10 percent of a sample of 1100 therapists relied on any professional publications in their work.[3] Another study examined 416 intake evaluations completed by various therapists. Only one of these evaluations involved a treatment plan demonstrating any awareness of relevant research.[4] Still another study found that the psychologists in its sample preferred to discuss treatment issues with their colleagues rather than read the professional literature.[5] Collectively, these studies suggest that therapists prefer chatty gossip over rigorous thinking—and these circumstances certainly amount to a crisis.

The eminent philosopher of science, Thomas S. Kuhn, defines the prevailing theories, methods, and procedures of a profession as its "paradigm." When the existing paradigm of a profession is no longer viable—as is the case in traditional psychotherapy—a crisis prevails and the profession must undertake a "paradigm shift." Otherwise, it jeopardizes its legitimacy as a profession. Once a profession has accomplished a paradigm shift, it "....will have changed its view of the field, its methods, and its goals."[6]

Paradigm shifts are not smooth transitions accomplished all at once with an easy consensus of opinion. Instead, these shifts require massive modifications in theory and practice. This motivates many psychotherapists to deny the need for such shifts. Candidly acknowledging the need for wholesale paradigm revision leaves psychotherapists feeling overwhelmed. Specifically, they feel overwhelmed by the rapidly approaching specter of professional obsolescence.

Indeed, collective obstinacy undermines the practice of traditional psychotherapy. Despite evidence that overwhelmingly demands a paradigm shift, the more familiar, better established paradigms remain deeply entrenched. As a result, traditional therapists continue to fiddle while their professional crises burn around them. Their capacity to withstand the heat of these fires, while remaining unresponsive to them, is truly remarkable.

Most likely, the impetus for a psychotherapeutic paradigm shift will come from an informed public demanding it. At this point, the public possesses greater potential for objectivity about psychotherapy than its practitioners do. As we look for a new paradigm, we need well-defined guidelines. What do the shortcomings of traditional therapy tell us about the paradigm that must replace it?

AN INSTRUCTIVE CASE

In discussing her long-term therapy, one client unwittingly revealed her isolation and described the counterproductiveness of her treatment.

> I like the regular contact. It helps structure my life. Now that the kids are gone and my husband travels so much, I have more contact with Dr.___than with anyone else. The problems aren't the main thing because we don't even talk about them most of the time. I just bring up whatever I want. I have no idea if it's going anywhere but I like the process.[7]

Faced with distressing changes in her marriage and family, this client needed more than the "process" of therapy—she needed tangible results. Because her roles as wife and mother had altered so much, a competent therapist would have involved her husband in the treatment. Together, they could have found ways to reorganize their marital and family life more satisfactorily.

An effective therapist would have asked the husband what initially attracted him to his wife, how did he court her, and why did he choose her as *the* woman he wanted to marry? Questions such as these recall feelings of warmth and tenderness for both spouses. A therapist could also have asked the husband how his wife might help him adjust to the changes in his life; and how could he help her with the changes in her life?

The husband's answers would have likely reassured his wife about her continuing importance to him. Warmed by the knowledge that her husband still needed her, the wife would have felt renewed by his praise and attention. A spouse who enjoys this kind of a marriage declines any offers of compensatory companionship from a rent-a-friend agency.

Because effective therapeutic intervention was not forthcoming in this case, the client developed an "addiction" to therapy as a compensatory relationship. Many traditional therapists attempt to rationalize compensatory relationships. They cite client statements about "feeling better" as a result of therapy; but any such short-lived relief is irrelevant to a client's long-term psychological welfare.

The previously cited case underscores the shortcomings of all individual psychotherapy: (1) Therapists appoint themselves to positions of undeserved importance in their clients' lives. (2) Without well-defined goals relevant to the clients' needs, therapy may indulge in aimless dialogues that wander from subject to subject. (3) Treatment disregards the clients' relationships with other people who are important to them.

Tempting as it is to indict incompetent therapists for this situation, psychotherapy's problems originate elsewhere. Beyond the limitations of its therapists, traditional therapy's problems ultimately correspond to the futility and counterproductiveness of its techniques. Consequently, psychotherapy requires the new direction of a paradigm shift.

New Directions

A Revised Client-Therapist Relationship

Therapists need to develop more humility about the limits of their knowledge and influence. As previously emphasized, therapists have no monopoly on the ability to assist psychologically distressed people.

Once they feel confident about what needs to be done, friends and relatives often aid clients more effectively than a therapist. Effective therapists commonly see clients who have other people in their lives who are important to them. As a result, a competent therapist can help those people to support and assist the client.

For example, when a family has been effectively mobilized to resolve the psychological distress of one of its members, it is the rare therapist who can compete with the wisdom and influence of that family. When clients are substantially aided by the collective efforts of their family, they direct their feelings of gratitude toward that family—not their therapist.

Unfortunately, too many therapists need to be needed and appreciated by their clientele; and, in fact, they often seem to have selected their calling because of such needs.[8] Psychotherapists who seek their clients' adulation and affection are disinclined to share those clients with others. When other people in a client's life assist him to overcome his problems, he may appreciate them more than the therapist. This kind of outcome leaves therapists who need to be needed less than elated.

An effective therapist structures therapy so that clients and families assign substantial credit to themselves for successful outcome. Such a therapist may be stretching the truth to some degree, but he does so on behalf of his clients. [9]

When clients and families give themselves credit for a positive outcome, they possess the confidence to deal effectively with future problems in their lives. Their self-reliance may not enhance a therapist's ego—or his cash flow. Nevertheless, when clients and families are confidently self-reliant, their psychological welfare has been significantly enhanced.

Clearly Defined Goals and the Need for Action

Clients who feel frustrated in their jobs, conflicted with their spouses, or overwhelmed by their children need a well-defined direction to resolve those problems. Persistent problems create increasing frustration, and increasingly frustrated people feel lost as to what to do about their problems.

Traditional therapy's "talking about" techniques neglect to specify well-defined goals; and they disregard the need to provide clients with specific courses of action. Instead, these techniques reduce clients to passivity. While all psychotherapeutic orientations agree that therapy should be a learning experience, client passivity interferes with efficient learning and discourages appropriate action.

Effective learning experiences in psychotherapy require a client's active participation. If a client is helped to do something about a problem, as opposed to just discussing it, therapy assists him more effectively.

Focus on Interpersonal Relationships

Despite the ill-chosen metaphor of "mental illness," psychological distress rarely remains within the people who contend with it. More and more authorities are rejecting the concept of mental illness as a myth.[10] To qualify as an illness, the condition in question must damage the body's physical tissue. Psychological distress does not satisfy this requirement.[11] To the extent that psychotherapists insist on continuing to use this ill-defined metaphor, they should at least think of psychological distress as an infectious condition. Psychological distress both influences, and is influenced by, a client's relationships with others.

For example, consider the situation of a married person who struggles with depression. The withdrawn, often sullen demeanor of this depressed person can alienate his spouse. Because there is little joy or happiness in relating to depressed people, their mate often withdraws from them. Spousal withdrawal usually creates more depression; and increasing depression encourages continued spousal withdrawal.

Thus, psychological distress often perpetuates itself as a result of vicious cycles that transpire between people. Effective psychotherapy must address itself to resolving these kinds of cycles, but individual psychotherapy rarely suffices. Attempting to change a *two person* relationship via *individual* psychotherapy is a hopeless task.

Psychotherapists cannot continue to focus exclusively on events that transpire *within* their clientele. Too often, this amounts to a futile and counterproductive kind of endeavor. Therapists need to address themselves to the relationships that exist *between* their clients and the other people in their lives who are important to them. The shift from focusing on events within clients to focusing on events between clients and others is not a moderate difference of *degree*; it is a major difference of *kind*. Indeed, such a shift is a paradigm shift.

Psychotherapy's need for a paradigm shift raises a number of important questions: Does a particular professional affiliation (psychiatry, psychology, or social work) increase a therapist's effectiveness? What are psychotherapy's major theoretical orientations and how did they develop? What do those orientations emphasize in therapy? Do theoretical preferences influence how therapists relate to clients? What kinds of errors do therapists commit, and what are their consequences? When psychotherapy works, what makes it effective? And finally, how can a therapist be evaluated?

The remainder of this volume addresses itself to these questions and others. Hopefully, it will assist readers to make informed choices about psychotherapy, and help them find competent therapists who effectively meet their needs.

PART TWO

PSYCHOTHERAPISTS AND TRADITIONAL PSYCHOTHERAPY

7

WHO PRACTICES PSYCHOTHERAPY?

A ll psychotherapists do not belong to one single, professional group. Instead, psychotherapy is practiced by a variety of professional groups, including, but not limited to: psychiatrists, psychologists, social workers, a myriad of different counselors, and marriage and family therapists.

While the previously cited professionals must be licensed or certified by the states in which they practice, some pretenders gratuitously call themselves "psychotherapists." They assume this self-appointed designation to circumvent their lack of legitimate credentials. There is no such thing as a licensed or certified "psychotherapist."

Though psychotherapist is the generic term for various professionals, practitioners should identify themselves according to their licensure or certification. This volume uses the term "psychotherapist" for ease of communication; but any therapist who publicly promotes himself as such is suspect.

As the number of therapists has soared over the past two decades, the episodic warfare between these professional groups has grown increasingly heated. Each group exag-

43

gerates claims about the advantages of its training and mode of practice; and simultaneously, they are inclined to indict the credentials and competence of other groups.

Psychiatry prefers to attack from a position of self-appointed superiority. Psychiatrists remind any and all that they are the "real doctors" in this business, and all others are merely imposters.

Psychologists boast about the breadth of their training in the behavioral sciences and research. They insist that this supposed breadth makes them uniquely competent.

Therapists who practice with a master's degree (most social workers, some psychologists, numerous counselors, and many marriage and family therapists) challenge doctoral level practitioners to produce any evidence that doctoral level training indicates greater competence as a psychotherapist.

As their interdisciplinary debates escalate, the shrill voices of the confronting professions sound more like a babel. The claims and counter-claims hurled back and forth can bewilder a potential client. Hopefully, the following comments will clarify some of this confusion.

PSYCHIATRISTS

Psychiatrists have completed the same basic medical education as other physicians (surgeons, internists, cardiologists, etc.). Prior to their training residency in psychiatry, psychiatrists emerge from medical school as well-educated medical practitioners. The psychiatric resident then turns his back on this medical legacy to specialize in an endeavor remotely related to the mainstream of medicine.

The transition from medical school to psychiatric residency is typically a jolting experience for a neophyte psychiatric resident. He is moving from an endeavor organized about the data and conceptualizations of the life sciences (biology and chemistry) into an endeavor organized about the data and conceptualizations of the behavioral sciences (psychology and sociology).

Some cynics have observed that "a psychiatrist is an individual trained in medicine which he does not practice, while practicing psychology in which he is not trained." Given the discontinuity between medical school and psychiatric residency, one wonders why psychiatrists choose their specialty? Their decision involves a major career change before having tested the waters of their first choice.*

Psychiatrists would have the lay public believe that they, and they alone, are qualified to respond to the total range of a client's needs. This range includes both physical as well as psychological conditions.

In theory, the collective position of psychiatry on this issue is correct. Clarification of actual psychiatric practice, however, is best obtained by asking psychiatrists when they last performed a comprehensive, physical examination? For most experienced psychiatrists, this is an embarrassing question. They would have to admit that they rarely use their skills as physicians in their psychiatric practice.[1]

When psychiatrists suspect that a client's emotional distress is physically determined, they do what any other competent psychotherapist would do. They refer the client to a neurologist, or endocrinologist, or urologist, or some other specialist who can respond appropriately to the client's needs.

Psychiatrists might still argue that they are better prepared to diagnose those physical conditions that can manifest themselves via psychological distress than are their non-medical colleagues. Here, the psychiatric establishment is really raising the issue of "false negatives."

False negative errors occur when a therapist regards psychological problems as unrelated to a client's physical condition; while, in fact, the client's physical status is a major factor in his psychological distress. These types of errors do occur, but not as often as the psychiatric establishment would have the American public believe.

It should also be emphasized that psychiatrists commit their own type of diagnostic errors. These errors are called "false positives." Many psychiatrists can erroneously assume that a client's psychological distress is physically determined when, in fact, it is not.

Given the enthusiasm with which American psychiatry prescribes psychotropic (mood and/or mind altering) medication, their false positive clients can be unnecessarily medicated. The effects of unnecessary medication can cause more psychological

---

*A urologist known to this writer once remarked: "I'm not sure what psychiatrists do, but I know they don't practice medicine."

distress than a client ever endured before he saw a psychiatrist. In testifying before a congressional subcommittee, Nicholas Cummings, a former president of the American Psychological Association, deplored the counterproductiveness of unnecessary medication. He cited the case of a 79-year-old woman who had been diagnosed with Alzheimer's disease. Cummings explained:

> Upon psychological evaluation, she was found to be taking 28 different medications—seven prescribed by several psychiatrists.
> A psychologist did an evaluation and asked that the patient receive a thorough medical evaluation. The psychologist had the patient removed from all medications except three. Within two weeks, there were no symptoms of senility, and she was, in every respect sound.[2]

To one degree or another, this woman's supposed Alzheimer's disease was really the result of inappropriately prescribed, psychotropic medication. When their medications do more harm than good, psychiatrists might feel quite awkward if asked: Is better living through chemistry really better living?

While in medical school and in their residencies, psychiatrists undergo a great deal of training in hospital settings. Hospitals have long been characterized by a well-defined chain of command—physicians issue orders to nurses, nurses issue orders to aides, and practically everybody tells the patient what to do!

As a result of their medical training, psychiatrists are inclined to assume substantial authority in their clients' lives. They are accustomed to hospitalized patients accepting their authority. Psychologically distressed clients who are not hospitalized, however, may feel perturbed by the eagerness with which their psychiatrist issues orders.

When dealing with a psychiatrist they consider arbitrarily domineering, clients often exhibit an emotional state called "reactance." Reactance refers to the readiness of all people to defy an authority figure they perceive as arbitrary.[3] A talent for creating client reactance interferes with psychotherapeutic relationships. Consequently, clients often find it difficult to view their psychiatric therapist as warm and genuinely understanding. In other words, the medical training of psychiatrists undermines their ability to establish a therapeutic relationship. Their faith in the sanctity of "doctor's orders" is not always reciprocated by their clientele.

PSYCHOLOGISTS

The majority of psychologists who function as independent providers of psychotherapeutic services possess a doctoral degree. Most of these doctoral level psychologists hold the Ph.D. degree (a minority of doctoral level psychologists possess Psy.D. degrees—Doctorate of Psychology—or other professional degrees).

The Ph.D. degree, however, is not a professional degree; it is an academic research degree. The American Psychological Association has long advocated the "scientist-professional" model of graduate training for clinical psychologists.* The "scientist-professional" model of graduate training emphasizes the value of research endeavors.

Legions of doctoral students in clinical psychology proceed through graduate school while concealing their real ambitions. They are discouraged from developing their skills as professional psychologists in general, and as psychotherapists in particular. Instead, they are expected to demonstrate their potential, first and foremost, as researchers. It is not enough that they be able to interpret, critique and utilize research— they must be able to *conduct* it. As a result, most doctoral-level clinical psychology programs sacrifice training in psychotherapy to an emphasis on research training.**

Because of their research training, psychologists often regard psychotherapy as an exercise in data collection. They "talk about" all kinds of issues in a client's life as they seek to acquire more and more data; but they often postpone decisions requiring client action. Thus, they advocate passivity in their clientele; and those clients are deprived of the opportunity to rapidly resolve their problems.

Many psychologists are also committed to subjecting their clients to psychological tests. Psychologists exhibit a fond affec-

---

*Clinical psychology is the specialization in psychology most often involved in providing psychotherapy services.

**Consequently, many psychologists feel so hostile about research that they spend the rest of their careers studiously ignoring it.[4]

tion for psychological testing because it is an enterprise unique to psychology. The other psychotherapy professions are not qualified to administer or interpret psychological tests.*

It is rare, however, that psychological testing leads to a well-defined course of treatment for any client. It does not tell a therapist how to most effectively meet a client's needs. Psychological testing usually confines itself to assessing what transpires *within* clients. It overlooks the significance of what occurs *between* clients and others important to them.

In their training, all clinical psychologists learn that psychological testing is appropriately confined to answering well defined questions (i.e., is this client mentally retarded, has that client lost contact with reality?). In fact, the range of questions to which psychological testing can accurately respond is severely limited. Many psychologists, however, are compelled to disregard the lessons of their training. Otherwise, they would endure substantial embarrassment by acknowledging the extent to which psychological testing is an irrelevant endeavor.

SUB-DOCTORAL THERAPISTS

Providers of psychotherapy services whose highest degree is a master's degree (some psychologists, most social workers, many marriage and family therapists, and a myriad number of other "counselors") exhibit a broad range of competence. In this writer's professional experience, some of the best and some of the worst therapists practice at a master's level.

Compared to doctoral level training, the training of master's level psychotherapists is usually less closely supervised. Typically, these graduate programs lack the funds to provide for the lower student-faculty ratios of doctoral programs. These circumstances, however, do not reduce the effectiveness of therapists who practice at this level.

Anyone who attempts to select a psychotherapist on the basis of professional affiliation encounters a maze of possibilities—but few good choices. Despite the number of different professional groups providing psychotherapy services, there is

---

*There are some psychiatrists, however, whose grandiosity is such that they are not deterred from frequently abusing psychological tests. Even though they are not properly trained, they use these tests and attempt to interpret them.

virtually no evidence indicating that any particular group (psychologists vs. psychiatrists, for example) is more effective in its therapeutic skills than any other group. Similarly, there is virtually no data available to indicate that psychotherapists trained at a doctoral level are more effective than those trained at a master's level.

Whether a therapist is a psychiatrist, psychologist, or social worker; and whether or not a therapist has a doctoral degree, is irrelevant to his psychotherapeutic competence. Indeed, the three most competent therapists this writer has directly observed include: a psychiatrist, a doctoral level psychologist, and a master's level marriage and family therapist (not ranked in any particular order).

Considering the inadequate training that most therapists undergo, it is understandable that no particular group of therapists is more effective than another. All of these groups share the same training and supervisory practices that are marginally effective at best. As a result, prevailing training-supervisory practices create a common denominator of mediocrity for all the therapy professions.

OVERVIEW

The professional organizations that represent psychotherapists downplay the issues and problems outlined in this chapter and Chapter Three. Instead, they vigorously lobby state legislatures and the U.S. Congress on behalf of their members' interests. These organizations are determined to increase the demand for psychotherapy services, and expand the supply of therapists who can provide those services.

For example, more than thirty states have passed "freedom of choice" laws. These regulations provide health insurance reimbursement to therapists previously ineligible for it. Obviously, freedom of choice laws significantly increase private practice opportunities for a large number of therapists. These regulations also provoke professional "turf battles" between different groups of therapists.

Freedom of choice legislation has mobilized psychiatrists to defend their sense of territory. In years past, they were the only therapists who received insurance reimbursement for their services. In response to the growing number of non-psychiatric therapists, organized psychiatry now encourages health insurance carriers to limit reimbursement for therapy services to "medical psychotherapy."

Not surprisingly, psychiatry defines medical psychotherapy as therapy provided or supervised by a psychiatrist. Fortunately, most health insurance companies reject this featherbedding ruse; they see no benefit in it for their subscribers.

Also, more than thirty states have passed mandatory mental health statutes. These provisions require health insurers to provide coverage for the treatment of formally diagnosed psychological distress. As with freedom of choice laws, mandatory mental health regulations significantly increase private practice opportunities for a large number of therapists.

While approximately sixty percent of the states have passed laws to benefit the practices of psychotherapists, a significantly smaller percentage require them to undertake continuing education. Only nineteen states mandate that psychologists participate in continuing education as a condition of maintaining their licenses to practice. Basically, the same situation prevails for social workers, marriage and family therapists, and the various groups of counselors. Psychiatrists must engage in continuing education more often because of their status as physicians.

Obviously, there is little encouragement for psychotherapists to stay abreast of recent research developments. Once they have departed graduate school, most therapists are not obligated to update their skills. Circumstances such as these invite rather cynical conclusions.

Compared to their interest in protecting the welfare of the public, psychotherapists seem more ready to pursue their own legislative priorities. Any state that has passed mandatory mental health coverage or a freedom of choice law, but disregards continuing education requirements for psychotherapists, has irresponsibly neglected the public's welfare.

More than considerations of professional affiliation, a therapist's theoretical orientation ultimately influences the therapy experiences of clients. We turn to those orientations now.

It is the customary fate of new truths to begin as heresies and to end as superstitions.

—THOMAS HUXLEY

PSYCHOANALYTIC PSYCHO- THERAPY AND INSIGHT

In the annals of intellectual history, Sigmund Freud stands as a giant. The influence of Freudian theory is found not only in contemporary psychology and psychiatry, but also in literature, art and cinema. Indeed, Freud deserves credit as the seminal force for all of the behavioral sciences (sociology and anthropology, as well as psychology and psychiatry).

Most significantly, Freudian theory established human behavior as an independent area of legitimate, intellectual inquiry. Prior to the development of the behavioral sciences, questions about the human condition fell into the domains of theology and philosophy. Freud rejected these classical disciplines for failing necessary standards of objectivity.

For Freud, the speculative methods of theology and philosophy undermined any attempts to understand human behavior. As a result, Freud sought to employ scientific methods of objective observation in the development of psychoanalysis. Whether or not he succeeded in this attempt is open to debate.

To say the least, Freudian theory created substantial controversy over the last ninety years. Freudian concepts of "penis envy" and "feminine hysteria" have invited harsh criticisms from feminists and academicians alike. Freudian theory has also been indicted for overlooking the impact of cultural forces on human behavior.

Nevertheless, the volumes of literature critical of this theory also testify to its profound influence. Even though legions of behavioral scientists have attempted to dismantle Freudian theory, they must admit that they cannot ignore it; the theory is too important and influential.

Any in-depth critique of Freudian theory is beyond the scope of this book. The merits of Freudian theory as a theory of personality may, or may not, be regarded as valuable. This chapter, however, will focus on the effectiveness of Freudian psychotherapeutic techniques (hereafter referred to as analytic therapy).

PSYCHE AND SOCIETY

Analytic theory assumes that psychological distress develops because of unresolved emotional conflicts originating in childhood. Analytic therapists insist that children are controlled by powerful, sexual and aggressive drives which are instinctually determined. These drives are an expression of that portion of the personality Freud called the id. The powerful drives of the id supposedly compel the child to seek their immediate gratification.

The social order, however, demands the control of instinctual drives in the service of society's welfare. Obviously, blatant promiscuity and rampant homicide would undermine stability and security in the social order. Therefore, one of the tasks of the social order is to socialize the child. An effectively socialized child has acquired control over the disruptive drives of the id.

Parents assume the primary responsibility for socializing their children. A child's formative relationship with his parents results in the development of what Freud called the superego. The superego demands compliance with parental expectations; and as a result, it is the personality's internalized sense of right and wrong. Disregarding the superego's prohibitions results in painful feelings of guilt.

Over the normal course of development, children acquire the

ability to control their instinctual drives in a socially approved manner. This control increases their capacity to function reasonably and logically. The capacity for reason and logic reflects that portion of the personality Freud called the ego.

A well-developed ego enhances the effectiveness with which an individual contends with the inevitable conflicts of the human condition. An inadequately developed ego is vulnerable to conflicts created by the demands of one's instinctual needs.

Analytic therapists regard the distressed client as an individual whose ego is inadequately developed. Such an ego attempts to manage the inevitable conflicts of the human condition by eliminating any awareness of them via repression. Repression allows people to overlook their conflicts by forgetting them. These conflicts are repressed because the client finds it too emotionally painful to acknowledge them.

For example, acknowledging a desire to share mother's bed, while disclosing fantasies of dispatching father with any convenient weapon, disqualifies one as a model citizen in the eyes of others. Disclosing these desires also provokes painful feelings of guilt. As a result, psychologically distressed clients are highly motivated to repress, or forget, such urges.

Repression And Intrapsychic Conflicts

According to Freudian theory, the repression of sexual and aggressive urges jeopardizes the ego's welfare. Repression heightens the intensity of the id's urges, which, in turn, threaten to overwhelm and shatter the ego. Analytic therapists employ hydraulic metaphors to describe these dynamics. For example, they might speak about the turbulent waters of adolescent sexuality threatening to break through the floodgates of repression and overflow the structure of the ego. When this happens, the personality must invest more and more energy into repression.

Energy used for repression is unavailable for more constructive endeavors. An increasing reliance on repression sabotages the efficiency of the ego. The personality is too preoccupied with inner conflict to respond effectively to the demands of the outside world. Because repressive defenses are not always entirely effective, the ego can endure excruciating anxiety.

When the pressurized urges of the id threaten to overwhelm repressive defenses, anxiety levels heighten. Anxiety is considered the hallmark of neurotic conflict. Analytic therapists assume that a client's anxiety level corresponds to the intensity of his conflicts. Substantially elevated anxiety levels indicate severe conflicts.

For the analytic therapist, a psychologically distressed client is inevitably beset by unrelenting conflicts. These conflicts reflect the oppositional forces of a client's drives, and the demands of the social order to harness those drives. Over time, a client's conflicts evolve to a point where they become a significant dimension of his personality. Once these conflicts are woven through the fabric of a client's personality, they are termed intrapsychic conflicts.

Intrapsychic conflicts exist outside of a client's awareness because of his use of repression. Analytic therapists want to identify those conflicts and examine them in a rational, logical manner. They assume that rational, logical examination of such conflicts enhances the ego's capacity to resolve them via insight. Insight prevails when a client understands his conflicts in depth and detail.

Insight is the ultimate goal of analytic therapy. Analytic therapists consider insight an emancipating experience for clients. Insight supposedly affords clients the opportunity to deal more effectively with their problems. Insight, or what might be called "enlightened understanding," also presumably eliminates the need to use neurotic defenses such as repression.

While insight is the terminal goal of analytic therapy, it is realized via examination of a client's mental content. A procedure called "free association" requires that clients describe all their thoughts and feelings. Clients also frequently report the content of their dreams to their therapist. The analytic therapist then interprets, or insightfully explains, the free associations and dream reports. Interpretation is considered *the* method for promoting client insight.

For analytic therapists, the most significant interpretations deal with their clients' unconscious minds. Analytic theory assumes that the human psyche is like an iceberg —most of it remains submerged within the murky waters of the unconscious. Supposedly, the personality we present to the world is a facade that responds to social pressures; this "public" portion is only a small fraction of the total personality.

THERAPISTS WHO KNOW EVERYTHING

Analytic theory assumes that most human behavior is unconsciously motivated—people do not really understand why they do what they do. Thus, this theory insists that self-deception is the enduring characteristic of the human condition. Analytic theory leads its practitioners to insist that clients cannot—of their own accord—understand their unconscious motives.

When analytic therapists attribute client behavior to unconscious motivation, they automatically qualify themselves as experts. By analytic definition, the therapists are addressing events which the clients cannot understand.[1] As self-appointed experts, however, analytic therapists create a curious paradox for themselves.

A client reports events of his day-to-day life to his therapist. The therapist assumes that those reports are distorted but he remains confident in his ability to bring objectivity to those distortions. The therapist, however, has no knowledge of the client's life independent of the client's distortions. Therefore, how can the therapist understand what the client cannot understand, when the therapist's understanding is limited to the distortions of the client?

In effect, analytic therapists tell their clients: "Even though you experienced it (some life event), you don't understand it. And even though I didn't experience it, your misunderstanding allows me to understand it better than you." Above and beyond their logical impossibility, these interpretive tactics suggest that the Mad Hatter would have enthusiastically embraced analytic theory.

The theory of unconscious motivation allows therapists to assume positions of enormous power and influence in their clients' lives. This therapy regularly informs clients that their therapist is infinitely more wise than they are. Analytic therapists establish their supposed expertise by disqualifying what clients say about themselves. One observer cited three examples of this tactic.

(1) **Patient:** I really love my wife.

Therapist: It seems to me that you are trying to hide the fact that you hate her.

(2)   **Patient:** My mother was terrible and I hated her.
Therapist: Perhaps what you are really trying to tell me is that you loved her too much.

(3)   **Patient:** I feel extremely generous today. I just donated $5,000 to the Allied Jewish Appeal.
Therapist: Might you have done this because you wanted to give Jews something to make up for the love you weren't given in childhood? If so, this would mean of course, that you gave not so much out of generosity, but out of a wish to get something.[2]

Because analytic therapists maintain their authority so cleverly, they almost always enjoy the upper hand with their clients. If a client requires a reminder about who the expert is, the therapist negates the client's statements. This procedure usually reduces clients to confused self-doubt. Well-indoctrinated clients rarely protest this pre-emptive tactic. They have learned that when their therapist corrects them, the issue at hand is one of unconscious motivation—and, obviously this makes the therapist *the* expert.

RESISTANCE

Analytic therapists expect clients to occasionally reject their interpretations. A client may not like what a therapist tells him about himself. He might emphatically deny any responsibility for creating his own distress. Or a client could want to cling to the status quo of his life, and avoid any necessity for change. Client responses such as these are called "resistance."

Analytic assumptions about resistance also support the therapist's reputation as an infallible expert. If clients disagree with the interpretations of their therapist, analytic theory assumes they are merely exhibiting their maladjustments. The therapist rarely—if ever—is wrong. Some clients just persist in self-deception and demonstrate it in their resistance.

Analytic therapists deal with client resistance via resistance interpretations. Clients are told that they are resisting the therapist's influence, and they are told why they are engaging in such resistance. Because of the insight they supposedly facilitate, resistance interpretations are considered effective for reducing client resistance. The therapist assumes that once a client understands his resistance, it will dissipate.

Analytic therapists regularly appoint themselves as the final authority in any differences of opinion with their clients. "Good" clients, who respond to resistance interpretations with appropriate awe and appreciation, are treated more charitably by analytic therapists. Supposedly resistant clients, who do not properly appreciate a therapist's wisdom, are not treated so charitably.

While analytic therapists credit themselves with the wisdom of a sage, resistant clients endure repeated reminders of how abysmally ignorant they supposedly are. Indeed, analytic therapists defend their self-appointed roles as experts with impressive tenacity. For example, consider the following dialogue between another analytic therapist and a client who was so bold as to question his wisdom.

> **Patient:** What you said about my being a latent homosexual doesn't click right with me. I mean I used to whittle sticks when I was a boy. After all, I was creating things out of the stick. I was carving it into a little boat mast or an arrow. So I think your interpretation is pretty wrong.
> **Therapist:** What it really is, is your own penis that you were cutting down.[3]

Unless this client responds more agreeably to his therapist's interpretations, he will endure more humiliating assaults on his self-esteem. The wise client learns not to dispute the self-conferred wisdom of an analytic therapist. Analytic therapy is structured so that clients rarely win these disputes.

MAY I KISS YOUR RING?

Obviously, this is not a therapy that advocates sharing and cooperation between peers involved in an egalitarian endeavor. Not only do analytic therapists unilaterally appoint themselves to the status of expert, they also expect clients to deferentially endorse their expert status. Clients who defy this expectation are told they are resisting what they need to understand. "Good" clients are also docile and obedient in their subordinate roles. They respond compliantly "yes, doctor; no, doctor; anything you say, doctor."

In fact, this writer has been guilty of using a misnomer throughout this chapter. Analytic therapists do not use the term "client;" they prefer the term "patient" (one might insist that "victim" is the most appropriate designation) This preference for "patient" underscores how analytic therapy can reduce clients to hesitant, self-doubting dependency.

The helpless dependency of clients complements their therapist's role as all-wise authority figure. The authoritarian features of this therapy are also reflected in the aloof style that analytic therapists insist is most appropriate for their work. They maintain a rather formal, emotionally distant relationship which they expect clients to understand and accept.

Analytic therapists expect clients to seek their acceptance and approval, but they rarely nurture or reassure them. Otherwise, they would regard themselves as indulging the childish immaturities of their clientele. When clients demand that their therapist abandon his distant role, this is called a "transference relationship."

Analytic therapists regard transference phenomena as absolutely essential events. Transference relationships supposedly reflect the dynamics of other unresolved conflicts in a client's day-to-day existence. For example, consider a male client, in his late twenties, who exhibits problems relating to older, male authority figures. It is expected that this client will bring those same problems into the therapy relationship.

As in cases of resistance, the therapist deals with transference issues via transference interpretations. A client is told that his need for acceptance and approval from the therapist is unrealistic, and that he moreover responds to other people in the same unrealistic manner. Not only do transference interpretations supposedly reduce client transference; presumably, they also assist a client in resolving other problems in his life.

CONTEMPORARY STATUS OF ANALYTIC PSYCHOTHERAPY

Occasionally articles in the popular media tout the "new" psychotherapies; but analytic therapy still enjoys substantial influence.

A 1983 survey of clinical psychologists indicated that 43 percent were analytically oriented in their therapeutic practices.[4] The analytic orientation was clearly the most preferred orientation. The second and third preferred orientations were endorsed by twenty-two percent and nineteen percent of the psychologists. At the very least, one must admire the resilience of analytic therapy. Like the proverbial Timex, "It may take a licking, but it keeps on ticking."

Analytic therapy can be most compellingly indicted because of its deeply entrenched resistance to change. R. R. Greenson, a well respected analyst, has noted that most contemporary discussions of analytic technique are antiquated; they draw upon papers that Freud published more than 70 years ago.[5] Over the past thirty years, analytic therapy has drifted away from the mainstream of the behavioral sciences. Far too many analytic therapists remain oblivious to the research that seriously questions the appropriateness of their techniques.

Indeed, analytic therapy is in jeopardy of deteriorating into an isolated cult. Analytic therapists can confine their professional lives to enrolling in their own training institutes, attending their own meetings, and reading their own journals. Insulated in this manner, they reassure each other that the more contemporary issues in the field (about which they only occasionally overhear) are irrelevant to their "deeper, more intensive" therapeutic work.

This kind of insulation defends the analytic community from even acknowledging, yet responding to, the crises in psychotherapy practice that demand a profound paradigm shift. As a result, analytic therapists are not about to substantially change the therapeutic practices that can be so damaging to their clientele.

At this point in time, many people assume that analytic therapy is merely an anachronism. For example, Haley has insisted, "As a force in the world of ideas, psychoanalysis died in 1957 and the funeral goes on in large cities, but I don't think it is an effective force any more."[6] As much as many might wish that this were so, reports of this system's demise are premature and indicative of wishful thinking.

As recently as 1989, the American Psychological Association celebrated a judicial verdict that allowed psychologists to enroll in analytic training institutes. Previously, only psychiatrists could undertake this kind of training (it should be clarified that this situation did not discourage many psychologists from zealously embracing analytic therapy). The enthusiasm with which psychologists applauded this development is bewildering; it makes as much sense as pharmacists advocating a return to snake oil.

THE REASON BEHIND ANALYTIC THERAPY

Despite its pervasive flaws, analytic therapy remains prominent and influential. There is a seductive logic about this therapy that is attractive to all people who prefer to regard themselves as clear-thinking, rational, and decisive.

It is altogether appealing to expect that the most distinctive of human characteristics—man's capacity to reflect about his own existence—is the vehicle to emancipate us from psychological distress. This is the kind of appeal that many people find so seductive. Any opportunity to celebrate wisdom's triumph over ignorance is always tempting and difficult to resist.

There are some clients who regard their long term, analytic therapy as a positive experience. The "good" analytic client has lived a life style where deferred gratification, while involved in some cerebral endeavor (such as undergraduate, graduate, and/ or professional school education) has been regarded as a necessary rite of passage. Ordeals, in general, are familiar to such a client; and the requirements of analytically oriented therapy are particularly familiar ordeals.

Often, "good" clients are motivated to avoid the responsibilities of adulthood. At one point in their lives, they become professional students; this endeavor effectively postpones the assumption of adult independence. At another point in time, they elect to undergo intensive analytic therapy, which can further postpone the assumption of adult responsibility—"I will have to wait on that decision until after my therapy is terminated." Indeed, clients who are inclined to can remain in analytic therapy as long as the maintenance of their self-doubt requires it.

9

Nothing changes more than the past; for the past that influences our lives does not consist of what actually happened, but of what men believe happened.

—GERALD W. JOHNSON

ANALYTIC THERAPY: THE FAILURES OF INSIGHT

Above all else, analytic therapy invites clients to understand themselves; but its formally engraved and elaborate invitations arouse expectations far beyond what it delivers.

Therapists who embrace analytic therapy cling to an unrequited infatuation with insight. They remain deeply entrenched in their assumption that insight must precede changes in behavior. The absence of experimental evidence to verify this assumption rarely tarnishes the reputation that insight enjoys in analytic circles.

Preoccupied with the pursuit of insight, analytic therapy disregards the everyday concerns of a client's real life. Here and now considerations of how effectively a client functions are ignored as irrelevant. Instead, obscure fantasies and esoteric insights consume the time and attention of client and therapist. A client who had been well-indoctrinated in this manner reportedly insisted, "I wish my wife and kids would just go away. They're interfering with my analysis."[1]

Important means-ends distinctions about

61

therapy had become sorely confused for this man. *Therapy is most appropriately the means toward some end; it is not an end in and of itself.* It also seems reasonable to expect therapy to enhance relationships with spouse and children. Following our guidelines for a new paradigm, therapy should not promote the deterioration of those relationships. Unfortunately, too many analytic therapists remain indifferent to concerns such as these.

Because of its obsession with insight, analytic therapy reduces its clientele to little more than cerebral beings who ponder ambiguous issues. Clients respond to vague questions, in pursuit of elusive answers, while seeking the supposed benefits of insight. At best, these endeavors are irrelevant to the resolution of a client's psychological distress; and at worst, they are counterproductive.

WHY: THE ETERNAL QUESTION

In their pursuit of insight, analytic therapists are determined to dissect the mental experiences of their clients. Thus, they become preoccupied with questions of "why," which they use as scalpels. Analytic therapy involves endlessly speculative questions such as: "I wonder why you really said that to your wife; why do you think you thought that about your mother; and could that mean you were actually feeling sexual interest, and if so, why?"

For clients, contending with questions of "why" is similar to growing mushrooms; one is kept in the dark and inundated with material politely called fertilizer. Bewildered by the esoteric topics on which they are cross-examined, clients struggle with escalating feelings of confusion.

The obscurity of "why" questions typically prevents clients from finding satisfactory answers. As clients stumble disorientedly in response to these circular queries, analytic therapists smugly enjoy their appearance of expertise. In the following example, the therapist persistently encouraged the client to doubt himself.

> **Therapist:** Tell me why you saw Paula last night.
> **Patient:** Oh I don't know. Just decided to, I guess.
> **Therapist:** Just decided?
> **Patient:** Well, Paula's OK. Why not Paula?

Therapist: The question is why Paula.
Patient: I really don't know.
Therapist: Think about it for a minute. It could be important.[2]

The critic of this procedure explained: "With each suggestion from Therapist that Patient 'think about it,' Patient grows more apprehensive about the importance of an unanswered question which may change his entire therapeutic history."[3] When analytic therapy creates these kinds of self-doubts, clients often conclude that their treatment must continue until such questions are answered. Analytic therapists, of course, are more than ready to applaud these conclusions.

Answers to questions of "why," even when available and valid, are irrelevant to effective therapy. These answers do not offer any course of action to resolve a client's distress. While analytic therapists may find questions of "why" intellectually stimulating for themselves, those questions disregard the needs of their clients.

Do Insights Solve Problems?

Too often, client problems stubbornly defy the supposed benefits of insight. For example:

> A woman who had been in counseling for over seven years, several times a week, claims to have derived greater insight, mastery, and comfort. She likes her therapy and feels better for being in it. But there has been no improvement in the problem she went in with—unsatisfactory relationships with men—and in some ways it is worse. Though she has accumulated greater understanding of her relationships with men, and though she has explored her entire childhood and all her encounters with men over and over again, she has been unable to use her knowledge to any positive end.[4]

Another critic of analytic therapy cited the case of a thirty-five-year-old male bed-wetter who was treated by Freud himself. After seven years of analytic therapy, a friend of this client inquired:

Friend: How's the analysis coming?

Client: Wonderful, very helpful indeed.
Friend: Have you stopped wetting the bed?
Client: No. But now I know why I do it.[5]

Examples such as these illustrate the irrelevance of insight to successful outcome in psychotherapy. Assuming that insight develops into specific behavior changes is a devout act of analytic faith. Analytic journals are littered with reports of clients whose distressed behavior persists despite their impressive insights.

Because analytic therapy insists that insight precede changes in behavior, it reduces its clientele to intellectual passivity. Clients are required to ponder and ruminate about their problems in the pursuit of insight. Pondering and ruminating, however, discourage clients from undertaking specific courses of action that could alleviate their problems.

In analytic therapy, questions of "why" encourage orgies of conjecture that incessantly breed more questions. The staggering number of unanswerable questions that ensues can fuel this circular activity indefinitely. When psychotherapy is organized around questions of "why," treatment proceeds in an almost never-ending, ad infinitum manner that approaches ad nauseam. As a result, the length of analytic therapy is sometimes measured in decades.

Health insurance companies commonly review the appropriateness of long-term psychotherapy. In one study, ninety percent of the cases needing review involved analytic therapists.[6] Half of the clients whose cases were under review saw their therapist between two and four times per week. The average client had accumulated 280 therapy sessions at the time of review. At least one client had been in therapy for 720 sessions.

These statistics suggest that analytic therapy can become a part-time job for some clients, or at least a very serious avocation for others. One must ask, if such therapy takes that long, can it be that effective? Beyond the first ten to fifteen sessions, there is no research evidence indicating that long-term therapy promotes any greater benefit than shorter term, more problem-focused therapy. Analytic therapists, however, are not deterred by such research.

The analytic therapist can always find another dream to examine, another fantasy to analyze, or another insight to explore. Long-term therapy, however, rarely serves the welfare of clients effectively. Too often, it encourages client dependency via a compensatory relationship (see Chapter Four). Clients who find themselves trapped in this potentially never-ending endeavor just might be underwriting the college education of a therapist's first-born child.

IS THE PAST MORE IMPORTANT THAN THE PRESENT?

Analytic therapists vehemently insist that the causes of psychological distress inhere in the formative history of their clients. Specifically, these therapists focus on the emotional conflicts of a client's childhood which remain supposedly unresolved. For example, one analytic therapist has emphasized:

> . . . the way to understanding remains unchanged. As in all that has gone before, understanding comes only after the early injurious influences have been laid bare and their effects on the past and present of the patient have been revealed.[7]

The limited accuracy with which analytic therapists make their historical interpretations is another limitation of this therapy. As Johnson's quote in this chapter heading emphasizes: The subjective, emotional past of all individuals is forever changing—all people are inclined to distort their interpretation of past events.

The existing research, regarding the intellectual development of children from birth to age six, also challenges the validity of historical interpretations in analytic therapy. This research indicates that adults cannot accurately recall meaningful events from that period of their lives.[8]

The inherent limitations of human memory prevent analytic therapists from determining what *actually* happened in a client's past. They can only interpret what they *believe* to have transpired in a client's history.[9] These intuitive impressions cannot be verified via any objective, reliable procedure; such procedures simply do not exist. The unavailability of such procedures poses burdensome problems for this therapeutic orientation. Too many of its historical interpretations qualify as wholesale speculation.

The analytic emphasis on personal history also suffers a particular bias. Analytic therapy not only focuses on the past, it preoccupies itself with traumas that allegedly occurred then. Analytic therapists persistently cross-examine their clients until they discover some event that qualifies as a formative trauma. As a result, clients may unwittingly invent some trauma to satisfy the theoretical convictions of their therapist.

Because of its bias, this therapy focuses minimal interest on formative experiences that have been positive and constructive. Rather than identify the psychological strengths and resources of its clients, it vigorously probes them for any evidence of maladjustment or pathology.

The case of a married female attorney in her thirties who sought the services of an analytic therapist provides an excellent illustration of the biases inherent in analytic therapy. In the very first session, the therapist was determined to obtain information about her client's major emotional relationships from birth to age six. This historical focus ignored the more contemporary status of her strengths.

By the age of thirty, she had earned two college degrees was a practicing attorney, was married, and had four children. Given this client's personal legacy of competence and achievement, her early childhood could not have been entirely traumatic. In fact, there was likely a great deal about her formative experiences that were positive and constructive.

Considerations of theory, however, led this therapist to disregard the client's history of competence and ignore significant events in her present-day life. At the end of this client's first session, the therapist knew virtually nothing about her husband, his occupation, his family background, or his education.

In the second session, the client disclosed a pattern of conflicts with her mother-in-law. She described her mother-in-law as " . . . the most castrating woman I've ever seen."[10] In the third session, the client reported a history of migraine headaches. She explained, "They began when I had our second child and Will's [her husband's] parents were visiting, staying with us."[11] In the fourth session, the client reported a pattern of conflicts between herself and her husband. She explained, "With my husband, if I want to argue or say something, I'm always afraid of getting him into trouble. When alone, I can be definite, outspoken, but with my husband, I wait for him to talk."[12]

Likely, contemporary conflicts undermined this client's welfare. Conflicted with her mother-in-law and alienated from her husband, one wonders what she did for emotional support? An effective therapist would have pulled this client and her husband into a closer alliance with each other.

Once closely allied, husband and wife would have been coached to obtain endorsement for their marriage from the husband's mother. Committed to the same goal, the client and her husband would have been motivated to support and encourage each other. Consequently, resolution of her contemporary conflicts would have enhanced this client's psychological welfare.

The theoretical dogma of analytic therapy, however, left this therapist preoccupied with the client's formative history. Unfortunately, these historical issues were superfluous compared to her more contemporary problems.

IGNORING CLIENT NEEDS

In the thirteenth session of therapy, the client explained:

> **Patient:** . . . I don't know how father ever paid for our education. When he needed money for our tuition, he would sell a few cattle and then in time replace them. When I was to leave for college, 80 cattle died and mother said I couldn't go, but father said I could and would go. Somehow he managed. We all worked summers. When Roberta [the client's sister] wanted a dress, she'd give blood to get the money. This is why I feel guilt—to be hostile to father after all he sacrificed.

> **Analyst:** We'll have to work on getting rid of this guilt and hostility.[13]

This client's perceptions of her father were balanced and reasonably objective. She could appreciatively acknowledge his sacrifices and support of her in the past. The client wanted to know what she could do to improve her relationship with her father. Her therapist, however, wanted her to "talk about" her feelings of hostility and guilt.

An effective therapist would have praised this client; she demonstrated the capacity to relate to her father compassionately. She should have been asked if her father knew how much she appreciated his previous encouragements? What would happen if she wrote him a letter thanking him for his past support? Surely, her father would feel deeply moved and very proud in response to such a letter. In turn, a daughter who enjoys the affection of a proud father experiences a special closeness with him. This kind of closeness rapidly diminishes feelings of guilt and hostility.

This therapist, however, disregarded the client's needs. Because he wanted her to understand her feelings, she was discouraged from initiating any course of action to resolve those feelings. Obligated *to think* about her insights, she was unable *to do* anything about her problems. This preoccupation with insight creates a phenomenon often called "paralysis via analysis."

Determined to pursue insight, analytic therapists immobilize a client's capacity to undertake constructive courses of action. Rather than assist their clients to solve their problems, they expect them to prostrate themselves before an altar of "enlightened understanding." Unfortunately, legions of analytic therapists sacrifice the psychological welfare of too many clients at that altar.

EXPLORATION OF MENTAL EXPERIENCES

Because of her therapist's indoctrination, the female attorney eventually lost the pragmatic, problem-solving attitude she had exhibited in the thirteenth session. For more than 140 sessions, treatment responded to therapist's agenda, rather than meeting the client's needs. In the 143rd session, the therapist said:

> **Analyst:** To continue the review, let's begin this hour by talking about how the pattern to mother operates in your present life.

> **Patient:** I thought that my cat phobia was all related to father, but now I think it is to mother because since we've gone into the feelings toward mother, it has greatly decreased. I think I was hostile to mother, not to father; and when father shot the tomcat for scratching Roberta, I thought: That is how one gets punished for hostility.

The cat scratched Roberta and Mabel was the one who told father about it. She told him the cat had nearly killed Roberta but actually the cat hardly even touched her. The poor cat. He had an open wound on his thigh and Roberta stepped on it accidentally. The cat's reaction was only natural. Afterward, father was angry at Mabel. Roberta has often been scratched by cats, three or four times, so she fears them too. So I think the cats represented my hostility to mother. They probably represent this today also in maybe all my hostilities. But, I also like cats, I displace all sorts of emotions. I couldn't show mother much love and affection either, so I showed it to the cats and dogs and somewhat to the animals. So if I put so much emotion into an animal, my love needs were more satisfied by the animals than by my mother. I was constantly with them. The ranch was big, and I had no playmates except the animals.[14]

First of all, any reader who diligently read every word of the previous monologue deserves accolades for remarkable persistence. Those who only skimmed it, finding it trivial and boring, deserve applause for impressive judgement.

Tempting as it is to ridicule this client for her trivial ruminations, it should be remembered that she had been well-indoctrinated by her analytic therapist. Outside of analytic therapy, this client's behavior qualifies as ruminating obsessiveness. Within analytic therapy, obsessiveness is considered necessary and desirable in the pursuit of insight.

Because of their unique talents for rationalization, analytic therapists can elevate ruminating obsessiveness to the status of a reputable endeavor. If a client is not preoccupied with the trivial and obscure before analytic therapy, he will likely be so preoccupied by the time he terminates it.

This client had also been well-indoctrinated about the significance of symbolism in analytic therapy. From a symbolic perspective, nothing a client says or reports can be taken at face value. Instead, almost any event or object that a client discusses is regarded as symbolic of something else.

In the previously cited example, the client's cat phobia was allegedly symbolic of her hostility toward her mother. Her memory of her father shooting the cat was supposedly symbolic of punishment. The client's affection for animals presumably symbolized her frustrated needs for parental affection and attention. However fascinating such conjecture may be for novelists, for legions of would be novelists, and for all of us who enjoy a good story, these symbolic interpretations were not verified by any independent evidence.

In formulating their symbolic interpretations, analytic therapists do not rely on any body of scientific research to verify them; such research simply does not exist. More than anything else, symbolic interpretations reflect the personal idiosyncrasies of the therapists who indulge in them. Ten different analytic therapists could make ten different interpretations of the same dream, thought or fantasy.

Describing the symbolic interpretations of analytic therapy as speculative is almost charitable. Despite the frequency with which analytic therapists invoke the phrase "the science of psychoanalysis," the terms "science" and "psychoanalysis" are best considered mutually exclusive.

Admittedly, there are instances where analytic therapists demonstrate agreement in their symbolic interpretations. For example, they interpret dreams about water as indicating a desire to return to the warm, watery environment of the womb. Despite the consensus between analytic therapists regarding the interpretation of a few universal symbols, this does not confer any degree of validity upon those interpretations. Such consensus merely reflects the clinical lore, passed from one generation of analytic therapists to the next, over the course of their training.

Even this brief overview indicates that analytic therapy fails to meet the minimum guidelines we established for a new paradigm. Insight prevails as the goal of treatment, and well-defined courses of action are neglected. Analytic therapy overlooks important features of the client's interpersonal relationships. And perhaps worst of all, analytic therapists set the standard of arrogance in their field. In many ways, humanistic therapy evolved to counter the cold and accusatory methods of Freudian doctrine.

10

"The most melancholy of human reflections, perhaps, is that on the whole it is a question whether the benevolence of mankind does most good or harm."

—WALTER BAGEHOT

CLIENT CENTERED-HUMANISTIC PSYCHOTHERAPY:

THERAPY AS ART

Carl Rogers published his best-known book, *Client-Centered Therapy*, in 1951. Over the next three decades, his client centered philosophy increasingly influenced psychotherapy practice and research. Additionally, the impact of Rogerian theory has extended beyond psychotherapy. Rogerian concepts have influenced educational philosophy in our school systems, personnel practices in some corporations, and guidance methods of school counselors.

At the time that Rogers published his 1951 book, analytic thinking dominated psychotherapy theory and practice. His dissatisfaction with analytic therapy motivated the development of his own system. Rogers disavowed analytic therapy because he considered it cold, impersonal, and excessively intellectualized. He regarded analytic therapy as unwilling to fully acknowledge the emotional domain of human experience.

For Rogers, emotionality is a positive experience that enhances the human condition.

71

He would insist that emotion provides the joy and celebration of human existence. Unlike analytic therapists, Rogers refused to condemn emotionality as a disruptive source of psychological problems. Most of all, he rejected the analytic position that intellect should regulate emotional experience.

Rogers' client-centered system was the first major theory of psychotherapy developed in the United States, and it reflects many of the core, democratic values of our culture. Rogers emphasized that therapists should relate to their clients as equals. Because he refused to reduce his clientele to a subordinate status, Rogers categorically rejected the term "patient;" he preferred the term "client."

Rogers also emphatically disavowed the bleak, pessimistic assessment of the human condition endorsed by most analytic therapists. His more positive, optimistic view corresponds to American culture's faith in the potential of mankind. For example, Rogers emphasized:

> One of the most revolutionary concepts to grow out of our clinical experiences is the growing recognition that the innermost core of man's nature, the deepest layers of his personality, the base of his "animal nature" is positive in nature—is basically socialized, forward-moving, rational and realistic.[1]

For Rogers, people develop psychological distress when they deny their feelings and emotions to avoid the anxiety aroused by acknowledging them. Rogerians emphasize that many clients preoccupy themselves with considerations of what they should experience. Simultaneously, they disregard what they really experience. As a result, Rogerians distrust intellectual processes. Rogers, himself, emphasized:

> One of the basic things which I was a long time in realizing, and which I am still learning, is that when an activity *feels* as though it is valuable or worth doing, it *is* worth doing. Put another way, I have learned that my total organismic sensing of a situation is more trustworthy than my intellect.[2]

Because of such sentiments, this theory has been criticized for its anti-intellectual bias. At the very least, client-centered therapists reject intellectual goals such as insight. Rather than pursue understanding, they are determined to promote emotional awareness. Clients are expected to look deep within themselves to identify supposedly inhibited feelings and emotions. Thus, Rogerians encourage their clients to develop greater capacities for introspection. Presumably, introspection facilitates what this theory calls "moment-to-moment awareness." Client-centered therapy focuses on the moment-to-moment status of a client's feelings. Clients are encouraged to share the depth and intensity of their feelings with their therapist. The depth and intensity with which these feelings are shared supposedly enhances emotional awareness. Rogers labeled this awareness "the experiencing of experience," and described it as a process where . . .

> . . . the client can let himself examine various aspects of his experience as they actually feel to him, as they are apprehended through his sensory and visceral equipment, without distorting them to fit the existing concept of self.[3]

THE THERAPEUTIC RELATIONSHIP

Client-centered therapists assume the responsibility for creating a safe, accepting relationship with their clientele. They insist that judgmental, disapproving therapists inhibit any client's capacity for introspection. Consequently, this system of therapy emphasizes the need to establish a "therapeutic relationship" with clients.

In a therapeutic relationship, a therapist consistently expresses empathy, congruence, and warmth. An "empathic" therapist perceives the experience of a client with such accuracy that he might almost be the client. Clients who regard their therapist as empathic feel understood by him. A "congruent" therapist accurately and effectively communicates his thoughts and feelings to his clientele. Clients describe a congruent therapist as sincere and genuine. Therapist "warmth" is exhibited to the extent that a client feels his therapist accepts him, and is committed to his welfare as a person.

Additionally, client-centered theorists emphasize that therapists should demonstrate empathy, congruence, and warmth, in an unconditional manner. Unconditionality requires that therapists maintain high levels of these conditions independent of how their clients respond.

Massive numbers of research studies have verified the absolute importance of these therapeutic conditions. Most therapists, regardless of theoretical orientation, agree: Effective psychotherapy necessitates an appropriate client-therapist relationship.[4] Until client-centered therapists examined these relationship factors via controlled research studies, there was no evidence available to verify any effectiveness of psychotherapy. Without their research, psychotherapy might have remained entirely lost in a tangle of theories and speculation.

Client-centered therapists assume that once the conditions of a therapeutic relationship exist, a client's awareness of formerly inhibited feelings increases. As a result, energy previously used to deny feelings is available for more constructive purposes. When he no longer maintains a vigilant guard over his feelings, a client lives a fuller, more satisfying life.

The presence of a therapist's empathy, congruence, and warmth also encourages increases in client self-acceptance. Presumably, clients enjoy elevated levels of self-acceptance because they imitate a therapist's acceptance of themselves. It is also assumed that clients decrease their dependency on others to verify their self-worth. As a result, they supposedly develop greater independence and autonomy.

The therapeutic conditions of empathy, congruence, and warmth are defined as both necessary and sufficient to facilitate therapeutic progress. The necessary and sufficient status of the these conditions means that once a client-centered therapist has established them, he needs only to maintain them. From then on, therapy proceeds in a client-centered manner, and the therapist assumes a non-directive role.

Non-directive therapists are disinclined to directly influence the course or focus of therapy. Otherwise, they fear they could compromise a client's sense of independence. Thus, clients supposedly determine the course and focus of their therapy. If they have established the proper therapeutic conditions, client-centered therapists trust their clients to move in a positive direction.

The following dialogue, between a CC-H supervisor and supervisee, illustrates their preoccupation with a therapeutic relationship.

Supervisor: Ed, how do you see D's therapy going?
Supervisee: Well, let's see. D seems less afraid to show and share her feelings now.
Supervisor: What leads you to that conclusion?
Supervisee: Well, she is less uptight. Has been for the last couple of sessions. (Pause) And she has been revealing more material that's close to her, tough to talk about.
Supervisor: So you see therapy moving toward D's bringing more of her important feelings up with you?
Supervisee: Uh-huh.[5]

The previous dialogue underscores how client-centered therapists regard the client-therapist relationship as an end in itself. Unfortunately, this dialogue reflects no concerns about the ultimate value to the client of "revealing more material." The supervisor and supervisee seemed pleased that this client was "less afraid to show and share her feelings." There was no consideration, however, of how such "showing and sharing" would alleviate her distress; nor was there any discussion of what motivated this client to seek treatment. Perhaps such oversights correspond to a level of conceptual sophistication that describes clients as "less uptight."

Humanistic Therapy

Rogers influenced the development of other therapy methods that share his emphasis on feeling and emotion. But unlike traditional client-centered procedures that emphasize increased awareness of feelings, the newer methods press clients to dramatically express their feelings in order to ventilate them. These more recently developed techniques are typically defined as "humanistic." A phenomenological approach that emphasizes the moment-to-moment status of a client's feelings is the most important characteristic shared by client-centered and humanistic techniques.

Given the paramount significance of feelings for these therapeutic systems, the ultimate source of those feelings—the body or the soma—is exceedingly important for humanistic therapists. Proponents of humanistic therapy emphasize, "We are a people largely dissociated from our bodies and terrified of feeling or movement that occurs in our bodies."[6]

Humanistic therapists are determined to correct this supposedly deplorable state of affairs. They pursue this end by promoting greater awareness of emotional experiences at a somatic level. Awareness such as this is preferred over any kind of intellectual awareness. Thinking is regarded as an experience that interferes with a client's intuitive feelings. Many humanistic therapists would agree that it is desirable for clients "to lose your mind and come to your senses."[7]

Finally, these therapists function in a more directive manner than Rogerians. It is common for humanistic therapists to specify exactly what is expected from clients in the course of therapy.

CHARISMATIC THEAPISTS

Above all else, therapists of both schools—from now on we will refer to client-centered and humanistic therapists with the abbreviation "CC-H"—are committed to pursuing emotionally close relationships with their clientele. They consider the personal qualities of a therapist more important than any techniques he employs. Characteristics like "existential authenticity" and "transparency of self" receive more emphasis than a therapist's technical skill. Presumably, an "authentic, transparent" therapist readily creates therapeutic relationships.*

CC-H therapists exhibit an abiding faith in the potentials of the therapeutic relationship. They are eminently confident that this relationship, in and of itself, resolves a client's problems. Rogers described a therapeutic relationship wherein . . .

> . . . my inner spirit has reached out and touched the inner spirit of the other [the client]. Our relationship transcends itself and has become a part of something larger. Profound growth and healing and energy are present."[8]

Any therapist who uses his "inner spirit" to promote "profound growth and healing" must be a charismatic figure. While

---

*The reader may have noticed that the terms "authentic" and "transparent" are not defined. Nevertheless, be reassured that no one knows what they really mean. CC-H therapists use these terms primarily because they sound authoritative.

CC-H therapists regularly disregard what a therapist should *do*, they nonetheless expect him to *be* charismatic. Moreover, any therapist who relies on his "inner spirit" to "reach out and touch" sounds more committed to faith-healing than psychotherapy. CC-H therapists often confuse these endeavors with each other. Their preoccupation with "healing" and "energy" can cause them to overlook pragmatic considerations of their therapeutic effectiveness.

Beyond their obligatory charisma lessons, CC-H theorists feel there is little else for therapists to learn. Consequently, CC-H supervisors are inclined to tell trainees, "You don't have to do anything—just be." Many graduate programs in humanistic psychology are deeply committed to nurturing the charisma of their students; simultaneously, they neglect to develop students' therapeutic competence.

For example, there is one humanistic psychology program that would readily enroll a 40-year-old-plus salesman, with little background in the behavioral sciences and no therapeutic experience, and apparently train him as a competent therapist in one calendar year. Presumably, he mastered "existential authenticity" and "transparency of self" with impressive zeal.

Beginning therapists often find CC-H philosophy attractive; it encourages them to indulge in a reassuring assumption: Effective therapists are characterized not by *what* they *do*, but by *who* they *are*. In other words, neophytes can disregard their limited experience as long as they qualify as authentic.

CC-H Therapy And Isolation

Like analytic therapists, CC-H therapists are also in jeopardy of developing into an isolated cult. There was a long period of time, in the 1950s, 1960s, and early 1970s, when CC-H thinking was found in the mainstream of psychotherapy research and theory. CC-H therapists conducted the research programs that identified the relationship between psychotherapy outcome and the client-therapist relationship. Since that time, however, CC-H therapists have rested on their laurels.

Now, CC-H therapists are isolating themselves from contemporary developments in psychotherapy. They enroll in their own training institutions, attend their own meetings and conventions, and read their own journals. Consequently, CC-H therapists have effectively barricaded themselves from influences outside of their own theoretical domain.

In their choice of career, most CC-H therapists are motivated by a sincere commitment to helping psychologically distressed individuals. It is understandable that they are attracted to a system that advocates respect for clients and promotes a peer-like relationship between client and therapist.

In commenting upon a similarly benevolent concern for the welfare of mankind, Winston Churchill once suggested that any man who has not become a socialist by the age of thirty has no heart. Churchill also observed that any man who continues to be a socialist after the age of forty has no head. Correspondingly, any therapist who has not identified with CC-H philosophy, at least in the early stages of his career, does not feel much. But any therapist who single-mindedly embraces CC-H theory as his experience accumulates does not think much.

CC-H therapists tend to be benevolent, well intentioned individuals. Nevertheless, they limit their levels of conceptual sophistication because of their distrust of intellectual processes. The remarkable naivete that CC-H therapists bring to their work profoundly limits their effectiveness, and alarmingly increases their chances of damaging clients. CC-H therapy is not as benign as it may appear. With regard to CC-H therapy, one must conclude that benevolence does more harm than good.

Competent therapists mature and evolve beyond an exclusive preoccupation with the conditions of a therapeutic relationship. They realize that while such a relationship is necessary, it is rarely sufficient to foster resolution of client distress. Effective therapy is more than an "art." Clients in therapy should be able to expect legitimately effective services. They should not have to endure some free-form emotional experience at the hands of a self-appointed artist.

11

One must not always think that feeling is everything. Art is nothing without form.

— GUSTAVE FLAUBERT

CLIENT CENTERED-HUMANISTIC THERAPY:

THE FAILURES OF INSPIRATION

CC-H therapy is a therapy of inspirational experience. CC-H therapists are to psychotherapy what evangelists are to religion. Consider the following therapy session where:

> . . . the therapist had experienced intense eye contact with the client. Suddenly there occurred in the therapist's stomach a sensation that he had become a part of the client's experience. It was as if the therapist and the client had left their bodies and were able to talk momentarily as transcended beings about the client's experience. This experience followed many sessions when the client had expressed wanting to feel understood. The client initiated more affective expression following this session.[1]

Visceral sensations shared with a therapist, while dissociated from one's body, certainly are inspirationally dramatic experi-

79

ences. While this previously quoted passage tempts one to assign therapeutic value to vertigo, it also raises the question of how long these effects last.

Clients can leave therapy sessions like the previous one feeling a profound sense of emotional inspiration. They can also experience this inspiration as immensely positive and gratifying. Unfortunately, such inspirationally induced changes in feeling evaporate all too quickly. Unless a client has been able to modify the life circumstances that distress him, his feelings gravitate back to familiar themes of pessimism and discouragement. Optimistic, positive feelings rapidly diminish in the face of distressing life circumstances that remain unchanged.

CC-H THERAPY: NICE IN THEORY

CC-H therapists fail to discriminate between conditions that are necessary for effective therapy and conditions that are sufficient. Logically, some condition may qualify as necessary for a particular outcome—but not, in and of itself, totally sufficient for that outcome. For example, oxygen is necessary for human life; but in and of itself, it is not sufficient.

Despite its importance, CC-H therapists regularly disregard this distinction. They ignore the likelihood that a therapeutic relationship is necessary—*but not sufficient*—for therapeutic progress. Consequently, CC-H therapists regard their responsibilities as limited to relationship formation.

CC-H therapists expect clients to embrace their enthusiasm for the joys and happiness of a therapeutic relationship. Simultaneously, they disregard the psychological welfare of their clientele. Clients expect resolution of the distress that motivated them to undertake psychotherapy; CC-H therapists only offer "existential encounters" in the pursuit of fond fellowship.*

CC-H therapists regard feelings as if they enjoy an existence all of their own, independent of a client's life circumstances. They fail to recognize that emotional experiences do not occur in a vacuum. In fact, emotional experiences respond to a client's perception of what is transpiring in significant sectors of his life.

---

* Admittedly, therapists of other orientations operate "rent-a-friend" agencies; but CC-H therapists act as if they own the franchise rights for those enterprises.

Feelings and emotions are basically feedback experiences. They provide information for the client about the effectiveness with which he is living his life. Quite simply, distressed people are responding to distressing life circumstances. If one's therapeutic goal is to change distressed feelings, then it is necessary to change the distressing life circumstances that cause those feelings. Unfortunately, however, too many CC-H therapists blithely ignore these considerations.

While neglecting their therapeutic responsibilities, CC-H therapists often seek to make clients over in their own image. They promote anti-intellectualism, effusive emotionality, and introspective self-preoccupation. As a result of CC-H therapy, the self-absorption of many clients leaves them oblivious to anything beyond their navels.

Self-centeredness bordering on narcissism is not the hallmark of a mature, well-adjusted individual. Clients need to realize their potential for responding empathically to other important people in their lives. Also, the capacity of clients to think and conceptualize deserves more than denigration.

THERAPY TO GET THE FEELINGS OUT

Because of their inspirational zeal, CC-H therapies include some procedures that will seem excessive to many. For example, primal analysis is a procedure that directs the attention of clients to their "emotional pain." This therapy encourages clients to "experience" that pain and "express it."

A primal therapist summarized the treatment of a 23 year old female:

> When Karen came for therapy, her chief complaints were being 100 pounds overweight, depressions with suicidal thoughts, and having to take care of many people in her life. . . . At the start of one session, I asked her to start lying on the mat in her most vulnerable position, which was on her back, begin to breathe deeply for a few minutes and then call for one of her parents. Since she began to call "Daddy," quietly, I urged her to shout his name louder and louder. . . . Within minutes, she was screaming with rage and anger at her father. At first her throat was closed and her screams choked.

Gradually, her throat opened and her voice deepened
as her anger and hate poured out.[2]

The therapist explained that as a result of these primal
procedures, the client developed awareness that he considered
impressive and significant: "She experienced the pain of the
realization that her father never loved her, and used her to take
care of him and her younger brother."[3]

One might legitimately ask how this therapist knew that the
client's father was so unloving and exploitative? The therapist
had never met the father; and he certainly never availed himself of any opportunity to observe the client and her father
interact. Nonetheless, this therapist confidently "knew" these
things about the client's father. The dogma of primal theory
afforded him this knowledge.

Primal theory dictates that all psychologically distressed
clients have been betrayed by the alleged incompetence of their
parents. The primal therapist insists that clients identify their
most intense feelings, and connect those feelings to one or both
parents. For example:

> ... If a patient is feeling hopeless he is told to hold one
> of his parents responsible, the one who made the child
> of his past feel hopeless; if a patient feels like crying but
> cannot, he is told to tell that in therapy to the parent
> that is responsible [the parent is not actually in the
> session]; if a patient does not feel like doing any work in
> therapy, he is asked to talk to the parent that does not
> want him to change or express his feelings; and, if a
> patient states how poorly he relates to others, he is told
> to tell that to the parent that made it difficult for him to
> relate to himself, and therefore to others.[4]

Given the primal therapist's convictions about the inevitabil-
ity of parental betrayal, therapy merely focuses on finding the
proper details to verify these *a priori* assumptions. Anyone who
doubts the facility of primal therapists to ferret out such details
is seriously underestimating their zeal. This therapy is determined to subject the parents of clients to the most vicious kind
of character assassination.

One can only shudder at the long-term future consequences
for clients who are treated in this manner. Once a therapist

engages in these cruel, irresponsible indictments of a client's parents, how will that client relate to his family in the future? What is the likelihood of such a client ever enjoying mutually supportive relationships with his family? After they dismantle any harmony or trust that a client might enjoy with his family, are primal therapists prepared to adopt that client? Seeking answers for these questions from a primal therapist is little more than an invitation for self-serving rationalizations.

This is a therapy that actively encourages clients to regress in a childlike manner. Regression rarely enhances any client's maturity or sense of responsibility. If yesterday's and today's problems are the fault of a client's parents, who will the client learn to blame for tomorrow's problems?

As a result of this therapy, clients can conclude that the only trustworthy person left on the face of the earth is their primal therapist. While such a conclusion may inflate a therapist's ego, it does not bode well for the welfare of clients.

Understandably, many people are tempted to dismiss the credibility of primal therapy via humor. Some critics have described primal techniques as "screaming your way to maturity." Nevertheless, these techniques demand more serious scrutiny. The potential of primal therapy to seriously damage clients is far too pronounced.

How Does It Feel?

Other CC-H therapists insist that because the ultimate source of all feelings is the body, clients should establish a greater familiarity with their physiques. Experiential movement psychotherapy seeks to increase a client's awareness of his physical self—his "bodily felt level experience." Many CC-H therapists enthusiastically endorse these kinds of procedures. They supposedly afford clients the opportunity to release emotional tension that has accumulated in some area of their bodies.

The client in the following case was a 36-year-old female who characteristically related to others in a detached, aloof manner. She felt compelled to maintain substantial emotional distance between herself and others. People who expected more closeness than she could tolerate rapidly elevated her anxiety level. Her therapist conducted the following session of experiential movement therapy:

Elaine, 36, began her individual movement psychotherapy session by lying quietly on her back. Her arms
and legs outstretched; her eyes were closed. After a
while, her eyes still closed, she rose to standing and
began to pace back and forth exhibiting two different
movement patterns. When she approached one end of
the room, she moved slowly, stumbling as though drunk
without seeming direction. As she moved toward the
other end of the room, her movement picked up mo-
mentum. Her pace became rapid and direct. She stomped
loudly on the ground as she moved. Her movement
pattern seemed to take on the quality of two distinctive
human forms. She was encouraged to visualize these
two forms until they became clear in her mind's eye
(the forms which emerged spontaneously were a floppy
rag doll and a stubborn, petulant young child). When
Elaine was clear as to the configuration of these two
characters she was asked to identify with each of these
forms in turn and to explore the relationship which she
could develop between them through movement. When
she completed this movement-image exploration, she
verbalized her experience.[5]

When examined closely, it becomes clear and evident that
experiential movement exercises are little more than inspirational theatrics. These exercises generate dramatic topics which
client and therapist can talk about intensely. Nevertheless, it is
difficult to understand how these exercises can resolve conflicts
about interpersonal closeness.

Client and therapist *may* achieve greater closeness with
each other as they discuss the dramatic topics of the session.
There is no basis, however, for concluding that such closeness
in the session translates to the client's relationships outside the
session, but experiential movement exercises do satisfy all the
requirements to enjoy the status of a placebo.

A psychotherapeutic placebo requires clients to engage in
some kind of unusual activity. Common, everyday experiences
like reading the daily newspaper, or walking the dog, will not
suffice. Such experiences are too familiar, and they do not
create an atmosphere of dramatic intensity as a result of their
familiarity. Accelerated pacing back and forth across the room,

however, that is episodically punctuated by awkward stumbling, certainly does qualify as an unusual activity.

A placebo also requires that clients receive a plausible explanation summarizing the therapeutic value of the unusual activity. The opportunity to release emotional tension from some area of the body certainly sounds plausible. In this period of preoccupation with stress, who would dispute the virtue of decreasing tension?

CC-H Ordeals

CC-H therapists exhibit a pronounced affinity for inspirationally dramatic placebos. Consider a CC-H therapist who encourages clients to vigorously assault a pillow with a tennis racquet.* Simultaneously, clients are told to yell angry epithets to people who have allegedly betrayed them.

Outside the state of California, at least, this is an example of unusual behavior. An explanation about the value of "getting into those heavy feelings," in order to alleviate their burden, could qualify as the plausible-sounding rationale to justify this procedure. Finally, there are legions of CC-H therapists who would endorse such methods.

More than being a mere placebo, this procedure could also assume the status of an arduous ordeal. Imagine a client who is energetically slamming a pillow with an obligatory tennis racquet (no doubt using a John McEnroe signature model). Simultaneously, he is screaming vile statements about the ancestry of those people who have incurred his wrath. Also assume that the client has been continuously involved in these endeavors for approximately five to ten minutes.

The client is contending with fatigue that rapidly approaches depletion. He perspires profusely, aches and pains rack his body, and his chest heaves with labored breathing. When the client eventually collapses in temporary exhaustion, his therapist enthusiastically asks, "There, don't you feel better now?" Unless this client is completely possessed by exceedingly poor judgment, he is compelled to answer "yes." Except for being a masochistic fool, he no longer wants to pound a pillow.

Once the client says that he feels better, he and the therapist can congratulate each other on the supposed significance of this

---

*Because the therapist respects his own nondirective orientation, the type of grip that clients employ is optional.

breakthrough. In future sessions, the client will observe the tennis racquet in the therapist's office, vividly recall his previous ordeal, and quickly reassure the therapist that he feels at least "OK."

The potency of a placebo is enhanced by therapeutic experiences that are an ordeal. The client—and the therapist— expect that potent medicine brings about powerful cures. By telling a client, "Hey, man, that was heavy stuff," a CC-H therapist confirms the illusory powerfulness of these experiences. Not wanting to rain on their own self-congratulatory celebration, it is unlikely that client and therapist consider the relevance of this placebo experience to the client's real-life distress.

Placebo effects can be so potent that clients are compelled to regard themselves as making progress in therapy. They embrace this conclusion even when there is no evidence available to justify it. Moreover, CC-H therapists can come to the same unsubstantiated conclusions about client progress for the same reasons.

Therapists who are critical of CC-H philosophy question the counterproductiveness of therapeutic procedures such as these. These procedures encourage clients to practice and perfect displays of petulant immaturity. As a result, the CC-H therapist who indulges in them is in jeopardy of condoning the impulsive ventilation of angry feelings.

Subsequent to these kinds of therapy experiences, clients could assume they possess emotional license for throwing childish tantrums whenever they encounter frustration. From a client's point of view, the alleged desirability of "getting the feelings out" has been sanctioned by a credible authority. When such rationalizations are available to clients, they are disinclined to resolve their frustrations appropriately. Rather than take responsibility for their behavior, they can regress massively and yell childishly at the object of their frustration—and then justify their impulsiveness as a "therapeutic experience."

While CC-H therapies listen to clients with a warmer, more empathic ear, they still fall short of meeting our requirements for paradigm change. Their goals remain as amorphous as those of analytic therapy, and equally unrelated to the client's needs for problem resolution. While focusing with great intensity on the client-therapist relationship, CC-H procedures continue to isolate clients from the interpersonal spheres of their real lives.

12

I pass with relief from the tossing sea of Cause and Theory to the firm ground of Result and Fact.

—WINSTON CHURCHILL

BEHAVIOR THERAPY: SCIENCE AND PSYCHOTHERAPY

While analytic therapy and CC-H procedures evolved out of clinical experience with clients, behavior therapy developed differently. It originated from experimental work conducted in the laboratories of academic psychology. Behavior therapists reject the subjective, intuitive characteristics of analytic and CC-H therapy. They view those other orientations as poorly defined and lacking sufficient laboratory evidence to verify their effectiveness.

For behavior therapists, the clinical practice of psychotherapy requires the support of laboratory evidence. Behavior therapists have invested substantial time and energy in obtaining such evidence. Consequently, they insist that their procedures are more scientific and objective than other systems.

All behavior therapists assume that patterns of psychological distress have been learned. Correspondingly, they also assume that those patterns of distress can be unlearned. For the behavior therapist, psychological distress manifests itself in a client's overt behavioral responses. Some clients exhibit an excessive frequency of some response

87

(i.e., anxiety or guilt). Other clients exhibit a deficiency of a different response (i.e., self-confidence or assertiveness).

Most psychologically distressed clients exhibit both undesirable responses that are excessive, and desirable responses that are infrequent. Basically, behavior therapy involves procedures designed to eliminate some response or increase the frequency of some other response.

Stimulus control is a concept fundamental to behavior therapy. Behavior therapists define all behavior, whether normal or maladjusted, as controlled by some particular stimulus. The motorist who stops his vehicle at a red light, the smoker who craves a cigarette after a meal, and the adolescent male who is sexually aroused while reading *Playboy* magazine are all examples of responses controlled by some stimulus. Behavior therapists seek to modify the patterns of stimulus control that maintain a client's psychological distress.

When psychological distress is no longer exhibited in the presence of stimuli that formerly controlled it, the behavior therapist considers treatment successful. For example, a formerly anxious flyer now boards an airplane without debilitating anxiety. Or a previously self-doubting salesperson now exhibits poise and self-confidence as he makes his sales calls.

THE GOALS OF BEHAVIOR THERAPY

The previous examples also illustrate how behavior therapists prefer to define therapeutic goals. They specify their goals in terms of observable changes in a client's overt behavior. The changes in the behavior of the formerly anxious flyer, or the previously self-doubting salesperson, are tangible and readily observable. In contrast, behavior therapists reject therapeutic goals such as "enhanced ego strength" or "self-realization." They doubt that these goals can be defined so that therapist and client know when they have been achieved.

Behavior therapists select specific responses from a client, call them "target behaviors," and endeavor to modify them. Examples of such target behaviors include the anxiety of the anxious flyer, and the self-doubt of the discouraged salesperson. The course of behavior therapy consistently focuses on the modification of selected target behaviors. Behavior therapy does not meander to whatever topic suddenly captures the interest of therapist or client.

ORIGINS AND TECHNIQUES OF BEHAVIOR THERAPY

Behavior therapy reflects the influence of three different perspectives in research and clinical practice. First, the work of Joseph Wolpe, who developed systematic desensitization, originated behavior therapy. Second, the research of B. F. Skinner, examining the control of behavior via reinforcement, broadened the scope of behavior therapy. Finally, the contributions of Aaron Beck, focusing on the cognitive processes of clients, expanded the clinical applicability of behavior therapy.

Wolpe regarded anxiety as fundamental to the psychological distress of most people. For Wolpe, the task of effective psychotherapy is to substantially reduce or extinguish (eliminate) anxiety. In pursuit of this goal, Wolpe developed a procedure called systematic desensitization. This procedure blocks anxiety responses by replacing them with relaxation responses. A client learns to relax in those situations where he used to feel anxious. As a result, Wolpe's procedures are also called counterconditioning.

Systematic desensitization, or counterconditioning, uses an anxiety hierarchy that is organized in a step-wise manner. For an anxious flyer, the hierarchy's first step might address the anxiety he experiences when he makes his flight reservations. In the final step of the hierarchy, the client could be seated on a plane as it takes off from a runway. Depending on the needs of the client, and the judgment of the behavior therapist, a hierarchy may include as few as ten or as many as fifty separate steps.

Once a client learns how to remain relaxed, the therapist directs him to vividly imagine each step in the hierarchy. When a client can visualize a particular step without experiencing anxiety, the therapist moves him to the next step. If a client experiences anxiety at any step in the hierarchy, the therapist repeatedly exposes him to that step until his anxiety to it is eliminated.

Fundamentally, systematic desensitization affords clients the opportunity to rehearse and practice confidence. Moreover, they do so in a situation where elevated anxiety no longer debilitates the efficiency of their behavior.

Skinner influenced the development of behavior therapy by virtue of his emphasis on reinforcement (reward). Skinner viewed both normal and maladjusted behavior as controlled by reinforcement. Given this assumption, behavior therapists attempt to determine what reinforcers maintain a client's maladjusted behavior.

For example, a mother might respond to her tantrum-throwing toddler with substantial affection and reassurance. In doing so, she inadvertently rewards the child's tantrums. Such a situation could develop because the mother assumes that her toddler is frightened or insecure. Once a behavior therapist identifies the reinforcement conditions maintaining these maladjusted behaviors, he proceeds to modify them.

A behavior therapist would teach the mother to systematically reinforce her toddler's responses of smiling and laughing. The mother would learn to respond with affection and attention whenever her toddler smiled and laughed. As a result, the frequency of the child's smiling and laughing should increase. Obviously, a laughing, smiling toddler cannot throw tantrums at the same time he is laughing and smiling. Thus, increasing the frequency of laughing, smiling behavior effectively extinguishes (eliminates) the tantrum-throwing behavior.

Behavior therapists also address themselves to the thinking patterns, or cognitive processes, of clients. They regard thinking patterns as responses subject to stimulus control. In particular, behavior therapists address themselves to how clients think about various situations in their lives.

For example, the discouraged salesperson who approaches a potential customer anticipates, "This guy is certainly going to shoot me down. What will I tell the boss back at the office?" Because of his anticipatory thinking, he labels these situations as "inevitable failure;" and simultaneously, he mentally rehearses his own rejection. Convinced that he will fail, he influences customers to confirm his expectations. As a result, sales calls can degenerate into anxiety-arousing experiences for this salesperson.

Behavior therapists teach their clients to think in patterns that lead to more constructive outcomes. For example, the salesperson could learn to think in terms of: "How many calls will I make before I get my first order from this guy?" With this procedure, the behavior therapist facilitates a relabeling of the situation. Rejections are no longer simply rejections; instead, each rejection is one step closer to success. Thus, the client no longer thinks of "failure" when making sales calls; now he has learned to think about "persistence."

Behavior therapists also use "behavior rehearsal" techniques to increase the confidence of their clients. Behavior rehearsal involves role-playing interactions between client and therapist. In these kinds of role-playing procedures the client is afforded the opportunity to learn more effective behaviors by actually practicing them. For example, the self-doubting salesperson could practice new sales techniques while the therapist pretends to be a customer. A particularly creative behavior therapist might require this client to "sell" him on the idea of terminating therapy.

EFFECTIVE BEHAVIOR THERAPY

Behavior therapists deserve credit when they design procedures that are legitimately effective. They can demonstrate sophisticated awareness of the stimulus conditions controlling a client's psychological distress. The effectiveness of behavioral techniques is especially enhanced when therapists respond to the interpersonal environment of their clients.

Clients, and significant people in their lives, often alternate between provoking and reacting to each other's behavior. As they modify the patterns of interpersonal influence that maintain the psychological distress of many clients, some behavior therapists demonstrate impressive ingenuity.

For example, B is an intelligent young woman majoring in economics at the graduate level. She was referred for therapy because of intense crying episodes and anxiety attacks.[1] B recently moved into the apartment of a male friend (Z). Removed from the apartment, she was able to function very appropriately. In the apartment, however, B rarely studied. Instead, she drifted into a "homebody role" that left her preoccupied with housework, preparing gourmet meals, and entertaining Z's friends.

When Z would announce his intention to leave the apartment—and then linger after his announcement—B could deteriorate into acute distress. She was often reduced to hysterical crying, while complaining about the volume of her work and insisting that she could not study while Z remained in the apartment. If Z still lingered in the apartment, B would completely lose behavior control. She would begin to strike Z and cry more intensely. Once Z finally left, B was able to compose herself and study productively.

The behavior therapist treating B viewed her as conflicted by her own sex role expectations. In the therapist's estimation, B was responding to conventional expectations requiring her to be helpless, dependent, and incompetent in the presence of a male. Moreover, the therapist regarded Z as conflicted in his expectations for B's behavior. Z was unsure if he wanted an independent, competent female in his life or a dependent, clinging female. Because of his ambivalence, Z could sometimes subtly reinforce B's hysterical-like symptoms.

Basically, B and Z alternated in provoking and reacting to each other's behavior. At any point in time, either one of them could influence the other's behavior; while moments later, the entire influence process could reverse itself. As a result, the behavior therapist wisely decided to include both B and Z in the course of treatment.

Z was taught to recognize episodes of B's appropriate behavior in the apartment, and how to reward them. As he did so, despite having some difficulty in changing his own behavior, B made progress. In fact, B made enough progress that she eventually decided to move into her own apartment where she continued to function well.

The inclusion of Z in B's therapy demonstrated the therapist's responsiveness to B's interpersonal context. To at least some degree, the therapist was able to enlist Z as an ally who was committed to B's welfare. By involving Z in treatment with B, the therapist avoided a power struggle.

If the therapist had not proceeded in this manner, a power struggle would have likely ensued between the therapist and Z. These kinds of power struggles do not serve the welfare of clients very effectively. The behavior therapist in this case deserves credit for avoiding this type of counterproductive conflict.

STRENGTHS OF BEHAVIOR THERAPY

The previous example illustrates the collective responsiveness of behavior therapists to research data. It may take them awhile, but behaviorists eventually modify their procedures in response to data that demand it. As a result, behavioral therapy possesses the potential to change and develop in new directions. This potential makes behavioral therapy a viable force in the future of psychotherapy.

Behaviorists deserve credit for moving from the speculativeness of "Cause and Theory," to the better defined considerations of "Result and Fact." The specificity with which they define their methods and goals increases the effectiveness of their procedures. At the very least, behaviorists are substantially less likely to harm their clientele. They are more responsive to client needs and less inclined to subject clients to "bait-and-switch" procedures.

Nevertheless, the impact of behavioral therapy is limited. Only a relatively small number of therapists are competent behaviorists. Competence as a behavior therapist requires a comprehensive background in learning theory. In academia, learning theory has been the exclusive domain of psychology.

The other therapy professions provide graduate students with minimal background in human learning. Consequently, the vast majority of competent behavioral therapists are psychologists. This does not mean, however, that all psychologists are competent behavior therapists. Indeed, only about twenty percent of clinical psychologists identify themselves as behaviorists. As a result, competent behavior therapists are not as available to clients as other practitioners.

13

On principle it is quite wrong to try founding a theory on observable magnitudes alone. In reality the very opposite happens. It is the theory which decides what we can observe.

— ALBERT EINSTEIN

BEHAVIOR THERAPY: THE FAILURES OF TUNNEL VISION

Agoraphobia may be defined as ". . . the inability or reluctance to leave home or to enter public places or vehicles, alone or accompanied, because of a fear of panic, anxiety, and anxiety related symptoms, or of fainting or otherwise losing control."[1] Typically, behavior therapy is considered the treatment of choice for agoraphobia.

Behavior therapists view the anxiety responses of agoraphobics as controlled by the stimuli of their physical environment. As a result, behavior therapists attempt to determine what physical stimuli precipitate a client's anxiety: Is it sunlight, could it be the unfamiliar faces of strangers, or might it be how far the client ventures away from home?

Once the stimuli that apparently provoke a client's anxiety attacks are identified, the therapist employs counterconditioning techniques to reduce that anxiety. The counterconditioning techniques are focused on the client's responses to the physical environment.

Preoccupied with the characteristics of an agoraphobic's physical environment, behavior therapists overlook important character-

95

istics of an agoraphobic's interpersonal environment. The vast majority of agoraphobics are married females. How they function as wives and mothers is substantially influenced by their symptoms.

Obviously, female agoraphobics readily gravitate to traditional roles as housewives. An agoraphobic female is not about to march assertively out of the family home in pursuit of her own career goals; her symptoms effectively prevent her from doing so. Her symptoms also influence how her husband and children organize their lives.

DISREGARDING FAMILIES

The other members of an agoraphobic's family adapt to her assumption of a traditional housewife role. Husbands of agoraphobics view themselves as reliable resources of calm strength for their wives. Children in an agoraphobic family frequently maintain a close relationship with their chronically anxious mother; they feel responsible for protecting and comforting her. Any attempt at alleviating the symptoms of an agoraphobic substantially influences her relationships with her family.

Indeed, research evidence indicates that behavioral therapy can create severe repercussions for an agoraphobic's marriage. As the condition of agoraphobics improved in response to behavioral procedures, their husbands often began to demonstrate symptoms of psychological distress.[2] In particular, the husbands frequently exhibited signs of anxiety and depression.

The progress of their wives in behavioral therapy threatened these men. If they were no longer needed as reliable resources of calm strength, they worried how they would relate to their wives in the future. Consequently, many husbands were motivated to sabotage the therapy progress of their wives. Because they felt apprehensive about how their marital relationships might be reorganized as a result of their wives' diminishing symptoms, the husbands found it difficult to accept these changes.

The investigator who reported these data advocated that behavioral treatment of agoraphobia must include marital therapy. Otherwise, the effectiveness of behavioral procedures for agoraphobia is severely compromised. In fact, one of the seminal figures in the development of behavior therapy (Joseph Wolpe) has acknowledged that agoraphobia is a response to marital conflict.[3]

Most behavior therapists, however, continue their preoccupation with the stimulus characteristics of an agoraphobic's *physical* environment. Simultaneously, they act as if they are oblivious to the stimulus characteristics of an agoraphobic's *interpersonal* environment. They persist in their tunnel vision despite the availability of research evidence that contraindicates it. When behavior therapists disregard this research, they neglect the welfare of their clients.

Because of their preoccupation with physical environments, behavior therapists can commit some serious errors in clinical judgment. They are still too inclined to define their methods in a very narrow and restrictive manner. As they do so, they seek to maintain as much of the scientific purity of the laboratory as possible.

For example, an agoraphobic's physical environment can be defined more objectively than her interpersonal environment. Physical environments can be measured in terms of time and space. Interpersonal environments are not amenable to such exacting measurements. Wanting to maintain their reputation as scientists, behaviorists too often preoccupy themselves with the physical environments of their clients and ignore their interpersonal environments.

For too long, the methodological tails of behaviorists have wagged their conceptual dogs. Behaviorists gravitated to those considerations in the lives of their clients that they could define objectively (the time and space of physical environments). Simultaneously, they failed to pay sufficient attention to the interpersonal environments of their clientele. The readiness with which behaviorists have embraced these theoretical limitations sabotages the effectiveness of their clinical techniques.

ISN'T A MOTHER A STIMULUS?

A behavior therapist reported the case of an unmarried 40-year-old female, who lived at home with her mother. This client worked as an editorial assistant and rarely dated. She sought treatment because of a distressing phobia about elevators. When forced to use an elevator, the client endured intense anxiety and fear.

The behavior therapist who treated this client employed systematic desensitization techniques. This therapist also realized that "...there was more to the phobia than a feeling of being trapped with no escape." The therapist explained that as the client . . .

> . . . completed the relaxation and desensitization procedure and was able to conquer the elevator fear, she began to achieve some insight into her other, more widespread phobia—that of leaving home, becoming independent, sexual, doing more stereotypic male things ("going up in the world," for example). We then . . . expanded our treatment and began to desensitize the patient to her more pervasive fear of breaking away from home and becoming more independent.[4]

This therapist's definition of stimulus control was excessively narrow and restrictive. Ultimately, the stimuli controlling the client's phobia were not merely elevators, nor her fear of leaving home and developing greater independence. Rather than some conflict confined within herself, the most significant stimulus controlling the client's phobia was her mother, who likely felt comfortable with the status quo of her daughter as a live-in companion.

As the therapist used desensitization techniques to reduce the client's anxiety about living alone, one must ask: What was happening to the mother's anxiety level? If her mother felt anxious about the client leaving home, the client must have worried about her. While worried about her mother's anxiety, desensitization procedures could not alleviate the client's distress. Simultaneously, the mother's anxiety likely increased as she worried about her distressed daughter's readiness to live alone.

From the mother's perspective, her daughter would not seem so distressed if she was really prepared to leave home. Until the client appeared confident about living alone, her mother was compelled to worry about her. On the other hand, as long as her mother worried about her, the client would feel anxious about leaving home.

Unfortunately, the therapist did nothing to help the client and her mother resolve this impasse. Treatment focused on what was happening *within* the client; it ignored what transpired *between* the client and her mother. Thus, client and mother may have taken turns provoking each other's heightened anxiety.

Had the mother been included in this therapy, the therapist could have assisted the client more appropriately. An effective therapist would have asked the mother: "How will you know when your daughter is ready to live on her own?" The answer to this question would have helped the client. Her self-confidence would have increased by knowing how to reduce her mother's worry.

Also, client and mother could have been directed to look together for the daughter's apartment. Involving the mother in this process would have increased the likelihood of her encouraging it. Moreover, therapy should have assisted the client and her mother to plan future activities together. Such planning would reassure the mother that her daughter was not about to abandon her.

Additionally, therapy could have helped the mother to expand her network of friends and activities. Thus, she would have found it easier to fill the void created by her daughter's move. This therapist, however, neglected the mother-daughter dynamics in this case.

As a result of ignoring the mother's influence, the therapist overlooked the stimulus that ultimately controlled the client's phobia. Consequently, she may have endured the same kind of loyalty conflict that therapists of other orientations can create. The client could find herself simultaneously pulled in two different directions—one by her mother, and the other by her therapist. This kind of loyalty conflict is counterproductive; it rapidly elevates a client's anxiety level.

Biofeedback And Stress Management

Biofeedback is a procedure that originated out of the premises of behavior therapy. Though it confines itself to physiological events, biofeedback attempts to increase the frequency of some responses while decreasing the frequency of others.

During the past 20 years, biofeedback generated considerable excitement in both professional journals and the mass media. Large numbers of therapists were very impressed by the clinical potential of biofeedback. Biofeedback seemed to possess substantial promise for treating disorders such as hypertension, migraine headaches, and bruxism (teeth-grinding while asleep).

Quite simply, biofeedback is a procedure that helps people to control some physiological response. It does so by providing them immediate information—or feedback—about that response. Behavior therapists have addressed themselves to responses such as muscle tension, finger temperature, and brain wave activity, to cite but a few examples.

The hardware of biofeedback was developed to provide information for clients about the status of such responses. For example, a client can learn to lower his blood pressure while responding to a therapist's instructions to "keep the hum going." The client hears this "hum" via headphones he wears in the session. The biofeedback equipment is programmed so that the "hum" sounds only when the client's blood pressure is at, or below, the desired level.

During biofeedback sessions, clients can exhibit remarkable facility for controlling a variety of physiological responses. The problem with biofeedback, however, is the fundamental problem with all other therapy techniques: Can the client's success in the session transfer and maintain itself outside the session?

After almost twenty years of excitement about the potential of biofeedback procedures, discouraging research casts doubts on its clinical effectiveness. Alan Roberts, one of the original members of the Biofeedback Research Society, has stated: "There is absolutely no convincing evidence that biofeedback is an essential or specific technique for the treatment of any condition."[5]

Roberts clarified his position by explaining: " . . . too many clinicians continue to believe what they want to believe about the specific clinical efficacy of biofeedback in the face of experimental evidence to the contrary . . . "[6] Roberts also acknowledged that biofeedback may be a positive factor in a comprehensive treatment program employing multiple techniques. He remains adamant in his primary position, however, that biofeedback cannot be regarded as clinically effective in and of itself.

Despite this verdict, biofeedback continues to enjoy sustained popularity. The professional journals of psychotherapists still feature advertisements for biofeedback hardware.

Indeed, the journal in which Roberts' review was published contained a full page advertisement for biofeedback devices.

Moreover, the manufacturers of biofeedback equipment are still found in the exhibition halls of professional meetings, where, they demonstrate their wares with unabashed pride. Any therapist who is considering the purchase of this hardware is advised to be cautious. Do not expect a forthright discussion from sales personnel of the research review cited in the previous paragraphs.

As biofeedback has maintained its undeserved reputation of effectiveness, it has also served as a catalyst for related procedures. Seminars in "stress management" have developed from the impetus created by the biofeedback movement. These seminars supposedly assist employees of corporate and public bureaucracies to cope more effectively with the stress of their working environments. Bureaucracies often respond enthusiastically to such seminars.

Bureaucracies may overwork and underpay their employees, afford them little input into decisions that influence their working lives, and episodically assault their morale. Simultaneously, they sponsor their seminars in stress management to prove their enduring commitment to the health and welfare of their workforce. Because stress management seminars impose the onus for change on their employees, bureaucracies are particularly enamored with them. The bureaucracy can continue to embrace its status quo, while simultaneously ignoring any need to change its organizational practices.

Biofeedback procedures, and management seminars both commit themselves to an exercise in futility. They seek to promote changes by focusing a client's attention within himself. Nevertheless, techniques such as these remain oblivious and unresponsive to the environmental circumstances that ultimately precipitate stress disorders. Stress does not occur in a vacuum; distressed clients or distressed employees are reacting to stressful environments. Techniques such as biofeedback and stress management advocate that individuals cope with stress instead of addressing its causes.

One cynic, well known to this writer, reacts rather intensely to the stress management seminars popularized by American bureaucracies. He metaphorically observes: "So we have a problem with malaria. Should we limit ourselves to determining the most effective dosages of quinine? Or should we drain the swamps and kill the mosquitos?" For this observer, bureaucracies are too inclined to overlook the "swamps" and "mosquitos" of their own bureaucratic environments. As they do so, they remain oblivious to the stressful circumstances they create for their own employees.

OVERVIEW OF BEHAVIOR THERAPY

Behavior therapists make credible efforts to specify well-defined goals—and goals that actually correspond to client needs—but they are too often shortsighted in how they define those goals. Like analytic and CC-H therapists who preoccupy themselves with what transpires *within* the psyches of their clientele, behavior therapists frequently overlook what transpires *between* their clients and other important people in their lives.

Preoccupied with physical stimuli and observable responses, it took almost twenty years before behavior therapists acknowledged the role of cognition (thinking processes) in human behavior. Moreover, there are still some influential figures in behavior therapy who vehemently protest the attention paid to cognition. Concern for the cognitive experiences of clients is criticized as a speculative process.[7] As a result, it is difficult to determine how long it will take before behaviorists *consistently* respond to the interpersonal environments of their clients.

If they are to effectively meet the needs of their clientele, behavior therapists must also undertake a paradigm shift.

PART THREE

THERPEUTIC RELATIONSHIPS

14

There isn't anything we can do about the situation so we talk about it.

—UNEMPLOYED BLACK MALE DESCRIBING AN URBAN GHETTO (NBC-TV, Nov. 18, 1986)

THERAPIST AS FRIEND AND FOE

As has been outlined in the preceding chapters, the various therapy orientations respond quite differently to psychological distress. Analytic therapists see insight as the answer to any and all problems. CC-H therapists try, in a variety of more or less dramatic ways, to enhance emotional awareness. Behavioral therapists address themselves to changing specific patterns of behavior.

Though therapists of different theoretical persuasions remain committed to their preferred techniques, the evidence cited in Chapter Two deserves review. Those who claim effectiveness for the traditional techniques of individual psychotherapy find no support from the available research (except for a few behavioral procedures used for a limited number of problems).

Instead, the extent to which clients regard their therapist as warm and genuinely understanding accounts for the apparent effectiveness of psychotherapy. This means that the client-therapist relationship is the most important factor in the outcome of psychotherapy.

Therefore, we now examine the different kinds of client-therapist relationships that

105

analytic and CC-H therapists create. This issue does not require separate consideration for behavior therapists. They typically attempt to follow the CC-H tradition while avoiding its dramatic excesses. Behavior therapists, however, define an appropriate therapeutic relationship as necessary—but not sufficient—for meeting client needs.[1]

THE BIG (ANALYTIC) CHILL

Research evidence indicates that analytic therapists are rather humorless, sternly serious people, who maintain substantial personal distance between themselves and their clients. After therapists undertake intensive analytic training, they respond less optimistically and supportively to their clients while dealing with them more authoritatively and defensively.[2] Consequently, analytic therapists are reluctant to express their own feelings, rarely answer personal questions, and almost never offer their personal opinions.[3] Even a well-respected analytic therapist has acknowledged the "phobic attitudes" of his colleagues about emotionality.[4]

Briefly disregarding any considerations of professional courtesy leads to a grim conclusion: Most analytic therapists exhibit all the warmth and genuine understanding of a wet sponge. These circumstances further reduce the effectiveness of analytic therapy. Exceedingly aloof, emotionally inhibited therapists cannot facilitate many placebo cures. The emotional distancing of analytic therapists demonstrates their indifference to relevant research. Though they may acknowledge the substantial evidence underscoring how the client-therapist relationship influences psychotherapy outcome in theory, they often neglect it in practice.

ACCUSATORY INTERPRETATIONS

Analytic therapists act as if the pursuit of insight affords them license to assassinate a client's character. For example, a respected analytic therapist reported the case of a client he considered grandiose and narcissistically immature.[5] In the therapist's opinion, the client expected others to indulge him with the same admiration and solicitousness that his mother did. Consequently, the therapist told the client that his mother had nurtured him into a miserable human being.

The client protested vehemently and angrily in response to the therapist's interpretation. For the therapist, the client's vehement anger verified his immaturity and narcissism. Eminently confident in the wisdom of his interpretation, the therapist disregarded the impact of his rude assaultiveness. He ignored the likelihood that his arrogance invited the client's anger.

Fundamentally, the issue here is not whether this client was actually grandiose and immature. The issue is whether bludgeoning clients with evidence of their problems really helps them. Analytic therapists seem to think that the answer to this question is "yes." Presumably, they undermine the self-respect of their clientele in pursuit of greater gains. Too often, however, the only gain realized from analytic therapy is the therapist's financial gain.

Another client, a recently divorced male in his mid-thirties, sought psychotherapeutic treatment. His divorce, which he did not want, left him burdened with feelings of loss and despair. He wanted to recover from the devastation of the divorce and achieve a renewed sense of direction for his life. Unfortunately, however, an analytic therapist neglected his needs.

Even though the client's marriage was done and over, his therapist wanted him to understand why it had failed. Referring to the breakdown of the marriage the therapist insisted, "Something must have happened; there must have been something you did."[6] The therapist persisted in his accusatory stance and asked, "Were you doing anything to aggravate the situation?"[7]

Despite the client's present distress as a divorced man, he was assaulted for his previous failures as a rejected husband. This focus could have been relevant had the client been considering remarriage, but he was not. Since his divorce, the passage of time might have eased this client's despair; but the therapist was not about to let him off that easy. He encouraged the client to vividly recall his marital failure and continue his suffering.

Despite the therapist's assaults, this client remained well-motivated in his response to treatment. He assumed the therapist's responsibility and attempted to direct the session more constructively. At one point he asked, "How do I get started again . . . ?"[8] The therapist, however, disregarded the client's question. Preoccupied with what he wanted him to understand, the therapist failed to develop any course of action to effectively assist him.

In fact, this client's despair had developed to the point where he was suicidal, but he did not disclose his crisis to the therapist. His reluctance is not surprising. Likely, the client doubted that this analytic therapist could help him with his despair. Because of the previous assaults he had endured, the client probably anticipated more questions about why he was suicidal. Rather than help him, this kind of insight would have threatened his welfare; he needed to find reasons for hope—not review his reasons for despair.

Two children had been born in the client's marriage. He was still a significant factor in the lives of his children; and they remained very important to him. The client could have been asked: what made him feel good about himself as a father; and how would his children continue to need him in the future?

Renewed awareness of the special bond with his children would have reduced this client's suicidal despair. Emphasizing his identity as a father would have helped to restore his sense of purpose and determination. The sad fact is, however, analytic therapists rarely respond this effectively to their clientele.

CLIENT DEFENSIVENESS

Analytic therapy is structured so that it inevitably provokes defensiveness from clients. Belittled and humiliated by their therapist's accusatory interpretations, clients are compelled to respond guardedly.

For example, a female client sobbed as she told her analytic therapist about her son's serious illness.[9] Despite the client's obvious distress, the therapist remained aloof and unresponsive, which prompted bewildered silence from the client. In response to the client's silence, the therapist insisted she was repressing the guilt associated with her unconscious death wish for her son. As would be expected, the therapist's interpretation left the client feeling resentful and defensive.

Analytic therapists often dwell continuously on the defensiveness of their clientele, which they have created. While reminding clients how they supposedly deceive themselves, the therapists themselves assume a position of smug superiority. Simultaneously, they reduce their clients to feelings of inferiority and self-doubt. Self-doubting clients, who contend with increasing feelings of inferiority, are more inclined to think they need extensive therapy. Not surprisingly, analytic therapists often describe such clients as insightful.

Analytic therapists expect clients to gratefully endorse their accusatory interpretations; they disregard how accusatory interpretations immobilize their clientele. A client's self-doubt, provoked by his therapist's character assassination, interferes with his capacity to plan and execute changes in behavior.

Preoccupied with defending himself against his therapist's indictments, problem-solving is a luxury that a client cannot afford. A therapist's interpretive onslaughts diminish a client's self-confidence, causing him to doubt any course of action he might undertake. In other words, this therapy creates a demand for its own services—its abuse of clients makes them more dependent on it.

Analytic therapy often deteriorates into ceremonies of degradation and rituals of confession. Clients are expected to indict themselves for any and all of their alleged shortcomings. Thus, not only do analytic therapists require their clientele to embrace insight, they also expect them to be humble as they do it. Humble clients more readily endure their therapists' talents for character assassination.

DISTRUST OF CLIENTS

Given their theory of resistance, analytic therapists doubt that clients really want to overcome their psychological distress. They view their clients as determined to cling tenaciously to their symptoms. Presumably, clients must be coerced into recovery as they kick and scream in protest while dragged toward enlightened understanding.

Because analytic therapists are so wary of their clients, they feel compelled to hover vigilantly over the therapy process. Everything clients say requires scrutiny for any evidence of maladjustment. Otherwise, they fear they could find themselves victimized by the supposedly infantile, neurotic needs of their clientele.

Analytic therapists regard their clients as clever manipulators who are not to be trusted. Thus, analytic therapy is often a grim, sober endeavor exuding all the liveliness of a post-mortem examination. Any client's spontaneous levity may provoke the ever-present, analytic question: "Why do you think you *really* said that?"

Analytic therapists often feel paranoid about their clientele. They frequently assume that clients are deeply committed to defying and embarrassing them. In this moderately distrusting, rather adversarial client-therapist relationship,

> the classical psychoanalytic model encourages confrontations and attacks upon the patient's resistance as if they were nothing but dangers to therapy and the therapist, and obstructions to be blasted away.[10]

One is tempted to conclude that a "no pain, no gain" mentality pervades this therapeutic orientation. Analytic therapists assign the same virtue to a client's psychological discomfort in therapy that some athletic coaches assign to the physical agony of training. In both situations, suffering is applauded as a laudable ordeal that supposedly strengthens character development. Perhaps analytic therapy deserves a reputation similar to cod liver oil and cold showers. Anything that unpleasant must make one a better person.

In analytic therapy, a client either agrees with the therapist or exits the therapy process. Though exiting the process may seem an eminently wise choice, too many clients lack the self-confidence necessary to terminate their ordeals. The indicting atmosphere of analytic therapy sabotages their self-confidence. When an analytic therapist is always prepared to disqualify what a client says, or further dismantle his self-esteem, how much self-confidence can he enjoy? Such practices reduce clients to a status that makes the term "second class citizen" particularly meaningful.

Despite the abuse they endure, some clients are motivated to prolong their already long-term therapy. Angered again and again by the accusatory interpretations of an arrogant therapist, clients can feel compelled to vindicate themselves. Thus, they persist in treatment determined to win at least one argumentative victory over their arbitrary opponent. Consequently, one wonders how many health insurance carriers underwrite two-person debating societies in the guise of long-term, analytic therapy?

RENT-A-(CC-H) FRIEND

In sharp contrast to the chill of analytic therapy, CC-H therapists are determined to relate to their clients as caring "friends." Determined to impress clients with their credentials as "authentic human beings," CC-H therapists effusively introduce themselves by their first names. Rather than accusing or criticizing, they act as if they and a client have been the closest of friends for years.

By the end of an initial session, many CC-H therapists want to hug a client good-bye. Presumably, hugging strengthens the bonds of their flourishing friendship. Some clients, however, view the effusiveness of CC-H therapists as artificially contrived, and they feel alienated from therapy as a result.

THERAPIST CONFUSION

When CC-H therapists pursue deeply understanding relationships with their clientele, they often commit themselves to a futile endeavor. A therapist who understands the psychological distress of a client, with such accuracy that he might almost be the client, creates a difficult dilemma for himself. Clients initiate therapy as a result of feeling bewildered and confused by their own psychological distress. Any therapist who limits himself to empathically understanding a client's feelings soon feels as bewildered and confused as the client. Overidentified with the client's emotional experiences, the therapist suffers a serious loss of objectivity about the client's life situation.

Nevertheless, CC-H therapists insist that a therapist's bewilderment and confusion are inevitable occurrences in therapy. They also think that this kind of disorientation should be "experienced" and "shared" with clients. For example, consider the following instance of empathic sharing between a therapist and a client:

> The client's pain was experienced concurrently by the therapist so that *each began crying and shaking* [emphasis added]. Many restless, angry sessions had preceded the intense resonance experience. Afterward for a time there were discomforting feelings, which were worked through leading to a new definition of closeness and love, which led to an increased level of trust, speed-

ing up the therapeutic process.[11]

When a therapist so profoundly identifies with a client's emotional state that he cries and shakes with him, he severely compromises his ability to assist that client. If a client concludes that his problems are serious enough to reduce the therapist to tears and shuddering, he can feel even more overwhelmed and hopeless.

Once CC-H therapists immobilize their capacity for problem resolution, they often resort to shallow palliatives to encourage their clientele. Suggestions to "trust yourself" and "be kind to yourself" are responses frequently invoked by CC-H therapists. Too often, this superficiality merely perpetuates the distress that motivated clients to undertake therapy.

Exhortations to "trust yourself" and "be kind to yourself" are, at best, hollow adages. Though CC-H therapists insist that this kind of encouragement is helpful, they actually resort to it when they are otherwise unable to aid their clientele. Moreover, the encouraging platitudes of this therapy are often counterproductive.

Ideally, clients should share trust and kindness with the people in their lives who are genuinely important to them. Trust and kindness as solitary experiences, or even when shared with an excessively central CC-H therapist, merely underscore the loneliness of many clients. CC-H therapists use these platitudes to create an illusion of their own competence. Bewildered and confused by the morass of client feelings they have provoked, they struggle to maintain credibility in the eyes of their clientele.

Determined to salvage some appearance of competence, CC-H therapists elevate ingratiation to the status of a psychotherapeutic technique. When they advise clients to "trust yourself" and "be kind to yourself," CC-H therapists are soliciting their loyalty and friendship. Clients who are loyal and friendly are less inclined to judge their therapist harshly. Despite the ineffectiveness of their therapy, loyal and friendly clients more readily endure a therapist's incompetence.

If they can assume that a client has developed a sense of affection for them, many CC-H therapists regard treatment as successful. While recalling small gifts or personal mementos that clients have bestowed upon them, these therapists share a sense of proud satisfaction with their colleagues.

Preoccupied with enjoying the esteem of their clientele, CC-H therapists disregard whether they are assisting them. Inspired by clients who gratefully appreciate their warmth and understanding, they effusively leap to unsubstantiated conclusions. They overlook the logical fallacy between "he likes me" and therefore "I helped him." In fact, the former does not guarantee the latter.

Sharing Isn't Everything

In CC-H therapy sessions, emotional sharing flourishes as a common pastime for client and therapist. CC-H therapists expect that introspective experiences, transpiring in an atmosphere of "emotional sharing," inevitably enhance the psychological welfare of clients. In such an atmosphere, clients are supposed to share their deepest, most private feelings with their therapist.

Nevertheless, experiences of emotional sharing are really peripheral and irrelevant exercises. The shared emotional experience between client and therapist merely reflects their relationship with each other. Such sharing fails to resolve the interpersonal conflicts that burden a client.

Genuinely important feelings exist between a client and significant others in his life—a spouse, children, parents, or friends. Traditional therapists are at a loss to modify these genuinely important feelings, how can they influence a relationship when they are seeing only one of the individuals?

Emotional sharing with a therapist may lead clients to substitute that experience for more important relationships outside of therapy. If other relationships have soured, this one is at least warm and trusting; and a compensatory relationship can provide clients a short-term sense of relief. Intensely dramatic dialogues, shared between clients and therapists, create the illusion that some significant endeavor is taking place. Nevertheless, it is rare that meaningful problem resolution develops from such dialogues.

When people feel paralyzed by a difficult situation, they are often reduced to talking about it; and their conversations can lead them into circular meandering. Dramatic exchanges between clients and therapists, wherein they "encounter each others' human vulnerability," fail to effectively assist clients. Merely talking about a situation reflects an inherent sense of futility.*

*This same principle is exhibited in academic and business settings when persistently stubborn problems are referred to committees. There, those problems will be repeatedly discussed in many meetings with minimal results. Nevertheless, organizational practices such as these create the reassuring illusion that somehow, someone will develop something resembling a solution.

15

I'll be judge, I'll be jury . . . I'll try the whole cause.

—LEWIS CARROLL

THERAPIST AS GOD

Because analytic and CC-H therapists approach the client relationship from diametrically opposed perspectives, it is perhaps surprising that they often obtain similar outcomes. Whether from fear of their authority or by succumbing to their charms, clients tend to fall under the spell of their therapist. Once lost in a therapeutic trance, clients forget what their therapy *should* do and treatment deteriorates into a compensatory relationship.

A client's compensatory relationship with his therapist overshadows the problems that motivated him to seek therapy. "Breakthroughs" correspond to experiences of insight or emotional awareness in the session; but those breakthroughs are rarely translated into problem resolution. Rather than address the client's needs, a compensatory relationship responds to its own goals. Thus, the client-therapist relationship can serve primarily to perpetuate itself.

ISOLATING THE INDIVIDUAL

Analytic therapy is almost exclusively an individual therapy; analytic therapists are disinclined to share a client's attention with other people. Analytic therapists prefer individual

115

therapy because it encourages transference relationships. Remember, these therapists assume that clients bring the same problems into treatment that distress them outside of therapy; thus, they expect clients to transfer their problems onto their therapist. As a result, "transference problems" can receive more therapeutic attention than the clients' real-life problems.

Because of their expectations for a transference relationship, analytic therapists appoint themselves to positions of substantial authority in the lives of their clientele. The analytic therapist acts as if his relationship with a client should be the most significant relationship in the client's life.

Analytic therapists admonish clients who distract themselves from the transference relationship. They commonly require that clients postpone important decisions in their lives (educational plans, marriage, job change). They consider these decisions distractions that diminish the importance of transference. Thus, clients must delay such decisions pending the therapist's permission to make them.

These kinds of restrictions create a curious dilemma. A client initiates psychotherapy because he can no longer tolerate his life situation and the distress inherent in it. Determined to create a transference relationship, his analytic therapist insists that nothing can change—the client cannot alter the circumstances that frustrate him.[1]

The client may protest the absurdity of these constraints, but the therapist remains confidently entrenched in his position. Reassured by the dogma of analytic theory, he knows that a protesting client is merely resisting the transference. Some clients are perceptive enough to see through this convoluted agenda, and they emphatically reject it as irrelevant.

For example, the following client felt alienated by the intrusiveness with which her analytic therapist interpreted transference phenomena. While describing the dream interpretations of her therapist, she explained: "He was never in any of my dreams, but the way he would interpret them, he was every character—like if I dreamed of a dog and wolf, he would say he was the dog and he was the wolf."[2]

This client refused the therapist's attempts at assuming an unwarranted role of significance in her life. She regarded him as presumptuous, and she concluded that he neglected her needs as a result of his own needs.

Erotic Curiosity

Clients may experience some erotic feelings about a therapist. Such feelings exist because of the atypical closeness that has evolved between client and therapist in an artificial setting. The analytic therapist demands that a client disclose her intimate fantasies and sexual secrets to him. Moreover, this is done in a unique relationship shared only between client and therapist. Outside of analytic therapy, the therapist's behavior could be considered a variation of voyeurism (a "Peeping Tom").

If a client were to disclose her intimate fantasies to her husband in this manner, her erotic feelings for him might well increase. Consider a situation where a woman spends fifty minutes disclosing her innermost sexual fantasies to her husband. This is done in a setting where the wife can sit or lie down on a comfortable piece of furniture.

The woman and her husband undertake this procedure in a quiet, tranquil setting where they will not be interrupted. As the wife discloses her personal erotica, her husband must listen attentively. Also, neither husband nor wife are allowed to touch each other for the fifty minute duration of this procedure.

Because passion restrained is often passion intensified, a procedure like this could rapidly accelerate levels of sexual interest between wife and husband. It is tempting to conclude that these free associative procedures would be more effective in the client's home than in a therapist's office.

In analytic therapy, the therapist intrudes into this scenario. Subjected to her therapist's voyeurism, a client might naturally wonder about her capacity to arouse his erotic interest. Understandably, the client is curious about this person to whom she discloses her most guarded confidences.

Analytic therapists often interpret a client's erotic curiosity as indicating transference. They attribute any erotic curiosity to the client's unresolved conflicts. This interpretive license makes the therapist more important in the client's life than he actually is or really should be. These analytic assumptions also ignore the artificially close relationship that the therapist has designed. Ultimately, a client's erotic curiosity develops because a therapist provokes it, and long-term therapy encourages it.

ANALYTIC ADOPTIONS

Analytic therapists often appoint themselves to positions of substantial significance in the lives of their clients, while disregarding their family situation. These therapists risk creating some major catastrophes. In the following case the young man who was the client . . .

> ". . . . was a student who lived at school all week and returned home to his mother on weekends. The time he spent at school was fraught with anxiety. He was extremely isolated, avoiding contact as much as possible because of the considerable anxiety he felt whenever he was with another person, whether the janitor, his classmates, his teachers, or anyone else he might encounter. He went right from class to his room, ate alone, and would walk considerably out of his way to avoid seeing anyone he might have to say hello to.
>
> Being home with mother on the weekends, while not particularly joyful either, was nonetheless rather a reprieve for him. He was relatively free from anxiety at home, and relaxed most of the day, often in front of the TV set. His relationship with his mother was described as involving seductive behavior on her part, but rejection when he got too close.
>
> Much of the therapist's efforts were directed toward elucidating the patient's strong erotic and symbiotic ties to his mother. It was expected that resolution of his core conflict regarding parental figures would be a central means of creating the change necessary for improvement in the other relationships in his life and a reduction of his intense anxiety at school.[3]

Obviously, this mother occupied a position of substantial power and influence in her son's life. She seemed to vacillate between overprotecting him and encouraging his independence and autonomy. Without at least some maternal encouragement, it is unlikely that this client would have been enrolled in a boarding school. The therapist sought to resolve the client's "core conflict regarding parental figures" by encouraging his acquisition of insight. This procedure, however, raises the question of how would the client's insight modify his mother's vacillating behavior?

As this client was acquiring insight, his mother probably understood that an insensitive therapist sought to steal her son. This would only be a logical conclusion on her part. Her son was talking a great deal about an important, influential figure in his life (the therapist). Suspicious of the therapist's influence, the mother likely increased her efforts at overprotecting her son. If this were the case, the son was compelled to cling ever more tenaciously to the therapist. Otherwise, he would remain excessively dependent on his mother.

In fact, this client became excessively dependent upon the therapist. Simultaneously, his psychological welfare was markedly deteriorating.

> The patient would plead with the therapist to "take me home and teach me how to live." He would tell the therapist that he was the only nice person in the world, literally the only one worth being with, and would combine this with strong complaints that the therapist wasn't helping enough, wasn't giving enough. The therapist began to feel flooded by the patient's demands, and frustrated by the patient's complete *unwillingness to reflect upon what he was expressing.*[4]

This analytic therapist assumed that the course of treatment unraveled because of problems within the client. He felt increasingly frustrated by the client's "unwillingness to reflect upon what he was expressing." This "unwillingness" conflicted with the therapist's expectation that the client would develop insight. The therapist insisted that the client's intense dependency prohibited his development of insight.

Nevertheless, by virtue of excluding the mother from therapy, the therapist invited the client's dependency. While the therapist wanted the client to develop insight, the client wanted the therapist to replace his mother. In view of the mother's substantial power and influence, the client needed an equally powerful figure to promote his independence and autonomy. The client also expected that his relationship with the therapist would duplicate his closely enmeshed relationship with his mother. The therapist's refusal to meet these expectations left the client severely frustrated.

Basically, the therapist sabotaged the course of this client's therapy. Without establishing an alliance with the client's mother, the therapist created a conflict for the client, who was pulled between his mother and the therapist. In this case, the client opted to align himself with the therapist. Thus, the client needed more support than the therapist was able to provide. Consequently, this case terminated less than favorably.

The client ended his relationship with the therapist and admitted himself into a psychiatric day hospital. This case suggests that any therapist who attempts to tear a client from his family should be prepared to adopt him. Therapists who are not prepared for such adoptions should work with a client *and* his family.

This case is all too close to the story of Robert Andrews that began this book. Its outcome could have been even more tragic.

THERAPIST AS BEST FRIEND

Some clients welcome the friendly, informal manner of a CC-H therapist; they regard their therapists's offer of immediate friendship as a flattering experience. A therapist who seems to hang on a client's every word, while putting forth substantial efforts to understand a client's emotional experiences as the client understands them, can rapidly assume a role of central importance in that client's life. Therapists who assume such importance invite compensatory relationships with their clients. Whether this centrality of CC-H therapists to their clients really serves their welfare is entirely another issue.

Many CC-H therapists act as if they are the only figures in a client's life qualified to share important feelings with him. They like to think of themselves as paragons of "openness" and "sensitivity." CC-H therapists use this assessment of themselves as a standard to determine whether others are sufficiently "open" and "sensitive." Anyone in a client's life who falls short of these standards may be labeled callous and insensitive. Rogers described such people in the following manner:

> With another person we recognize that what he is saying is almost certainly a front or a facade. We wonder what he really feels, what he is really experiencing, behind this facade. We may also wonder if he knows what he really feels, recognizing that he may be quite

unaware of the feelings he is actually experiencing. With such a person we tend to be cautious and wary. It is not the kind of relationship in which defenses can be dropped or in which significant learning and change can occur.[5]

CC-H therapists often view their clients as victims of others who hide their feelings behind a facade. Typically, however, they know very little about the other people in their clients' lives. Their limited knowledge in this regard encourages them to form compensatory relationships with their clientele.

Often, clients are highly motivated to protect a compensatory relationship with their therapist. Once their therapist volunteers himself as a personal ally, clients may feel less than enthusiastic about sharing him. The involvement of someone else in a therapy session could provide a therapist with another perspective about a client's problems. Informed input, from a third party, can dispel various myths that have been the basis of a compensatory relationship.

For example, once a therapist meets a client's spouse, he may learn that the client is not really a beleaguered victim. The therapist can also understand that the spouse is not actually the villain he seemed to be. Despite a client's helpless appearance, the therapist may see that he exercises more power and influence than previously apparent.

Therefore, clients can unwittingly conspire to maintain their therapist's belief that others have sabotaged their welfare. Consequently, CC-H therapists often distrust the capacity of anyone, other than themselves, to respond supportively to their clients. As a result, they make themselves excessively important to their clientele.

HE NEEDS ME

CC-H therapists act as if their charisma, and only their charisma, can alleviate a client's distress. For example, a CC-H therapist was discussing the treatment of a particular client. In summarizing the client's needs the therapist emphatically concluded, "He needs a relationship with me." CC-H therapists regularly leap to such conclusions about their clientele; and, most remarkably, they do so while blithely ignoring their own grandiosity. As a result, one must wonder if CC-H therapists prefer large offices; they likely need them to accommodate the expanse of their egos.

Because of the significance that CC-H therapists readily assume in the lives of their clientele, a client can regard such a therapist as uniquely important. He can feel awed by a therapist's allegedly positive influence in his life, and doubt that it will ever be matched by anyone else.

While these kinds of circumstances move CC-H therapists to feigned expressions of modesty—"Yes, my inner spirit *seems* to have touched him"—one must ask: How easily do clients say "good-bye" to such a significantly central figure? Once a "good-bye" has been said, how much will those clients mourn? Moreover, to what degree do problems of saying "good-bye," and subsequent mourning, serve the best interests of clients?

CC-H therapists would do well to understand that after clients terminate therapy, they should forget their therapist as rapidly as possible. Doing so encourages clients to enjoy relationships that are open and spontaneous (instead of being reserved by appointment time). The emotional exchanges of open, spontaneous relationships allow people to define themselves as equals. Such relationships also have a future.

An excessively central therapist, as too many CC-H therapists are, does very little to ultimately promote the welfare of a client. The therapist's centrality to the therapy process, makes too many therapeutic changes dependent upon the therapist's presence and influence. Outside of the therapy session, removed from the immediate influence of a CC-H therapist, a client's progress can rapidly dissipate.

Again, the quality of the therapeutic relationship between client and therapist is not the ultimate issue in therapy. That relationship is only a means to an end, not an end in and of itself. Ultimately, the effectiveness of therapy is determined by whether a client's progress *in* a session is transferred *outside* the session. Such transfer is most appropriately directed to a client's relationships with other important people in his life.

In CC-H therapy, compensatory relationships predispose client and therapist to merely commiserate with each other. While doing so, they bemoan how difficult and unfortunate the client's situation is. Convinced that no one understands him as well as his therapist, a client can conclude that the therapist is a "special human being."

Impressive as they may sound, gushing testimonials about a therapist's reputation as a "special human being" demand skepticism. This kind of adulation contains the seeds of its own discrediting. The significance of a "special human being" is such that a client readily develops a dependency on him. Hero-worshiping dependency discourages independence and self-confidence; thus, it rarely serves the psychological welfare of clients very well.

SERVING THE CLIENT'S WELFARE?

Though their demeanor is relatively benevolent, CC-H therapists are not necessarily more sensitive to what their clients need. Additionally, the kind and gentle appearance of CC-H therapists can be deceptive. They impose their agenda on clients as often as therapists of other orientations, but they exercise their authority more indirectly.

In response to Rogerian theory, CC-H therapists assume that clients should direct the course of their own treatment. They also remain convinced that effective therapy requires clients to explore and vent their feelings. Thus, CC-H therapists know how they want their clients to respond to therapy, but they are disinclined to tell them. CC-H therapists resolve this dilemma by *subtly* leading their clients into introspective experiences.

Careful examination of audio tapes from Rogers' therapeutic work indicate that he insidiously coerced his clientele. When clients introspectively focused on their feelings in the manner he expected, Rogers responded more attentively, in a warm, accepting, empathic style. When clients did not exhibit an introspective style, Rogers became more distant, moderately cold, and less accepting of them.[6] These kinds of responses effectively influence clients to comply with their therapist's expectations.

More often than not, CC-H therapists exercise their influence unwittingly; they are unaware that they are doing it. While this consideration preserves the benevolent reputation of CC-H therapists, it raises other problems. Given the readiness with which CC-H therapists deceive themselves, they bring little objectivity to their therapeutic endeavors. As a result, they limit their capacity for empathic understanding; and they compromise their ability to assist clients.

It must also be emphasized that the unintentional influence of CC-H therapists does not lessen its effects. CC-H therapists direct the course of therapy subtly, but effectively, by selecting which client responses deserve their close attention and empathic concern. Clients who wallow in the sensory residue of their feelings are responding to their CC-H therapist's influence.

Indeed, one must conclude that the nondirective, client-centered features of CC-H therapy are more of a myth than a reality. Make no mistake: CC-H therapists control the therapy process far beyond what they understand or acknowledge.

WITH FRIENDS LIKE THIS . . .

On some occasions, CC-H therapists appear not to care very much for their clients. They demonstrate this disaffection despite their self-proclaimed commitment to "the inherent value as a human being" of nearly everyone! A bioexistential therapist, who is also very concerned about a client's relationship with his body, reported the following case:

> Albert entered therapy over a year ago at a time of going through a separation and divorce, as a tall, schizoid, very intellectualized and affect-lame, passively angry man whose self-concept as a child was "a brain in a jar on a shelf." He did not work well in Gestalt-type dialogues or any psychodramatic-like procedures attempted [other examples of CC-H procedures designed to encourage the ventilation of feelings]. He would get to the edge of feelings, come out of the dialogue and direct analytical, intellectualized comments to me.[7]

This therapist did not particularly care for Albert; his response to therapy deviated significantly from the therapist's preferences. The therapist preferred that Albert focus on his feelings and their sensory-visceral correlates. Unlike his client-centered colleagues, this humanistic therapist overtly expressed his expectations. Nevertheless, Albert disregarded these expectations; he remained determined to "direct analytical, intellectualized comments" to the therapist.

Clients who ignore their therapist's preference regarding the focus of therapy are also disinclined to properly appreciate their therapist's wisdom. Possibly, this therapist felt compelled to assassinate Albert's character because he frustrated him; Albert had neglected to endorse the therapist as a sage. The characterization of Albert as a " . . . schizoid, very intellectualized and affect-lame, passively angry man," was less than an enthusiastic endorsement of his value as a human being.*

Albert must have possessed some personal strengths that would have been a positive basis from which to build in therapy. This therapist, however, did not appear to see any strengths in Albert; and he certainly did not report them. Given the intensity of his negative reaction to Albert, and his decision to continue treating him, the appropriateness of this therapist's clinical judgment is open to question. One suspects that Albert would have responded more positively to a compassionate, empathic therapist.

Nonetheless, this therapist continued his course of treatment with Albert; and during one session in particular, Albert was described as . . .

> . . . extremely distraught that the woman with whom he is living will not "commit herself." He says that she has recently accused him of trying to control her, hold her down, "thwart her independence," and is preparing to move out to her own apartment. He reports paranoid ideation. When she types in the next room, he wonders what man she is writing a secret love letter to, etc.
>
> I ask him to assume a position in front of a foam rubber mattress with his knees bent sufficiently to be on the balls of his feet but not up on his toes, his pelvis dropped all the way back, and to reach out with his arms and, breathing long and deeply, to stand there until he has to fall. After less than a minute in this position, a look of stark terror comes over his face and he emits a snarling roar and falls onto the mattress,

---

*This is an example of a therapist using diagnostic labels as a weapon. Too often, therapists use such labels to assault the self-respect of their clientele. When therapists indulge their arrogance in this manner, their smugness is usually hidden behind a facade of professionalism. Consequently, diagnostic labels should probably be classified as concealed weapons.

beating it with his fists, sobbing, and screaming, "I hate them all (mother, former wife, current lover) and I won't fall in love!"[8]

Some observers might interpret Albert's fall as merely his inevitable capitulation to the law of gravity. Albert, however, knew that he should find profound importance in this event. Otherwise, he could find himself repeatedly falling on his face until he properly appreciated its existential significance.

Any physical ordeal, supplemented by a plausible sounding rationale, could have provoked Albert's experience of intense feelings. Requiring him to vigorously run backwards around the therapy room might have sufficed. He could have been told that this was an effective method for "getting back into important feelings of the past." More than anything else, the therapist's expectations influenced Albert's expressions of feelings. The therapist's somatic procedures merely created an atmosphere of dramatic intensity that enhanced his influence.

It is also appropriate to question the relevance of Albert's emotional experiences in therapy. He was contending with a long and difficult history of unresolved conflicts with females. One might well wonder how beating a mattress, while sobbing and screaming, could effectively assist Albert in resolving these problems? As a result of dramatically ventilating his feelings, were his conflicts resolved? How would the inspirational impact of these emotionally charged events in the session, constructively influence his situation outside the session?

Preoccupied with the emotional experiences of their clients, CC-H therapists rarely consider questions such as these. Instead, they assume that their procedures are effective as a matter of blind faith.

16

Ignorance is preferable to error; and he is less remote from the truth who believes nothing than he who believes what is wrong.

—THOMAS JEFFERSON

THERAPIST AS INTERLOPER

Because of their focus on the individual, traditional therapists overlook their clients' relationships with parents, marital partners, children, and friends. Whether they attend to their clients' insights, or feelings, or behavior, they exhibit an almost universal lack of interest in the social network that sustains—or fails to sustain—the client. Even more alarmingly, that lack of interest may deteriorate into disrespect.

Traditional therapists commonly disregard the impact of individual therapy on other people in a client's life. Correspondingly, they also ignore how those people react to that impact. Other important people in a client's life can feel threatened by the prospect of therapy changing their relationship with that client. Because individual therapy excludes those other people, it is difficult for them to approve a therapist's methods and goals. As a result, it is understandable that other people in a client's life can feel motivated to sabotage a therapist's work.[1]

Too often, individual psychotherapy leads clients into painful loyalty conflicts. Important people in their lives can pull them in one direction, and an excessively central thera-

127

pist pulls them in another. When the therapist's influence prevails in this therapeutic "tug-of-war," clients can find themselves alienated from significant others in their lives. This kind of alienation ensues because clients and therapists organize their relationship around the premise that "the enemy of my enemy is my friend."

When clients and therapists act as if influences outside of therapy threaten their relationship, the loyalty they share dramatically increases. This heightened loyalty often inspires therapists and clients to form a close alliance, and indict others in the clients' lives. In turn, these indictments disrupt the clients' relationships with people who are important to them.

TAKING SIDES

Given the close, therapeutic alliances that CC-H therapists create, they are particularly prone to disrupting a client's relationship with others. For example, it is always easier to prolong a conflict, especially with a disaffected spouse, if one enjoys the support of a sympathetic ally. Determined to qualify themselves as caring friends in the eyes of their clients, CC-H therapists often accomplish little more than to escalate marital conflicts.

When one spouse in a conflicted marriage ventures into CC-H therapy, the other spouse is often described as unwilling to undertake treatment. This reluctance invites therapeutic speculation about the absent spouse; it supposedly establishes a *prima facie* case of how severely inhibited his "caring" must be.

A CC-H therapist typically accepts as fact his client's report of the other spouse's disinterest in therapy. Because of his nondirective passivity, he rarely takes the initiative to personally contact a spouse who has been described as uninterested. Instead, he assumes that therapy and feelings are unimportant to a therapeutically absent spouse.

CC-H therapists are particularly intolerant of others who appear to reject their values about therapy and feelings. Thus, they can do a great deal to polarize existing value conflicts between spouses. CC-H therapists align themselves with their spouse-client, and provide support for this allegedly beleaguered victim who is so unfortunate to be married to someone uninterested in therapy. As a result, what might have been typical spousal conflicts, within a normal range of frequency and intensity, can deteriorate into chronically severe problems.

Even though they have not seen a therapeutically uninterested spouse, CC-H therapists confidently make conclusions about him. They can know he is the kind of person who conceals his feelings behind "a front or facade." He does not offer the kind of relationship "in which defenses can be dropped or in which significant learning and change can occur." They can also conclude that their victimized clients have no choice but to be "cautious and wary" in such a relationship.

In response to these conclusions, clients gratefully endorse the wisdom of therapists who seem so perceptive. As a result, therapeutically uninterested spouses should be advised not to provoke feelings of rejection in CC-H therapists. Once they feel rejected, their facility for brutal character assassination should not be underestimated.

If a CC-H therapist concludes that his client has significantly "outgrown" a therapeutically uninterested spouse, he can undertake a rescue mission. In order to save his client, the therapist seeks to extricate him from a supposedly oppressive relationship. Therapist and client create a close alliance with each other organized around the goal of extrication.

Once therapist and client have organized themselves in this manner, the allegedly uninterested spouse is systematically excluded from the therapy process. No matter how motivated the excluded spouse may be to save the marriage, the decision has been made—the marriage is over.

In one case known to this writer, an excluded husband eventually committed suicide. The wife in therapy had become closely aligned with a CC-H therapist. This therapist engaged in both subtle, and not-so-subtle character assassinations of the client's husband. The wife came to the conclusion that the marriage was no longer viable. The therapist responded supportively to the client's decision, with all the warmth and genuine understanding at his disposal. The therapist was determined to support the wife's decision; it underscored how he had apparently enhanced this client's levels of awareness.

Committed to a sympathetic alliance with his client, the therapist made no meaningful attempt to resolve the spousal conflicts in this case. He failed to do so, quite simply, because he did not know how to do so. The therapist regarded his credentials of "human authenticity" as sufficient for establishing his competence as a therapist. Unable to resolve these spousal conflicts, the therapist rapidly concluded that this marriage was hopeless.

When he learned of the other spouse's suicide, the therapist was moderately but only briefly distressed. Disregarding his own divisive influence, he rationalized that his client had "outgrown" the spouse who committed suicide. Any attorney who was familiar with this case might have advised this therapist to feel grateful that lawsuits are rarely filed from the grave.

ANALYTIC INTRUSIVENESS

This kind of divisive influence does not limit itself to CC-H therapists. For example, consider the reaction of a husband to his wife's analytic treatment, and then listen to the therapists's response. The husband emphatically protested,

> "The therapist is too smart, too influential. I am angry that they discuss me and decide for me. I am furious that the analyst said that she can't talk to me about her analysis.[1]

The therapist dismissed the complaints of the husband as those of a " . . . little boy, shut out of the grown-up's world."[2] Obviously, the response of this analytic therapist was grossly inappropriate.

One might well wonder what gave this therapist license to engage in such cruel, character assassination? Did this man really deserve ridicule for his worry and concern about how his wife's therapy would influence their marital relationship? The intensity of this husband's reaction underscores how divisively analytic therapy can intrude on the spouses and families of clients.

Analytic therapists attempt to rationalize the chaos and trauma created by their therapeutic practices. They insist that "the therapist, of course, must be guided by the interests of the patient, which may run very counter to those of the spouse or parent."[3] This attempt at differentiating between the welfare of a client as an individual, and the welfare of a client's family as a collectivity, is grossly artificial and exceedingly ill advised.

As a social animal, man's welfare as an individual is inextricably bound to the welfare of other people who are important to him. Nevertheless, these therapists insist that therapy can be helpful even though it ".... may drive a kind of wedge between the spouse or parent and the family member in treatment."[4] The logic of this position is not particularly convincing.

How does a client endure conflicts with spouse or family and still enjoy what these therapists blithely call "the promise of a happier life"? Interpersonal conflict causes people substantial psychological distress. An effective therapist seeks to resolve those conflicts—not exacerbate them.

Despite the willingness of these therapists to candidly discuss the problems their practices create for clients and families alike, they expressed no willingness to modify those practices. They did make a feeble attempt at minimizing the problems they precipitate for clients and families. They suggested that the intensity of these therapeutically created problems tends to "mellow" over the course of treatment. Nonetheless, they also cited the case of:

> One woman, who believes that her husband withdrew from the family and rarely listened to her during the years he was in analysis, has now taken a full-time job away from the family following his termination [of therapy]. She shows her wish for revenge in her comment, "Now I leave and I can't always listen to him whenever *he* wants *me* to."[5]

This outcome sounds more tragic than it sounds like any "mellowing" process. Perhaps this man's involvement in analytic therapy also led him to conclude, "I wish my wife and kids would just go away. They're interfering with my analysis." Was this man really enjoying "the promise of a happier life," once he was alienated from his wife, and his children were estranged to some degree from their mother?

PARENT BASHING

Psychoanalytic theory traces adult personality conflicts to trauma inflicted, usually by parents, during a child's formative years. Legions of analytic therapists are determined to repair this parental damage. Consequently, they explain in vivid detail how their parents supposedly failed them. Parents, and other family members, are subjected to repeated episodes of character assassination.

Given the disregard of analytic therapists for verifying the accuracy of their historical interpretations, clients' parents are convenient scapegoats. All kinds of client problems can be blamed on the parents. Analytic therapists frequently indict, and even convict the clients' parents for alleged misdeeds of the past. The parent's cannot defend themselves; they are usually excluded from the inquisitions that condemn them. Like all good inquisitors, analytic therapists prefer to conduct their endeavors behind closed doors.

When analytic therapists indulge in their unwarranted indictments of parents, they are using "blame-and-change" maneuvers. These maneuvers can persuade clients that therapy *blames* your parents in order to *change* you. A related study demonstrated that blame-and-change maneuvers are alive and well in psychotherapy.

When therapists described various members of their clients' families in the articles of a journal, more than 90 percent of the descriptions were negative, and less than 10 percent were positive.[7] The family members were portrayed as intellectually dull, critical and intrusive, and cold and withholding to cite but few examples. Especially alarming is the fact that the therapists arrived at these conclusions without ever having seen the people whose character they irresponsibly assassinated.

Other, more enlightened therapists reject blame-and-change maneuvers as merely amounting to "parentectomies."[8] Parentectomies—cutting clients away from parents—can cause serious harm. These procedures often lead clients into feelings of bitterness and alienation about their families.

Convinced that they have been regularly betrayed by their parents, for example, clients deal with them more guardedly. Bewildered by an adult child who seems defensive and moody, parents become distant and aloof. In analytic therapy, clients then describe their parents as remote and unapproachable, and the therapist explains the origins of the enormous burdens they presumably bear. In response to these interpretations, clients gratefully acknowledge their therapist's supposed wisdom— and the therapists enthusiastically applaud their clients' apparent perceptiveness. The French call this kind of situation *folie à deux*—meaning shared madness—but too many therapists call it psychotherapy.

Once analytic therapy is terminated, how does a client work out future relationships with parents and family? Who mends the ties that a therapist's accusations have torn? And, if worse comes to worse, how will a client replace those important relationships when they have completely deteriorated under the hypercritical scrutiny of an analytic therapist?

Other than referring clients to analytically oriented group therapy, which is typically no more than a mediocre family substitute, analytic therapists do not answer these questions very well.

THE STORY OF DAN

Dan, a sixteen-year-old student enrolled in the tenth grade at a midwestern boarding school, was referred to an analytic therapist. Dan was contending with academic problems and conflicts with his peers. He was described as possessing . . .

... an extraordinarily strong motivation for a high level of academic success, which had recently been disrupted by frequent squabbles with his peers. Dan frequently accused the other youngsters of ridiculing him, an accusation that the teachers asserted was often "made up." In fact, Dan often "makes fun of himself" and "verbally abuses his peers," and then cried when they reacted.[9]

The therapist also explained that Dan had a slightly deformed arm. Over the course of his therapy, Dan . . .

... spoke a great deal of his father, always in idealized terms, and never mentioned his mother. For example, he described his father as having worked his way up the socioeconomic ladder to become a "director of research," as "super-orderly" and "super-sociable," and as a harsh disciplinarian intolerant of weakness: "By my father there is no such thing as fear."[10]

In summarizing this case, the therapist emphasized: "Dan's description of family life revealed a father who demanded total success from Dan as a means of validating his own [the father's] worth."[11] In other words, the therapist was convinced that Dan's father saw Dan merely as an extension of himself.

Dan's therapy was organized around four assumptions made by his therapist. First, the therapist assumed that Dan had long been disappointed in his relationship with his father; a disappointment he repressed. Second, the therapist assumed that Dan's defective arm was a topic his father would not discuss. Third, the therapist assumed that Dan's father provided little encouragement regarding Dan's physical handicap. Finally, the therapist assumed that Dan's father possessed personality problems so severe that he failed to recognize his son's individuality.

These assumptions were no more than unverified, intuitive impressions. The therapist made these conclusions about Dan's father despite the fact that he had neither met nor even spoken to him. Dan may have needed expressions of confidence and emotional support from his father. But he did not need the conflicts and distress likely created by the therapist's assassination of his father's character.

BLAME AND CHANGE MANEUVERS

Dan's therapist was determined to pull him from the darkness of his supposed self-deception into the light of insightful understanding. The therapist never doubted that insight would serve as an emancipating experience for Dan. If Dan could only understand how his father had supposedly betrayed him, his problems would be resolved.

The therapist disregarded the likelihood that accusing the father damaged Dan. Rather than harming Dan, the therapist thought himself involved in pursuing the "truths" responsible for Dan's distress. In this pursuit, the therapist ignored how his indictments could influence Dan's future relationship with his father.

Had Dan concluded that his father was a callous, selfish man, who saw his son only as an extension of himself, how would he relate to his father in the future? At sixteen years of age, Dan still needed the guidance and emotional support of a father. Once he knew of his father's alleged betrayals, who would provide the guidance and emotional support he needed in the future—his therapist?

Fortunately, Dan resisted his therapist's attempts at indoctrinating him. Over the course of his therapy, he clearly indicated confidence that his parents loved him. This confidence apparently allowed him to conclude that his therapy was a waste of time and energy. As a result, he fired the therapist.

The therapist did not regard Dan's course of therapy as successful. He attributed the negative outcome of this case to obscure technical errors he committed in his method of interpretation. The therapist never doubted the value of assassinating the father's character. He merely confined his reservations to *how* he proceeded in this endeavor.

Dan's therapist may have underestimated the value of Dan's therapy. As he defended his father against the therapist's onslaughts, Dan could have become even more aware of the many ways in which he valued his father. Defending his father necessitated that Dan focus on those characteristics of his father that he considered positive.

If Dan discussed his therapy with his father, they may have shared incredulous anger with each other at how incompetent the therapist was. The bonds of loyalty and esteem between two people can be substantially strengthened when angered at the same third party. Moreover, a father is compelled to feel a strong sense of pride and admiration for a son who has tenaciously defended the father's character. Thus, the therapist may have encouraged a closer relationship between Dan and his father than had existed previously.

It is sobering, however, to consider the consequences of therapy when an adolescent is unable to resist the kind of indoctrination pursued by Dan's therapist. Once an adolescent client is convinced that a parent is an insensitive, selfish figure who has betrayed him, how will that adolescent resolve normal conflicts with the parent in the future?

Therapy can leave adolescents with pronounced feelings of bitterness and betrayal about their parents. Once saddled with such a legacy by a therapist, how well does an adolescent adjust to the future course of his life? If adolescents cannot trust their own parents, who can they trust?

BEHAVIORAL BLAMING

A behavior therapist reported the case of a divorced, childless, twenty-eight-year-old tax attorney, who felt "nervous, confused and unfulfilled'."[12] This client ("Sam") was described as an individual who had always excelled in school. Nevertheless, he had no close friends; and he typically felt uncomfortable in the presence of other people. Sam sought therapy to overcome his claustrophobia.

In the second session, the therapist sensed unresolved conflicts between Sam and his parents. The following dialogue ensued:

> **Therapist:** So with that background let's just suppose that little Sam had a temper tantrum. How would Mom and Dad react?
>
> **Sam:** Well, they certainly wouldn't like it.
>
> **Therapist:** Would they beat little Sam, lock him up, verbally reprimand him, or what?
>
> **Sam:** Oh, I would say they'd do all of it. My dad used to hit first and my mother was called "crab" because she would pinch my sister and me when she was riled.
>
> **Therapist:** And all of this gives you no cause for anger or resentment?
>
> **Sam:** Are you deliberately trying to create a feeling of antagonism in me? Do you want to hear that I hate my parents?
>
> **Therapist:** Only if it's true. I feel that you deny your own emotions and that you find anger especially threatening. I'm trying to put you in touch with your anger so that you can learn to express it in a socially acceptable way. With your background, I would find myself hating and resenting certain things about my parents while, at the same time, loving other qualities and attributes. But I wouldn't deny the negatives, and while focusing on them, I would feel aggressive if not rather murderous.[13]

As the previous dialogue illustrates, blame-and-change maneuvers are not confined to analytic therapists. Behavior therapists also attempt to resolve a client's distress by indicting his family. Sam was not particularly impressed by the evidence against his parents; thus, he emphatically declined to endorse the therapist's indictments. To his credit, this particular therapist was sensitive and flexible enough to retreat from his overt indictments of Sam's parents.

The therapist then proposed that Sam and his parents meet

with him in a family therapy session. Sam was less than enthusiastic about this proposal and he rejected it. Even though the therapist had abandoned his indictments of Sam's parents, he had already sown the seeds of Sam's concerns. Sam probably continued to worry whether the therapist would treat his parents properly and compassionately.

Basically, Sam doubted whether family therapy could result in a positive outcome. Likely, he was concerned that the therapist might pour gasoline on the already smoldering coals of familial conflict. The family explosiveness that could result struck Sam as neither desirable nor constructive.

Both Sam and Dan assertively resisted their therapists' divisive influences; they refused the invitations to indict their parents. But without any watchdogs to monitor therapists, this outcome is not guaranteed. Children, in particular, need protection from parent-bashing, but parents are routinely excluded from their child's therapy sessions.

Blame-and-change maneuvers do not resolve interpersonal conflicts between clients and their families. These tactics intensify and escalate those conflicts; and they leave clients alienated from their families. Committed to promoting a client's independence, analytic therapists too often applaud alienation from family as a favorable outcome.

Émile Durkheim, the 19th century French sociologist, outlined the manner in which alienation jeopardizes the psychological welfare of all people.[14] Alienation is associated with elevated rates of psychological distress in general, and an increased likelihood of suicide in particular. Durkheim's work was first published in 1897. Apparently, many therapists have not heard about Durkheim's work. They continue to disregard the counterproductiveness of alienation between client and family; and as they do so, they neglect the welfare of their clients.

17

One hug from a family member is worth a hundred from a therapist.

—CARL WHITAKER

THERAPIST AS SUBSTITUTE PARENT

When children are physically ill, their parents know what to expect from medical practitioners. They take their children to a physician who diagnoses the child's illness, prescribes appropriate medication, and possibly orders some other therapeutic regimen. Though parents participate in this process, their participation is relatively passive and peripheral. They expect a physician to "fix" the child's physical ailment; their involvement is limited to insuring their child's compliance with the physician's orders.

Parents also expect that psychotherapeutic treatment for their children corresponds to medical care. Parents assume that a psychotherapist "fixes" psychological distress like a physician "fixes" physical ailments. Thus, without an invitation to participate in their child's therapy, most parents distance themselves from it. It would be inappropriate to fault these parents as uninterested in the welfare of their children. Instead, they are disinclined to do anything that would interfere with a therapist's work.

Unfortunately, too many psychotherapists readily endorse the mythical virtues of pa-

139

rental noninterference. Parents are led to believe that therapists are experts whose special skills will help their children.
Supposedly, these experts can resolve a child's problems without parental involvement. Reassured by an appearance of expertise, most parents assume a passive role in their child's
therapy.

Parents are told that participating in their child's therapy
could lead to undesirable consequences. Therapists who work
with children act as if the efficiency of their endeavors necessitates a confidential relationship with their clientele. As a result, parents are expected to maintain substantial distance
from their child's treatment.

One child therapist explained her rationale for excluding
parents to a mother:

> What a child actually does in his therapy must be
> between him and me. Only then will he feel free to
> bring to me those things that he has secreted in little
> grubby hideaway holes in his mind or that he has
> interred more spoorlessly for fear that they will frighten
> or destroy.[1]

A therapist who engages in a practice such as this disqualifies
parents from helping their own children. Indeed, whether it be
overtly or covertly, the therapist is defining the parent as less
than competent.

Not surprisingly, then, the outcome research related to the
effectiveness of individual therapy for children is sobering to
say the least. A study of clinic-based therapy, as opposed to
research-based therapy (see Chapter 2), reported that 52 percent of the children neither improved nor regressed, 45 percent
improved, and 3 percent deteriorated as result of treatment.[2]
These results indicate that individual therapy for children is, at
best, a 50-50 gamble regarding improvement. This same study
also found that changes in parental behavior increased the
likelihood of a positive outcome for their children, but it never
mentioned the inappropriateness of excluding parents from
their child's therapy.

Parents who are excluded from their child's therapy can feel
left in the dark. They know that the therapist evaluates them;
but they remain unaware of how they are evaluated and what
is expected of them. Faced with a situation that requires paren-

tal decisiveness, such parents may hesitate and appear incompetent. They wonder what they should do, doubt what they could do, and postpone what they otherwise would do. These kinds of circumstances lead parents into feelings of confusion and self-doubt.

Confused, self-doubting parents continue to struggle with the unchanging, often escalating problems of their offspring. Consequently, individual therapy for children and adolescents frequently leads to counterproductive outcomes.

Prevailing methods of psychotherapy for children and adolescents are organized around the same analytic, client centered-humanistic (CC-H), and behavioral procedures used for adults. Compared to other procedures, however, play therapy techniques are unique to children. Play therapists have used their techniques with children for over forty years. They regard the spontaneous play activities of children as possessing impressive therapeutic value.

PLAY THERAPY

Play therapy is assumed to possess therapeutic value because . . .

> . . . play is the child's natural medium of self-expression. It is an opportunity which is given to the child to "play out" his feelings and problems just as, in certain types of adult therapy, an individual "talks out" his difficulties.[3]

This is a therapy that shares a great deal in common with CC-H procedures. The opportunity for children to "get their feelings out" is considered a valuable, therapeutic experience. Also, play therapy supposedly helps distressed children because, "The presence of an accepting, understanding, friendly therapist in the playroom gives him a sense of security."[4]

Additionally, the play therapist . . .

> . . . respects the child and his ability to stand on his own two feet and to become a more independent individual if he is given the opportunity to do so . . . [the therapist] is understanding him and accepting him at all times regardless of what he says or does. Thus the therapist gives him the courage to go deeper and deeper into his

into his innermost world and bring out into the open his
real self.[5]

Inspirational as this rhetoric may sound, its assumptions demand closer examination.

However desirable it might be for a child to enjoy a sense of
security with a play therapist, it is altogether more desirable
for a child to enjoy that sense of security with his parents. The
manner in which conventional play therapy is structured precludes this outcome. Too often, play therapists interfere as
interlopers between parents and their children. If they are to be
anymore than mere interlopers, they must address themselves
to the feelings of security that exist between children and their
parents.

Children who enjoy a sense of emotional security with their
parents are children whose psychological distress is more readily
resolved. Too many play therapists fail to promote feelings of
emotional security between children and their parents. Instead, they are determined to solicit those feelings for themselves.

As they attempt to create a sense of emotional security
between themselves and their clients, play therapists often hug
and hold children. One play therapist described how she physically held a seven-year-old boy:

> He came to the playroom each time and climbed straight
> into my lap. No dubiousness. No hesitance. This was what
> he wanted. Contact with me *as though I were his mother*
> [emphasis added]. To be held by me quite simply.[6]

In fact, this therapist was *not* the child's mother. The therapist seemed to recognize that her client needed this kind of
warm, affectionate interaction with his real mother. Nevertheless, the therapist did nothing to promote a warmer, more
affectionate relationship between this mother and child. While
hugging and holding this boy, the therapist merely compensated for the presumed deficits in his mother-son relationship.
She sought to give him the warmth and affection that his
parents allegedly could not.

When play therapists act as if they are more prepared to
meet a child's needs for affection than are his parents, they
undermine that child's psychological welfare. Affectionate ex-

changes between a child and his parents are far more important than such exchanges between a child and a therapist. Consequently, play therapists who hug children should be regarded as abusive. They are abusing the bonds of affection that should rightfully prevail between parent and child.

Though traditional psychotherapy enjoys various degrees of placebo effectiveness, the same cannot be said of play therapy. A review of the research literature examining the effectiveness of play therapy is sobering to say the least. There is no evidence that play therapy increases academic and intellectual achievement, resolves specific behavioral disorders, enhances interpersonal functioning, or facilitates personal adjustment. Commenting on the status of play therapy research, a reviewer stated:

> This is a disheartening state of affairs for those who feel strongly about play therapy. The data lead to a puzzling paradox. Why is it that clinical wisdom regarding the value of play therapy is unsubstantiated by the empirical results? Is a clinical activity being utilized whose value is at least suspect?[7]

Clearly, the research evidence indicates that the value of play therapy ranges from suspect to nonexistent. This research also compels one to regard the "clinical wisdom regarding the value of play therapy" as a clinical myth. Quite simply, there is no available research allowing play therapists to claim that their procedures are effective.

Health insurance companies commonly refuse to cover treatments which they regard as experimental. They refuse to do so pending the availability of research evidence to verify the efficacy of those treatments. In the case of play therapy, it is clear and evident that these methods have never evolved beyond the experimental stage. Consequently, the time has come for health insurers to seriously review their readiness to reimburse play therapists for their services.

THERAPIST AS CHAUFFEUR

While therapists who treat adolescents rarely use play therapy, they can make the same errors that play therapists commit—both create compensatory relationships with distressing regularity. For example, consider the therapist's excessively central significance in the life of the following client.

A nineteen-year-old male was referred for individual psychotherapy. He was described as socially isolating himself via self-imposed confinement in his home. This client appeared to have long been immersed in a hotly contested power struggle with his parents. Because his parents made the initial contact with the therapist, the client considered him his parents' agent and distrusted him as a result. In fact, however, the therapist was very sympathetic to the client's situation. The therapist explained:

> Contact with this boy's parents showed a very controlling and manipulative pattern of interaction with their son. The client, unable to give vent to his resentment, had instead evolved the strategy of maintaining an air of aloofness and detachment to protect himself from his parents' over-controlling behavior.[8]

Nevertheless, the client remained adamant in his refusal to see the therapist in his office.

Determined to demonstrate his sympathy for the client's supposed plight, the therapist suggested they go for a "drive." The client agreed to this suggestion and therapy was initiated in the therapist's vehicle. The therapist also explained:

> In fact, during the first year of therapy, going for a "drive" together was the only mode of interaction permitted by the client. Nonetheless, this had the important advantage of involving him with the real world of visiting museums, seeing movies, and attending sporting events, a step which he would not have been able to take without the security afforded by the therapist's companionship.[9]

While navigating about in his therapeutic taxi, this therapist created a sympathetic coalition between himself and the client. Moreover, this coalition was effectively aligned against the client's parents.

Once the therapist assumed his role as the client's sympathetic ally, he negated any capacity he might have had to resolve the conflicts between the client and his parents. Quite simply, no one can resolve a two-party conflict if they are perceived as a loyal ally of one of the parties. In such circumstances, the ally loses any appearance of objectivity. Consequently, this therapist escalated the intensity of the conflicts between the client and his parents.

A competent therapist would have addressed himself to resolving such conflicts, and promoting more gratifying relationships within the client's family. Trips to museums, seeing movies, and attending sporting events could have been legitimate therapeutic experiences had the client shared them with his parents. These experiences, however, were confined to the client's relationship with the therapist. As a result, the therapist appointed himself to a role of undeserved significance in the client's life.

Deeply committed to his role as a surrogate parent, the therapist became an enviable standard of comparison against which the parents were now forced to compete. As too many play therapists do, this therapist fired the client's parents while creating a compensatory relationship with the client.

The long-term consequences of this therapist's intrusiveness were very disturbing. After more than a year of therapy, the divisive relationship between the client and his parents remained unchanged. The therapist neglected his responsibility to repair the rapidly deteriorating relationships within this family.

Without a truce prevailing between this client and his parents, their mutual frustration likely predisposed them to escalating power struggles. Continued power-struggling with his parents must have sabotaged this client's attempts at independence and leaving home. He probably invested more time and energy in power struggles than in establishing his independence. And without sufficient independence to leave home, the client felt trapped and compelled to pursue more power struggles.

Because the therapist ignored this impasse, he could not resolve it. Thus, the meter on the therapist's therapeutic taxi likely continued to tick away for many more months.

ADOLESCENTS AND INDIVIDUAL THERAPY

When considering the appropriateness of individual therapy for adolescents, one must ask: Can any therapist actually compete with the bonds of affection and loyalty that exist between parents and their adolescent? Do therapists really think that they exhibit a greater regard for their teen-age clientele than their parents do? Are therapists actually prepared to make the sacrifices for their adolescent clients that their parents will?

Therapists who consistently answer "yes" to these questions require treatment for their grandiosity. The welfare of adolescents necessitates that therapists work *with* their parents — not against them. When therapists align themselves against an adolescent's parents, they overestimate the impact of individual therapy.

Any therapist who assumes that individual therapy negates parental influences is exhibiting colossal naivete. When therapists seek that outcome, they are inviting power struggles which they usually lose. Quite simply, therapists cannot compete with years of emotional bonding, and shared experience, that exist between adolescents and their parents.

Therapists who assume that such negation of parental influence is desirable—regardless of whether or not it can be accomplished—are irresponsibly cruel and callous. Despite the accusations that many adolescents direct at their parents, they do not want to really disown them.

Developmentally normal processes of increasing independence necessitate that adolescents episodically indict their parents. As they do so, they seek enough distance between themselves and their families to establish a sense of their own individuality. All parents, no matter how competent and compassionate they are, endure these episodic indictments from their adolescent offspring.

Too often, therapists are so naive that they fail to see the indictments of parental figures for the dramatic smokescreens they really are. Instead, many therapists overreact and assume that they must save such an adolescent from the allegedly negative influence of a parental figure. Therapists who undertake such rescue missions are in jeopardy of creating more problems than they will ever solve.

Adolescents who make these indictments really want no more than a new kind of relationship with their parents. Specifically, they want a relationship that is reorganized around a recognition of their greater independence and autonomy. They do not want to sever future relationships with their parents. Emotionally intense as adolescents are when they indict their parents, they are merely demonstrating their emotional zeal.

This is the same zeal they bring to bear on so many other of their life activities.

The fundamental loyalty of adolescents to their parents should not be underestimated. Unless they know that the psychological welfare of their parents is "OK," most adolescents cannot feel "OK" about themselves and their own lives. Therefore, effective therapists address themselves to resolving conflicts between teen-agers and their parents. Most importantly, an effective therapist does not encourage the escalation of those conflicts.

WORKING AROUND THE PARENTS

James is a foster child enrolled in a forty-five day residential program at a therapeutic, summer camp. The camp's pastoral setting in the White Mountains of New Hampshire provides a beautiful, tranquil environment. The program of the camp is organized around behavioral procedures. Goals are defined in terms of observable changes in a child's overt behavior. Programs of systematic reward are employed to modify the behavior of the campers. Contracts that specify well-defined behavioral goals are outlined for each camper.

Often, these contracts are written in a metaphorical manner that is ingeniously creative. James' contract read:

> I am a wonderful boy but I have a broken heart. This heart of mine has been broken many, many times. But I haven't given up. Sometimes my broken heart gets in the way and I do things which make people mad, particularly my foster parents.

> But I want to get along, be a good kid with my foster parents, and do things right. But most of all, I want shoes! I am going to start to fix my heart and get help from my foster mom and foster dad. I am going to earn hearts for listening, being cooperative and not being silly. I can earn up to 15 hearts a day. Fifteen little heart stickers will bring me one whole heart sticker. Five big whole heart stickers earns me one pair of shoes. Can James have a big, mended heart? We'll have to wait and see.[10]

James and his foster parents signed the contract. It was reviewed weekly by the camp's professional staff. James' foster parents also reviewed the contract during their two visits with him while he was at camp. If James' heart has been "mended" at camp, one must ask if it will remain mended when he returns to his foster home. Will the behavioral progress acquired at camp exhibit itself in the familiarity of the foster home?

Had the camp taught James' parents how to give "hearts," it would have increased the effectiveness of this procedure. Unfortunately, however, this camp limited parents to peripheral participation in its program. Consequently, these parents could have overlooked their child's progress because they did not know what to expect.

Another boy came to camp who exhibited the symptoms of a sullen, subtly stubborn victim. He often refused to eat, he rarely participated in sports activities, and he never defended himself. After six weeks at camp, this boy was appropriately assertive. He joined in various sports and earned the respect of his peers. His impressive gains transpired in a peer group organized by professional staff. This boy left camp with pleasant memories of positive experiences in his peer group.

The professional staff of the camp attributed substantial power and influence to this boy's camp experiences. The staff assumed that these experiences would be potent enough to resolve difficult circumstances in his home. When he was about to depart from camp, his counselor told him:

> When you go home . . . you know that when you eat well, when you act strong, you may not get as much attention. But just remember, you are a full-fledged member of the Stallions [the boy's peer group while at camp].[11]

Well intended as this counselor's advice was, it still raises some distressing questions. How influential are pleasant memories of positive experiences with a peer group? Can they sustain this boy's behavior changes when that peer group is no longer available to him? Originally, this boy was oppositional and defiant in his home. These behavioral symptoms were modified in the camp. Ultimately, the effectiveness of this therapeutic camp must be determined by whether its behavioral gains generalize to a camper's home.

In this particular case, the "Stallion" exhibited impressive progress when he initially returned home; by Thanksgiving, however, ". . . he slipped sharply. . ."[12] To the counselor's credit, he recognized that this boy might well regress. Nevertheless, the camp's therapeutic program was not organized to prevent this kind of regression. The camp experiences, by virtue of how they were structured, were not as therapeutically potent as the professional staff assumed.

This therapeutic camp was organized so that the camp and its professional staff received the credit for "fixing" a child. The camp program was not structured so that parents developed an increased sense of confidence in themselves as parents.

Removed from the supportive, therapeutic atmosphere of the camp, some children could regress to former patterns of inappropriate behavior. What are parents to do under such circumstances, especially when they are forced to view their child's progress in camp as unrelated to anything they did? Such parents could respond to a regressing child with a passively resigned attitude of "here we go again."

A child who is regressing does not need a passively resigned parent. Rather than a discouraged parent, this child needs a confident parent who can take charge of the situation, and rapidly bring the child's regression under control. Confident parents, by virtue of their confidence, can do a great do a great deal to stabilize the behavior of their children.

A child who regards his parents as confident in themselves is a child who knows what to expect in the course of family life; family life is not a chaotic experience for such a child. A consistent and stable family atmosphere significantly enhances any child's psychological welfare. Consequently, if it had addressed itself to enhancing the confidence levels of parents, this therapeutic camp would have achieved more effective outcomes.

ENLISTING PARENTS HELP

Parents should not have to compete with therapists who immodestly establish themselves as paragons of wisdom and kindness in the eyes of their clientele. Instead, parents should be *the* paramount figures of wisdom and kindness in the lives of their children. Parents should also be *the* significant sources of emotional security for their children, not some intrusive therapist.

Additionally, the welfare of youthful clients is not well served when therapists assassinate their parents' character. Such practices saddle youthful clients with feelings of bitterness and betrayal in future relationships with their parents. Therapists who burden their youthful clientele with this kind of legacy create a situation where that clientele may appear to need more therapy.

When a therapist appoints himself as a semi-permanent fixture in the life of a youthful client, he no longer serves as a problem solver; instead, he intrudes as a problem perpetuator. While an effective therapist resolves conflicts between clients and their parents, a problem-perpetuating therapist too often escalates them.

When therapists exclude parents from their child's therapy, they are acting as if those parents are malevolent figures in the lives of their children. It is inevitable that all parents make mistakes in raising their children; there is no such thing as a perfect parent. It is the rare parent, however, who sets out with premeditated malice to sabotage the psychological welfare of his children. The vast majority of parents love their children deeply and genuinely want what is best for them. Though parents do err, their mistakes are not malevolent.

An effective therapist promotes affectionate exchanges between parents and their children. Moreover, an effective therapist does so by seeing parents and children together as a family. This way, a therapist can mobilize parent-child relationships to enhance a child's feelings of trust and security.

Trusting, secure parent-child relationships characterize families that have been empowered with collective feelings of self-confidence. Effective therapy for children and adolescents addresses itself to creating these feelings of familial empowerment. Empowered families in general, and self-assured parents in particular, feel confident in their ability to effectively problem solve on behalf of their children.

Once empowered, families contend successfully with future developmental changes in the lives of their children. They do not need a therapist to negotiate each new developmental change confronting the family.

18

Common sense is not so common.

—VOLTAIRE

THERAPIST AS SUBSTITUTE SPOUSE

Therapy for children fails when it excludes parents from the process. It flounders not only because it exacerbates existing family conflicts, but also because it neglects to enlist parental support for the child's psychological welfare.

The same is true when dealing with marital problems. Individual psychotherapy, regardless of its theoretical orientation, will not suffice. Any individual therapy assumes that only the client experiences problems with the marriage. The problems or conflicts certainly do not involve the client's mate. Presumably, the mate is merely a victim of the client's unresolved conflicts. Psychotherapeutic reasoning such as this can only be regarded as colossally naive.

Individual psychotherapy disregards the valuable input that a mate can bring to treatment. This kind of input can assist the client and enhance the marriage. Traditional therapy, however, encourages therapeutic alliances that can cause more problems than they solve. A sympathetic coalition between client and therapist may

151

widen the rift already dividing a couple.

THE ANALYTIC FORMULA

In pre-feminist times, husbands commonly sent their "nervous, somewhat unbalanced" wives for treatment. The analytic therapist, who was usually a male, typically concurred with the husband's diagnostic impression. The therapist would also confer professional legitimacy upon a husband's opinion via a formal diagnosis.* A course of long-term analytic therapy would then be undertaken with the wife.

While these wives examined the alleged inadequacies of their feminine egos, their husbands remained well protected from analytic scrutiny. They enjoyed their sense of sanctuary because both therapist and husband "knew" who had the problem—the female client did. Some observers of the therapeutic scene would insist that practices such as these are still too common.

Nonetheless, most analytic therapists are very reluctant to bring spouses together in therapy. They insist that such a practice contaminates the transference relationship between client and therapist. In truth, analytic therapists not only protect the transference relationship when they refuse to see spouses together; they also conceal their own ineffectiveness. Analytic therapists lack the skill to manage spousal conflict that spontaneously erupts in their offices.

Remember, this is a very passive, exceedingly cerebral, profoundly reflective therapy. Intellectual passivity is not well received by spouses engaged in active marital combat. In fact, combative spouses embrace insight with the same enthusiasm with which they embrace each other.

Analytic therapists fail to understand that designating a particular spouse as *the* client is an arbitrary decision. More sophisticated therapists regard the relationship that exists between spouses as the object of treatment—not one particular spouse or the other. Indeed, research evidence indicates that

*Diagnoses are very important to analytic therapists. They often use diagnostic labels to assassinate the character of clients who frustrate them. Outspoken clients, who ridicule a therapist's speculative interpretations, can be labeled a "narcissistic character disorder." Once so labeled, any protests from such a client are dismissed as the whining of an immature personality, preoccupied with self-adulation, while demanding to have his own way.

analytic therapy is ineffective in resolving marital or familial conflicts.

In one study, clients who presented complaints of marital and/or family discord exhibited little tolerance for individual, analytic therapy. These clients were apt to terminate therapy in a manner that their therapist considered "premature."[1] Apparently, they were impatient with the striking limitations of this therapy to effectively meet their needs.

The outcome of the previously cited study is not surprising. Analytic therapy addresses only half the problem, and its principle tool—insight—is strikingly ill-suited to the task. The insight of one spouse rarely resolves a pattern of marital conflicts. When one spouse is insightful, the other spouse may find it difficult to adjust. Excluded from his spouse's therapy, he does not know what to expect. Unfamiliar circumstances can cause anxiety for everyone; and changes in a marriage— even when positive—can seem very unfamiliar.

Motivated to restore some comforting sense of familiarity to their marriage, the "non-insightful" spouse unwittingly invites the insightful spouse back into former patterns of interacting. Because married clients usually spend more time with their spouse than their therapist (admittedly not always!), the temptations of familiarity often prevail. Thus, the influence of insight rapidly diminishes when confined to one spouse.

Nevertheless, it rarely occurs to analytic therapists that clients and their spouses are mutually involved in precipitating and maintaining each other's maladjustments. This is another conceptual shortcoming that severely limits the effectiveness of analytic therapy.

THE INTERPERSONAL THEORY OF ANALYTIC THERAPY

A contemporary version of analytic theory emphasizes that interpersonal relationships are the appropriate focus for analytic therapy. Interpersonal relationship theorists insist that distressed people respond to distress in their interpersonal life—their problems are not confined to conflicts within their psyches. Instead, the intrapsychic conflicts of any client correspond to his state of interpersonal satisfaction or frustration.

This orientation wants clients to insightfully understand their conflicts with other people. Recent research has indicated that a client's interpersonal conflicts are relevant to therapy. The accuracy with which a therapist interpreted such conflicts moderately influenced therapy outcome.[2]

Encouraging as this research may seem, its interpersonal emphasis remains confined to theory alone. This emphasis is not meaningfully integrated into the actual practice of therapy. By virtue of how it is organized, individual therapy limits a therapist to "talking about" interpersonal relationships.

If the resolution of interpersonal conflicts really influences psychotherapy outcome, then a great deal of individual therapy is a burdensome waste of time. In therapy, effective resolution of interpersonal conflicts necessitates the participation of significant others with whom a client is conflicted. Analytic therapists, however, overlook the futility of most individual therapy. Even though important people in a client's life are typically excluded from the therapy process, analytic therapists disregard the consequences of their practices.

CC-H THERAPY AND INTERPERSONAL CONFLICT

CC-H therapists also lack well-developed skills for conflict resolution. When CC-H therapists attempt to see conflicted individuals together (spouses, parents, children, etc.), they often fail miserably. Candid exchanges of feeling between conflicted individuals accomplish little more than to dramatically escalate their conflicts.

Nonstop screaming between individuals who are less than enchanted with each other is not a constructive therapeutic experience for anyone. Even CC-H therapists are distressed by sessions involving conflicted individuals that escalate out of control. Nevertheless, the nondirective passivity of CC-H therapists sabotages their attempts at resolving interpersonal conflicts.

CC-H therapists frequently see one spouse in therapy, while they refer the other spouse to another CC-H therapist. When conflicted spouses undertake individual treatment, they often attempt to enlist their respective therapist as an ally. These attempts are not surprising. Each spouse can feel convinced that they have been victimized by the insensitive selfishness of their mate. What may be surprising, however, is the frequency with which spouses succeed in their recruiting campaigns.

Preoccupied with the feelings of their clients, CC-H therapists rapidly lose their objectivity. Consequently, they readily
volunteer themselves as sympathetic allies for distressed
spouses. Often, it does not take long for a therapist to conclude
that a client's spouse is insensitive and selfish. Once a therapist
comes to this conclusion, he has certainly demonstrated that he
understands a client's experience as the client experiences it.
He may also conclude that his client is an "authentic human
being" who merely wants a genuine relationship with the other
spouse.

Assuming that clients demonstrate the same "authenticity"
with their spouse as with their therapist is a profound leap of
faith. Without actually observing spousal interactions on a
firsthand basis, it is exceedingly difficult for any therapist to
accurately infer how a client interacts with a spouse.

If two spouses see different CC-H therapists at the same
clinic, some interesting, professional transactions can ensue.
The two therapists who treat these spouses can involve themselves in bitter, frustrated exchanges with each other. Each
may feel compelled to enlighten the other about his apparent
shortsightedness. Each therapist is convinced that his colleague
is overlooking important issues in dealing with his respective
spouse-client. Each therapist knows this is true because his
own client has convinced him of it.

Therapists who create this kind of dilemma for themselves
suffer the effects of myopic thinking. They rarely understand
that their professional conflicts merely reflect their clients'
spousal conflicts.

Once enlisted as a loyal ally for his spouse-client, a CC-H
therapist may eventually conclude that his client has "outgrown" the other spouse. The euphemism of "growth" allows a
therapist to conveniently ignore his own incompetence. He can
disregard how he failed to resolve the conflicts between his
client and his client's spouse.

When spouse-clients know they have "outgrown" their spousal counterpart—because a therapist has verified this circum-
stance for them—divorce is often inevitable. The illusion of
"growth," however, abates the intensity of mourning for a failed
marriage. As a result, the CC-H therapist is not a therapist who
failed to resolve marital conflicts; he is a therapist who facilitated "growth."

If both CC-H therapists are overcome with feelings of charity and fairness for each other, and for each other's spouse-client, they can decide that both spouse-clients simultaneously "outgrew" each other. The euphemism of "growth" creates an illusion that everyone has won, and no one has lost. The spouses have not failed, and the therapists most certainly have not failed; everyone enjoys an illusion of "growth."

Effective conflict resolution necessitates that therapists influence the patterns of interaction between conflicted individuals. Such influence allows therapists to lead them into new patterns of interacting with each other. Without this influence, they merely continue to exchange their accusations and counteraccusations.

CC-H therapists, however, rarely respond this actively to their clientele. They are profoundly disinclined, and exceedingly ill-prepared, to exercise directive influence in therapy. By virtue of their passivity, they often reduce themselves to helpless spectators while their clients struggle with escalating conflicts. As a result, they neglect the needs of their clients who contend with marital stress.

A BEHAVIORAL APPROACH

Ann, a thirty-five-year-old mother of two who worked part-time and was married to a dentist, sought the services of a behavior therapist. She was described as exhibiting " . . . . feelings of depression, severe and seemingly pervasive anxiety, lack of incentive, inability to function independently, and marked feelings of helplessness and inadequacy."[3]

The client, who was the third-born of three children and the only daughter, had been raised in a large Midwestern city. Her father died as a result of a heart attack when she was fifteen years old. After graduation from high school, Ann remained at home until her early twenties; then she married her husband just prior to his entering the Navy. His assignment necessitated their moving to the west coast. This departure from home resulted in Ann developing an acute anxiety reaction.

Ann also suffered episodic anxiety attacks and periods of depression over the next few years. She was treated psychiatrically, primarily via medication, on four separate occasions. When she recently moved into a new home with her husband

and children, Ann became acutely distressed. In the second therapy session, the therapist also learned that she responded sensitively to criticism, particularly her husband's.

Given the idiosyncratic characteristics of Ann's developmental history, an effective therapist would question how that history influenced her once she married and left home? It was known that she was the youngest of three children, and her mother's only daughter. One might wonder how close Ann and her mother had been by virtue of her status as an only daughter?

Subsequent to her father's death, a pattern of intense closeness probably developed between Ann and her mother. Because of their mutual grief, such closeness would be expected. Mother and daughter probably pulled closer together in order to comfort and support each other. Moreover, one would want to know if Ann was the last child to leave home? If this was the case, her departure from home could have created difficult adjustments for her mother.

Considerations such as these could begin to account for why marriage and leaving home were such difficult transitions for Ann. Married and separated by substantial geographical distance from her home, she likely worried about her mother; and her mother also likely worried about her. Worried about the welfare of her family in general, and her mother in particular, it must have been difficult for Ann to adjust to her status as a newlywed wife.

It seems reasonable to conclude that Ann was contending with long-standing conflicts between her identities as daughter, wife and mother. Specifically, Ann may have been unsure about which identities she should regard as priorities in her life. Quite possibly, she identified herself more as a daughter than as a wife and mother.

A daughter who is very worried about her lonely mother can find it difficult to embrace her role as a wife. To the extent that she is happily married, she could also feel guilty about her unhappy mother. Conversely, if this daughter-wife is distressed and anxious, her mother could think that her daughter still needs her.

Parents who feel needed by their children—even adult children—are energized by a sense of purpose and determination. Any parental problems are often put on hold as they single-mindedly pursue the welfare of their child. Consequently, Ann's symptoms may have protected her mother. As a result of her symptoms, Ann could have transformed her mother from a lonely, withdrawn person into an alert, active mother motivated by the knowledge that her daughter still needed her.

The circumstances outlined in the previous paragraph occur with remarkable frequency. In response to such circumstances, an effective therapist organizes a daughter-wife and her husband into a cohesive alliance with each other. Then the wife and husband can respond more effectively to this kind of situation.

An effective therapist would direct the wife and husband to demonstrate mutual concern for the wife's mother. They could write her joint letters, call her on the phone together, go visit her, or invite her to visit them. Moreover, the wife would be told that her mother needs reassurance that the wife is happily married.

This kind of therapeutic intervention reorganizes the relationships between wife, husband, and wife's mother. The mother is no longer cursed with a son-in-law callous and cruel enough to steal her daughter. Instead, she is blessed with a son-in-law kind and considerate enough to demonstrate concern for her welfare.

A mother readily endorses the marriage of a daughter who has been wise enough to marry such a caring man. In turn, the psychological welfare of the wife-daughter is no longer sabotaged by painful loyalty conflicts and corresponding anxiety. Once she knows that her mother accepts her status as a wife, her identity conflicts are resolved. The wife is no longer compelled to display symptoms that lead her to identify herself as a helpless daughter.

Sadly, Ann's therapist disregarded all the issues and questions outlined in the previous paragraphs. Make no mistake, these issues and questions never even occurred to this therapist; they are too far removed from the theoretical domain of behavior therapy. Consequently, the therapist was not in a position to assist Ann effectively.

DISREGARD OF INTERPERSONAL INFLUENCE

Between the third and seventh sessions, the therapist became aware that Ann " . . . . did very little by herself, managing to arrange her life so that friends and relatives were quick to reinforce her dependent behavior."[4] This comment raises more questions than it answers. One must wonder which relatives were reinforcing her dependency, and what were they gaining from it?

The therapist speculated that someone in Ann's life was attempting to sabotage her therapy. As long as the therapist confined himself to individual therapy for Ann, it was doubtful that he could find out who was sabotaging her treatment, and why it was being done.

Between the eighth and twentieth sessions, Ann made moderate gains in her degree of independence and overall level of relaxation. The therapist's relationship with Ann had developed to where his approval was very important to her. He explained, "Ann is obviously very dependent on me, a fact that undoubtedly enhances my ability to instigate and reinforce her behavior between sessions."[5]

The therapist's comments force one to question whether Ann's therapy had deteriorated into a compensatory relationship? Was a warm and genuinely understanding therapist compensating for the absence of those very qualities in other sectors of her life?

Individual therapy limited the therapist's information about the patterns of interpersonal influence in Ann's life. In particular, he still had no firsthand information about her husband. He clearly exercised significant stimulus control in Ann's life, but the therapist knew little about him.

Between the twenty-first and twenty-sixth sessions, Ann's anxiety level progressively diminished, and she was able to spend more time at home by herself. In one particularly important session, Ann and the therapist focused on her identities as wife and mother. The therapist explained that Ann " . . . . came to the conclusion that she *wanted* to be a homemaker but that she could not yet do so comfortably and successfully."[6] The therapist assumed that her ambivalence about this issue originated from unresolved conflicts within herself.

One might also question, however, whether someone else was withholding permission from Ann to be the "homemaker" that she wanted to be. An effective therapist would want to know how Ann's husband felt about her preference to be a homemaker? At this point in therapy, the prognosis varied substantially according to whether there was agreement, or conflict, between Ann and her husband on this issue. As a result of the therapist's decision to see Ann individually, he could not obtain this important information.

Between the twenty-seventh and thirty-fourth sessions, Ann became more assertive and less inclined to cling to her negative self-image. The frequency of therapy sessions was reduced from twice a week to once a week. Between the thirty-fifth and fortieth sessions, Ann's self-confidence dramatically improved; and she developed a strong sense of optimism about her future welfare.

Her husband apparently experienced problems adjusting to her recently developed assertiveness. At this point in treatment, the therapist considered the advisability of including Ann's husband in her therapy, but he eventually decided against it. Unfortunately, his decision disregarded the influence the husband exercised in Ann's life.

THERAPY BY CHANCE VS. THERAPY BY DESIGN

In assessing Ann's prognosis at this point, her therapist emphasized: "A lot will depend on whether her husband will become receptive to her growing independence."[7] An effective therapist would have assumed responsibility for bringing about this outcome. This therapist, however, forfeited his opportunity to obtain this end when he decided not to see Ann's husband.

As a result, the therapist could only hope that the vicissitudes of good fortune would somehow influence the husband's behavior. This is therapy by chance, as opposed to therapy by design. An effective therapist designs therapeutic procedures to obtain a certain outcome; he does not abandon such outcomes to chance.

From the forty-first session until therapy was terminated after fifty-one sessions, Ann reported increased coping skills, improved self-confidence, and she took greater pride in her personal appearance. In summarizing this case, the therapist at least acknowledged the significance of marital issues. He explained:

A married individual's difficulties are often enmeshed

in relationship issues with the spouse. In Ann's case, her husband had grown accustomed to dealing with a passive, dependent person. The increase in her assertiveness and overall independence necessitated a readjustment in their interactions with each other, and for a time it appeared that conjoint sessions might be needed. But Ann wanted to work things out without the therapist's direct involvement, and fortunately she and her husband were able to do just that.[8]

This therapist betrayed his own theoretical background. Behaviorists insist that a therapist should be able to directly observe changes in a client's behavior. This therapist could only accept Ann's reports about marital changes as a matter of blind faith. He relinquished the opportunity to directly observe Ann as a wife in relation to her husband. Behaviorists have long been inclined to indict other therapists for such therapeutic shortsightedness. It is ironic, to say the least, when they commit these kinds of errors themselves.

The outcome in this case does not reflect any straightforward impact of behavior therapy procedures. More than anything else, Ann benefited from a compensatory relationship with her therapist. He assumed the status of a warm, pleasant, understanding figure in her life; and as such, he provided her with encouragement that had otherwise been unavailable to her.

If Ann encountered future problems, she would have felt compelled to return to the therapist. He had acquired the status of problem-solver in her life. Effective therapy would have created feelings of mutual reliance and cooperation between Ann and her husband. This outcome would have helped Ann to contend with future crises more effectively, while decreasing the likelihood of her returning to therapy.

In fairness, it should also be emphasized that—unlike cases cited elsewhere in this book—Ann's therapist did her little harm. Any existing interpersonal conflicts in her life were not intensified and worsened as a result of her therapy. Her already fragile self-concept was not further undermined by her therapist.

Nevertheless, the course of Ann's therapy did not proceed in a particularly efficient manner. The necessity for fifty-one sessions to apparently resolve Ann's problems is not an impressive standard of psychotherapeutic efficiency. As other clients do, Ann likely terminated therapy "feeling warm and appreciative toward her therapist."[9] Her therapeutic gains, however, would have been substantially enhanced if she had terminated therapy feeling "warm and appreciative" about her husband.

If afforded the opportunity, Ann's husband could have evolved as a major source of support and encouragement in her life. Consequently, she would have enjoyed a closer, more trusting relationship with him. Her course of treatment, however, reduced the likelihood of this outcome. The therapist was an excessively central figure in her therapy while her husband was too peripheral.

19

THERAPIST AS SAVIOR

L ife offers far too many tragedies. Through no fault of their own, people can become victims of disease, natural disaster, or crime. Some of these tragedies involve villains who recklessly or maliciously disrupt the lives of innocent people. Other tragedies highlight heroes or saviors who manage to either stave off disaster or ease its effects.

Human emotions are always engaged by tragic situations. Our hearts ache for the victims, burn with anger at the villains, and delight in the saviors who intervene. As a result, such stories are a staple of human communication from great literature to the daily news.

People sometimes assume the roles of victim, villains, and savior independent of any tragedy. Human relationships can revolve around these roles when their circumstances are less than tragic—sometimes far less. Whether art imitates life, or life imitates art, the human condition can assume the characteristics of a TV soap opera. These formularized entertainment packages require a victim to tug at our hearts, a savior to elicit applause, and a villain at whom we can vent our spleen. In real life, the roles of victim, villain, and savior are usually quite inter-related with each other.

163

When people respond to a victim's plight, they can feel good about themselves as a savior. Moreover, two people can organize a relationship around the roles of savior and victim. For example, a disgruntled employee and his sympathetic co-worker can readily assume these identities.

Once two people have designated themselves as victim and savior, the identity of each demands that the other persist in his role. A victim needs a savior, and a savior needs a victim. The disgruntled employee reassures his sympathetic co-worker that he really is a savior; the co-worker reassures the disgruntled employee that he really is a victim.

The roles of victim and savior are also legitimized by the presence of a villain. Without the presence of a villain, victims cannot suffer properly and saviors feel unneeded. An arbitrary supervisor, however, can reassure the disgruntled employee and the sympathetic co-worker that they should remain closely aligned.

Borderline thoughtlessness or insensitivity from a villain allows victim and savior to commiserate with each other. New instances of alleged unfairness feed their drama and allow them to justify their roles. Thus, victims and saviors avoid the boredom that might otherwise develop from their repetitious exchanges. Consequently, victims and saviors need a villain, and they will not be elated if a villain attempts to unilaterally abandon his role. Such selfishness on the part of a villain threatens victim and savior with the loss of their identities.

When a villain participates in the interactions between victim and savior, a triangle has developed. Regardless of who plays what role, the results are the same—the triangle feeds off of itself. Victim and savior search for new evidence of the villain's bad faith, and the villain rarely disappoints them. Angered by the eagerness with which savior and victim censure him, the villain manages to verify his malevolent reputation.

Triangulated relationships between victims, villains and saviors persistently resist change. Victims cling tenaciously to their identity as a victim; they are unwilling to sacrifice the sympathy and support that their victim posture affords them. Saviors are also deeply entrenched in their identity; they do not want to lose the appearance of altruism. Villains perpetuate their identity in the pursuit of vindication; their anger, borne out of humiliation, compels them to persist in this pursuit.

If any one participant in the triangle attempts to change his role, he threatens the other two participants with a sense of loss. In such triangles, then, any individual impetus for change is typically outnumbered two to one.

THERAPIST AS SAVIOR

Individual psychotherapy can also organize itself around the triangulated exchanges of victim, villain, and savior. Therapists often like to define themselves as saviors. The altruistic reputation of this role appeals to their need to help people. As a result, many therapists label clients as victims to enhance their own savior reputations. The savior-therapist then designates someone else in the client's life as a villain, and a loyal alliance between therapist and client rapidly develops.

For example, a therapist can label an agoraphobic a victim of her fears and anxieties. He then appoints himself as a savior for this agoraphobic victim and undertakes a course of individual therapy with her. Until a therapist came into the agoraphobic's life, her husband regarded himself as his wife's savior. Husband and wife could both agree that he was her reliable resource of calm strength. A therapist's involvement in an agoraphobic's life, however, can create a situation where the husband feels displaced.

Displaced husbands, whose altruistic reputations are rapidly declining, feel less than elated with the therapist who displaced them. It would not be surprising if these husbands expressed some bitter, critical comments about the therapist. In turn, an agoraphobic wife feels distressed by her husband's comments and reports them to her therapist.

The therapist often takes offense at these attacks on his reputation. He regards himself as an altruistic figure in an agoraphobic's life, and he is bewildered as to why he suffers such attacks. When he feels unjustly attacked, a therapist can swell with self-righteous indignation. Nevertheless, most therapists maintain a facade of calm, professional composure; and explain to an agoraphobic that her husband is victimizing her.*

---

*Such a facade allows a therapist to maintain an appearance of professional superiority. This image might otherwise be tarnished if he were to express his anger overtly. Nevertheless, if the therapist is inclined to exact more revenge on the husband, he can diagnose him as a "narcissistic character disorder."

From a therapist's perspective, anyone interfering with his good works must be a seriously maladjusted individual who is highly motivated to sabotage the client's therapy. Thus, a husband no longer enjoys the reputation of a benevolent savior; the therapist has redefined him as a malevolent villain. This definition also significantly influences the husband-wife relationship, because of the therapist's reputation as an expert.

Once a client understands that her husband is really a villain, she responds more distantly and defensively with him. A husband who endures a malevolent reputation—while contending with a distant, defensive wife—is understandably motivated to protest his reputation. His elevated frustration can also provoke rather vehement protests. In turn, the vehement protests of a frustrated husband can provide both therapist and client with further evidence of the husband's alleged malevolence.

For example, a frustrated husband could angrily denounce the therapist saying, "That quack isn't helping you at all." As a result, therapist and client can consume a good deal of their sessions talking about the supposed malevolence of the client's husband. They could decide that he is not the kind of man with whom "defenses can be dropped." Instead, he is the kind of man who forces people to feel "cautious and wary." They might also conclude that the husband is acting like "a little boy shut out of the grown-up's world." This kind of compensatory alliance usually accomplishes little more than to fuel continuing protests from the husband.*

Triangulated problem cycles are not limited to the treatment of agoraphobics. The reader need only review the previous chapters to find one case study after another corresponding to this cyclical pattern. These kinds of self-perpetuating cycles allow traditional therapists to justify long-term therapy. They can do so because of the apparent intractability of a client's problems. Simultaneously, these same therapists often ignore their own role in creating those problems.

LONG-TERM VICTIMS

Clients often initiate therapy feeling burdened and discouraged. The psychological distress that undermines any happi-

---

*In the opinion of one attorney, who is a perceptive observer of the therapeutic scene, "This isn't therapy; it's gossip."

ness or satisfaction in their lives also undermines their self-confidence. They frequently blame themselves for not being resourceful enough to overcome their distress. Benevolent therapists, however, inform clients that they are not incompetent; instead, a client learns that he is a victim who is being sabotaged by a villain.

Obviously, the virtuous appearance of a victim holds greater appeal than the reputation of an incompetent. Consequently, victims are disinclined to give up their martyrdom until a therapist offers them a better alternative. An individual therapist, however, often cannot provide a better alternative for a victim, until he no longer regards the victim as being victimized by a villain. The therapist is like any other savior convinced of a villian's malevolence: in his estimation the victim is resigned to his noble but beleagured status.

In the course of individual therapy with a victim, a therapist is at a serious disadvantage when it comes to seeing a villain as less malevolent. He must depend on the victim's reports about a villain to change his perceptions. A victim, however, wonders whether a therapist wants to hear any positive reports about a villain. A therapist defined the villain as a villain; he might disagree if a victim reports that the villain possesses some redeeming value as a human being.

Therefore, a client continues to define himself as a victim until a therapist tells him otherwise. A therapist, however, is reluctant to unilaterally redefine a client's victim status. Before he does so, he expects the client to demonstrate that he is no longer being victimized. As a result, therapy can deteriorate into a long-term endeavor while both client and therapist wait for each other to redefine a client's victim role. Consequently, individual therapy often locks clients into hopeless situations that their therapists have created.

When therapy fails to alleviate a client's psychological distress, therapists can feel as frustrated as clients. Frustrated by a client's unchanging victim status, a therapist can shift the focus of treatment and conclude that a client is victimizing himself. In other words, if a therapist cannot help a client by blaming other people for his problems, his frustration compels him to blame the client.*

*Analytic therapists are most inclined to indict clients in this way, but therapists of other theoretical persuasions also indulge in this tactic.

Once indicted, the client endures *both* the malevolent reputation of a villain and the beleaguered status of a victim. Saddled with this dual burden, clients might conclude that they were better off before therapy when they regarded themselves as merely incompetent.

BREAKING THE VICTIM/VILLAIN CYCLE

Obviously, effective therapists neither volunteer themselves —nor accept induction—as saviors. Any therapist who makes this kind of mistake sacrifices his objectivity, and this sacrifice usually leads him into a situation where he is more a part of the problem than its solution.

Competent therapists reduce the conflicts between victims and villains by identifying who is fanning the flames of their heated conflicts. For example, distressed marriages rarely collapse beneath the weight of their own burdens. Rather than fall apart, failed marriages are usually pulled apart by one or more saviors who "assist" the victimized spouse.

An effective therapist recognizes that a client who embraces the victim role is typically supported in this act by a villain and savior. Changing these interpersonal patterns necessitates the participation of both victim and villain. The victim cannot change his identity unless the villain changes, and the villain cannot change his identity unless the victim changes.

Effective therapy promotes simultaneous changes in the identities of both victim and villain. Once these simultaneous changes are realized, the therapist organizes the *former* victim and villain to change the savior's identity. Unless the savior's identity is changed, he could pull the former victim and villain back into their old roles.

Victim and villain would be directed to demonstrate dramatic cohesiveness with each other, and thank the savior for his previous "help." Moreover, they would explain that such help is no longer necessary. When victim and villain form an alliance with each other, the forces for change are favored by a two to one margin.

In other words, an effective therapist helps people to write new scripts for themselves. As conflicted clients develop their skills as scriptwriters, a competent therapist responds as an encouraging editor. Client and therapist work together to find plots more conducive to mutual appreciation and harmony. Simultaneously, the therapist responds to the client's needs for dramatic intensity.

In these kinds of circumstances, clients learn that the proper script allows him tremendous freedom to test out new roles. Because sudden, dramatic plot shifts can arouse uncertainty and anxiety, the therapist reassures the clients that they can start by pretending.[1]

When the timing is appropriate, the therapist reminds the client that not only can anybody pretend practically anything, practice also affords him the opportunity to become remarkably talented at what he is pretending. Indeed, the time may come when clients are unsure as to whether the changes in their relationship are real or simulated—but they can act in accordance with whichever outcome most effectively maintains those changes.

20

Sentence first—verdict afterwards

—LEWIS CARROLL

THERAPIST AS PROSECUTOR

In 1896, Sigmund Freud specified a formative history of incest as the causational factor responsible for neurotic disorders.[1] By the end of the 19th century, however, Freud shifted his position to insisting that patient reports of incest were merely fantasies motivated by their unconscious desires. Critics of Freud have argued that his revised opinion served to suppress awareness of the prevalence and significance of intra-familial sexual abuse for the next seventy to eighty years.[2] The previous decade, however, has seen an increasing emphasis on the extent of childhood incest and its subsequent effects on adult functioning.[3-5]

Incest resolution therapies have developed to counter more conventional treatment that allegedly overlooks the effects of childhood sexual abuse. Despite persuasive evidence to the contrary,[6] therapists who designate themselves "incest-resolution therapists" argue that child sexual abuse has reached epidemic proportions.[7] These therapists also contend that the trauma of childhood sexual abuse motivates victims to forget—or repress—the horrible experiences they presumably endured.[8] It is moreover assumed that psycho-

171

therapy can alleviate the effects of repression, and assist victims of childhood sexual abuse to recover previously repressed memories of their abuse.[9,10]

RESEARCH RELATED TO REPRESSION

Surprising as it may seem, a careful examination of the relevant scientific data finds practically no support for the concept of repression. A 1974 review concluded that any evidence verifying the existence of repression was characterized by its conspicuous absence.[11] In 1990, the same reviewer emphasized that he was yet to find any data indicating he should revise his earlier findings. This reviewer concluded, "Despite over sixty years of research involving numerous approaches by many thoughtful and clever investigators, at the present time there is no controlled laboratory evidence supporting the concept of repression . . . "[12]

Additional research indicates that if repression does occur in response to trauma, it is an exceedingly rare event. For example, one study in particular examined the reactions of five to ten-year-old children who had witnessed the murder of one of their parents.[13] Not one of these children exhibited any evidence of repression; instead, they continually struggled with painful and intrusive recollections of what they had witnessed.

A related case study reported the reactions of a three-year-old girl who had been kidnapped, sexually abused, and left to die in a mountain outhouse.[14] When found and later interviewed by the police, she was able to describe what had happened, and identify the perpetrator in a line-up. The perpetrator ultimately confessed, thereby verifying the accuracy of the child's description. Obviously, then, this case presented no evidence whatsoever of repression despite the brutal trauma endured by the child.

LIMITATIONS OF MEMORY

In response to the research outlined above, Incest-resolution therapists cite a study of 450 clients who reported sexual abuse histories.[15] When asked if there was ever a time when they could not remember their abuse, 59 percent of this sample responded "Yes." These data have been interpreted to indicate that 59 percent of sexual abuse victims "went through periods of amnesia when they were not aware of their prior abuse."[16]

In fact, however, such conclusions are ill-advised because the entire sample of this study was in therapy. As a result, the therapists may well have convinced these clients that repression is a common experience associated with sexual abuse; and in turn, the clients reported experiences of repression merely in response to their therapist's influence. These same problems also undermine the reliability of a frequently cited 1987 study which reported that 28 percent of a sample of incest survivors reported severe memory deficits.[17]

A more recently published study interviewed 100 women whose history of sexual abuse, 17 years earlier, was verified by hospital records.[18] This study reported that 38 percent of the sample—none of whom were in therapy—did not remember their previous abuse at the time of the interview. These results, however, do not necessarily support conclusions regarding the assumed prevalence of repression.

Ordinary memory decay, or everyday examples of forgetting, are an inevitable fact of life. For example, 14 percent of a sample of 590 people known to have been involved in injury producing automobile accidents did not recall the accident a year later.[19] A related study interviewed 1500 people who had been discharged from a hospital within the previous year. More than 25 percent of this sample did not remember their own hospitalization a year later.[20] Instead of repressing their sexual abuse, some of the subjects who did not report it may have simply forgotten it.

When they were sexually abused, the subjects in the study cited above ranged in age from one to seventeen years. The exact percentage of the women who were less than five years old when abused was not reported. This is also a significant oversight because we can only speculate regarding what portion of this sample could not remember their abuse because they were too young when it occurred to recall it. In other words, it is necessary to discriminate between the effects of normal childhood amnesia, and the supposed mechanisms of repression.

Research addressing human memory consistently indicates that after the age of ten, people rarely remember events that occurred before the age of three or four.[21,22] In another study, for example, very few subjects who were younger than four years of age at the time of John F. Kennedy's assassination could remember any information regarding where they were when they learned of it. The majority of subjects who were age nine and older in November of 1963 were able to recall some first-hand information associated with JFK's death.[23]

Obviously, then, the accumulated data related to long-term memory clearly indicates that people rarely remember much that occurred before the age of four; and moreover, memories from between the ages of four and eight tend to be quite unreliable. When clients report that psychotherapy has allowed them to uncover memories for events that supposedly occurred before eight years of age, they are most likely reporting the effects of therapist influence rather than memory retrieval.[24]

BIASES OF INCEST-RESOLUTION THERAPY

The potential for psychotherapists altering and/or distorting the memories of their clients cannot be underestimated. Dr. Elizabeth Loftus, of the University of Washington, experimentally investigated this issue.[25] She used some of her laboratory assistants as confederates in an experiment to determine if it was possible to create childhood memories for events that had never occurred. Loftus' confederates selected a target person in their own family who was younger than them, and requested their participation in a memory experiment. The confederates asked the target subjects if they remembered being lost in a shopping mall when they were five years old.

Initially, the target subjects denied any such memory; but then they were asked to try and remember anything they could about this supposed incident. Within two days, the target subjects began to report memories related to this fictitious episode. For example one of them said, "That day I was so scared that I would never see my family again. I knew I was in trouble." The next day he thought he recalled a conversation with his mother: "I remember Mom telling me never to do that again." Two days later, this same subject reported, "I sort of remember the stores." In fact, however, this subject had never been lost in a shopping mall at the age of five. His persuasive statements to the contrary simply demonstrate the degree to which all people can sorely confuse imagination and memory.

Despite the significance of Loftus' research, the tenacity with which some therapists pursue verification of their theoretical convictions related to incest should not be underestimated. For example, a California psychologist reported blatant examples of biased assumptions regarding the prevalence of childhood sexual abuse.

> In the past two years, many patients have told me that previous therapists have presumed that they must have been sexually molested as children. If the patient had no such recollection, that was taken as evidence of severe "repression," or that the molestation must have happened very early in life, causing unusually great harm. Such therapists employed similar logic if the patient recalled a pleasant, loving family life. Such therapists repeatedly attempt to elicit fragmentary memories or fantasies, often with the aid of hypnosis, to confirm their preconceptions. Several patients told me their therapists went so far as to say, "I am certain you were molested because you have all the classic characteristics of adults molested as children."[26]

The potential for these kinds of tactics to result in mistaken conclusions regarding sexual abuse is alarming.

For example, when clients feel depressed—perhaps by questions suggesting that their own family profoundly betrayed them or in response to other circumstances—that depression increases the probability of their remembering their parents as rejecting and relying on negative controls.[27] When clients report these memories to their therapist, they may encounter lavish praise for "the impressive commitment to your 'recovery';" this outcome obviously motivates them to search for more anecdotes of parental betrayal.

The anecdotal speculations exchanged between uncertain clients and overconfident therapists can eventually converge into commonly shared theories leading to the same conclusion —the client suffered episodes of formative sexual abuse which remained repressed until uncovered by the therapist. In fact, however, recollection of such memories often respond more to current mood states than it involves any accurate recall of past events.[28] Thus, verification of these "memories" typically relies more on imagination than actual experience—and as a result, fiction can prevail over fact in incest resolution therapy.

UNCOVERING OR INDOCTRINATION?

In May of 1991, a private mental health facility in a Detroit suburb publicized the start of a "Process Group for Survivors of Sexual Abuse/Incest," designated as "Thrivers." This treatment experience was described as " . . . an entry group; this is appropriate for individuals who sense they were sexually abused yet have no clear memories as well as for people who remember, yet are not fully associated with the feelings." When clients enter a group such as this wondering whether they actually endured a history of abuse or incest, how long will it take before they are convinced that they really suffered such betrayals?

Given the influences of conformity and compliance that characterize any group, clients in an incest resolution group can feel coerced. If they decide that their formative history does not include sexual abuse, they run the risk of being ostracized as denying deviants. In these situations, the group pressure associated with a persistent focus on sexual abuse can motivate clients to invent memories that are more imaginary than real. Obviously, then, these circumstances also create fertile ground for a bountiful harvest of mistaken diagnoses indicating childhood sexual abuse.

In the fall of 1991, *Time* magazine printed a story titled "Incest Comes Out of the Dark." A *Time* reporter wrote a sidebar for this article graphically summarizing her own history of substance abuse, overeating, disappointing relationships, hyper-responsibility, and betrayal by a previous therapist who sexually exploited her.[29] She attributed all of these problems to the sexual abuse allegedly perpetrated by her mother over the course of her formative development. She lamented how her mother still refused to acknowledge the alleged sexual abuse, and implied that this situation drove her to " . . . finally giving up my mother." She also spoke of more recently having undertaken " . . . five weeks of intensive treatment and many hours of outpatient therapy."

Three weeks after the previously cited article appeared, *Time* printed a letter in response to the reporter's first-person account from her sister. The letter read:

> With the publication of my sister Barbara Dolan's article 'My Own Story,' our mother has essentially been tried and convicted of actions she thought were those of a loving, carefully protective mother. Fifty years after the fact, my sister has blindsided the reputation of our 83-year-old mother, who had no intent to harm. My sister did not have the courage to discuss this matter face-to-face with our mother, choosing a cowardly solution, the pen, so she would not have to view the destruction of a life. Where is the justice in this? What about my sister's responsibility for her own life? How did *Time* magazine stoop to this level of sensationalism?[30]

The reporter insists that she suffered repeated episodes of sexual abuse at the hands of her own mother. Her sister argues that while their mother may have been misguided, her behavior was not willfully abusive. This tragic situation raises the question of who is reporting fact, and who is reporting fiction? This writer is not so presumptuous as to assume that he can decide this matter. Nevertheless, the issues of this case certainly raise the possibility of a grossly mistaken diagnosis of sexual abuse.

In fact, the reporter's case presents more questions than it answers; but the questions it poses are so important that they demand serious attention. For example, did the therapist solicit biased information to confirm her or his expectations? Were the client's reports twisted to fit the therapist's preconceived assumptions? Could the therapist's influence have led the client into significant memory distortions? Was the diagnosis of incest a wholesale distortion, contaminating real events with imaginary events?

PROBLEMS OF DEFINITION

The accuracy with which therapists can diagnose a formative history of incest also suffers from persistent definitional problems. Quite simply, the question of exactly what constitutes incest is not well-defined. In response to the influence of the growing incest resolution literature, the popular media considers incest as including but not limited to "fondling, rubbing one's genitals against a child, and excessive or suggestive washing of a youngster's pubic area . . . "[31] Obviously, there is little about these criteria that qualifies them as reliable definitions increasing the accuracy with which a history of incest can be diagnosed. Given the gross subjectivity of these criteria, the rate of diagnosed incest could soar precipitously depending on who interprets the data.

Incest resolution therapy identifies incest as the central experience in the lives of clients.[32] As a result, it typically assumes that all the problems of clients originated with the formative betrayals they presumably endured. Consequently, this therapy can overlook contemporary client problems that develop as a result of contending with the vicissitudes of adult life. Despite the prevalence of substance abuse, depression, anxiety, and marital conflicts existing independent of any history of incest, incest resolution therapists seem determined to attribute these problems and others exclusively to their clients' assumed histories of formative betrayals.

The emphasis on the centrality of incest in this treatment model corresponds to its unidimensional thinking. How clients function as spouses or parents, for example, is assumed to directly reflect their apparent history of incest. Thus, clients are designated as passive objects suffering the persistent effects of pathogenic histories. In turn, this designation of passivity discourages clients from viewing themselves as active participants who influence—as well as are influenced by—the day-to-day events of their lives.

Rather than recognize their potential for self-sufficiency, incest resolution therapy attributes substantial fragility to its clients. One such therapist, for example, emphasized, "I always regard myself as the advocate for the child in my patients." [33] To the extent that incest resolution therapy relates to clients as fragile children, it can underestimate their strengths while subtly discouraging them from viewing themselves as competent adults.

CONSEQUENCES OF INCEST RESOLUTION THERAPY

The following case vignette outlines the counterproductive effects associated with inappropriately defining incest as the central issue in a client's life.

On one occasion when he was six, Clifford was fondled by his uncle. After he first recalled the incident during counseling in his early twenties, his therapist suggested he join a self-help group for victims of sexual abuse. Clifford began attending group meetings once a week. By the time he started therapy with me, he was still in the group, had received counseling for more than eight years, and had never moved beyond his outrage at his uncle, now dead. I saw Clifford for more than three months before he finally agreed to look at the other aspects of his life. Only then did he reveal that his father had died when he was twelve, that he had a mentally retarded sister, and that he had had four affairs during his nine-year marriage—all with members of his self-help group.

As critical as Clifford's encounter with his uncle was, it did not occur in a vacuum and should not have been allowed to overshadow everything that happened before and after, yet because his identity as a sexual abuse victim was constantly reinforced by his former counselor and his group, it not only remained the central focus but automatically was blamed for everything that went wrong in Clifford's life. [34]

Clifford's case demonstrates how incest resolution therapy can leave clients seriously misdirected. His treatment of eight years amounted to a counterproductive outcome because it created problems for him that otherwise would not have existed. Distracted by his therapeutically defined status as a sexual abuse victim, Clifford overlooked the significance of more pressing issues in his life.

These practices of incest resolution therapy also correspond to a larger issue in psychotherapy: Is treatment more effective when it seeks to compensate for the presumed deficits of a client's formative history? Or is treatment more effective when it attempts to capitalize on the strengths that clients demonstrate in the here-and-now?[35]

COMPENSATE OR CAPITALIZE

The issue of a "compensate" versus a "capitalize" focus in

psychotherapy is relevant to the case of the *Time* reporter. To say the least, this woman presents a variety of impressive strengths. By virtue of her career as a journalist, it appears safe to assume that she is well-educated (it seems unlikely that *Time* magazine hires high-school drop outs for its journalistic staff). She writes with qualities of such vigor and flow that those with lesser talents could feel envious of her style. Moreover, she has realized substantial success in her career; her status as a reporter for *Time*—a publication of international prominence—underscores her journalistic competence.

Compared to the "compensate" emphasis of incest resolution therapy, a "capitalize" focus would have addressed the personality strengths of the *Time* reporter responsible for her impressive accomplishments. Additionally, a capitalize focus would have identified the contemporary problems with which she was struggling, and then assisted her in bringing her strengths to bear on those here-and-now problems. This kind of capitalizing approach to treatment leaves clients feeling empowered by emphasizing their competence as adults rather than dwelling upon their supposed fragility as children.

Incest resolution therapists attempt to rescue their clients by providing them an idealized relationship designed to compensate for their history of alleged betrayals. Responding to clients in this manner can lead them into unrealistic expectations regarding the continuing centrality of their therapist in their lives. These circumstances make therapists more important than they should be by inviting their clients' dependency; and in turn, clients over-identify with their presumed status as incest victims. If the therapist is to continue relating as a savior to the client, the client must remain a victim; otherwise, the client would not need the therapist's savior services. Thus, in order to perpetuate the significance of their therapist, clients could be motivated to cling to their identities as victims.

FAMILY POLARIZATION

Incest resolution therapy emphasizes the supposed benefits of emotional catharsis. Therapists actively promote intense expressions of client pain and anger for purposes of "getting the feelings out." Faith in the value of such ventilation is frequently premised on "blame-and-change" assumptions which incest resolution therapists often embrace with a vengeance. More often than not, clients are encouraged to direct their expressions of bitterness and resentment toward the significant others who allegedly betrayed them, but these "ventilating" tactics can create more problems than they solve.

For example, incest resolution therapy appears to have seriously polarized the relationships between the *Time* reporter and her mother and sister—and perhaps even others in her family. Admittedly, a variety of recovery groups are available to this client; but such groups run the risk of reinforcing her status as a victim via a preoccupation with the betrayals she allegedly suffered in the past. Additionally, resorting to recovery groups for social support discourages clients from attempting to repair and restore relationships with their families.[36] Participation in these groups can encourage clients to substitute them for familial identification and support. When such outcomes transpire because a mistaken diagnosis of incest, the results are tragic, to say the least.

CONCLUSIONS

Two well-respected research psychologists have challenged the assumption that adult survivors of formative sexual abuse constitute a unique population requiring special therapeutic expertise.[37] They contend that when this population is compared to other clients, whose disorders originated subsequent to nonsexual or adulthood sexual traumas, there is minimal evidence to support assumptions regarding the atypicality of victims of childhood sexual abuse. Consequently; these critics question the effectiveness of treatments that respond to unique causes of trauma (a supposed history of sexual abuse) compared to treatments that address the effects of such trauma.

To belabor the obvious, responsible therapists are obligated to avoid rushing to judgment when diagnosing a formative history of incest. Nevertheless, it may be difficult for incest resolution therapists to adopt necessary safeguards in their diagnostic endeavors. For those who align themselves with an incest resolution model of therapy, rethinking their position could strike them as a retreat into the past. Moreover, therapists whose professional identities and incomes depend largely on their reputations as "incest resolution experts" might find it particularly difficult to objectively assess the pitfalls of their orientation. The welfare of innumerable clients, however, dictates that clinicians respond to their needs while checking their own theoretical assumptions, which may be seriously biased.

If psychotherapists disregard the necessity for approaching issues of incest more cautiously, the consequences of their oversights could extend beyond the considerations of treatment effectiveness previously outlined. Neglecting professional responsibilities related to these issues could eventually result in legions of attorneys taking legal action on behalf of families who regard a therapist as having defamed or slandered them.[38] Unfortunately, such litigation may be necessary for persuading incest resolution therapists to abandon their treatment practices which too often lead to counterproductive outcomes.

PART FOUR

THE GOALS OF PSYCHOTHERAPY

21

"You see an analyst?"
"Just for fifteen years."

— DIANE KEATON AND WOODY ALLEN

ANALYTIC GOALS:
BAIT-AND-SWITCH
IN PRACTICE

B ecause of their preoccupation with transference phenomena, analytic therapists neglect the problems clients present at the start of therapy. Instead, they manufacture artificial problems in addition to the issues that distress their clients.

When analytic therapists emphasize the priority of transference relationships, their grandiose presumptuousness is more evident than they would like. In effect, they tell clients: "You thought you had one problem when you first came to see me. Nevertheless, before we can resolve *your* problem, we first have to deal with *our* problem—you must insightfully understand how you relate to me." In other words, analytic therapists insist that clients make therapy more important than the problems that motivated them to seek it.

These kinds of procedures illustrate how this therapy is a veritable master of "bait and switch" tactics. Other therapy orientations employ such tactics episodically, but analytic therapy gives them a particularly unique dimension. Consider again the female attorney

185

whose analytic treatment was discussed in Chapter Nine. In the eighteenth session of therapy, the client reported the following dream:

> **Patient:** . . . . I was having sex with Will [her husband] and enjoying it very much but also at the time I had the feeling that there was no one there, that I was alone and only sleeping and dreaming—as though saying to myself: There you are. How stupid can you be, dreaming of sex with your husband and he isn't here. Then Will did come in and I said to him, "She (meaning myself) is asleep" (laughs). Then the phone woke me up, and I was mad and said to the person on the phone, "Why call now? I was having a nice dream." The woman who phoned said, "What were you dreaming?" and I said very coyly, "Oh, nothing."

> **Analyst:** Again we see the sexual wish. Here it is very frankly expressed but also inhibited from full satisfaction at the last minute, so to speak. This could, of course, still be the defenses against erotic wishes in the transference. In the associations there is the wish to be close and also the wish to comfort Will. It may be that you want to be close to me and have me comfort you. I agree that you are less embarrassed about the erotic component and are handling it well. Also by transferring the father pattern to me you are learning that you can tell me about sex with your husband without embarrassment, which you have felt toward father. I'm accepting of your sexuality where you felt father was not."[1]

This client's conflicts about sexuality required resolution between herself and her husband. Mutual feelings of apprehensiveness about closeness and sexuality likely influenced the client *and* her husband. When spouses take turns arousing each other's anxiety and vulnerability, resolution of their problems necessitates they both participate in therapy.

This analytic therapist, however, was exceedingly presumptuous. He assumed the client could resolve her conflicts only by relating to him as an accepting, nonjudgmental father figure. In making his assumption, the therapist inappropriately appointed himself to a position of prominence in the client's life. Moreover, the therapist's intrusive assumption—the client wanted his comfort and closeness—disregarded her conflicts with her husband.

This therapist's presumptuousness about his alleged significance in the client's life was counterproductive. It accomplished little more than to decrease the likelihood of her resolving her conflicts. She was distracted by a totally artificial issue—her supposed transference with her therapist. Baited by the expectation of resolving problems with her husband, she was switched to an irrelevant focus on her relationship with the therapist.

THERAPISTS AND SUPERVISORS: LEARNING BY EXAMPLE

Trainees in analytic therapy encounter bait and switch tactics in their contacts with supervisors. A trainee undertook therapy with a seriously depressed female client. During supervision, he described the client's condition as rapidly deteriorating to where she was suicidal.

The trainee explained to his supervisor that he felt lost and confused about what he should do. He also indicated that he felt disappointed in the quality of supervision previously provided for this case (this must have been an unusually bold, courageous trainee). The trainee expected a course of direction to deal more effectively with this client, but:

> At this point, the supervisor (apparently abruptly) changed the subject, by inviting the therapist [the trainee] to discuss with him how they felt about each other, in the light of a year's supervisory work and the fact that they were, at that moment, being observed. The supervisee was clearly taken aback by this change of direction. He responded angrily, demanding that attention be paid to the fact that he didn't know what to do about his patient and wasn't getting any help. He launched into an attack, suggesting that the supervisor's focus on the supervisory relationship was motivated by the fact that "I've got a flipped out patient and we both don't know what the ___to do."[2]

The trainee had responded to the bait of supervision: These

experiences will enhance your competence as a therapist. The supervisor, however, sought a change in the trainee's agenda; he invited the trainee to discuss their supervisory relationship (the switch). This trainee was not very flattered by the invitation and he emphatically declined it.

Nevertheless, the trainee never received the assistance he requested; and one can only wonder what happened to the client's welfare as a result. One might also question how often other trainees are "switched" by such supervisory procedures, and when these "switches" are successful, what is their impact on the clients of those trainees?

Supervisory practices that focus on the transference phenomenon between supervisor and trainee fail to develop well defined courses of therapeutic action. These practices are well designed, however, to conceal the incompetence of an ineffective supervisor. An analytic supervisor can speculate about obscure features of his relationship with a trainee, and both he and the trainee can feel impressed by the former's supposed perceptiveness. As a result, the supervisor's image as a sage remains untarnished.

Because analytic therapists endure "bait and switch" tactics in their training, they learn how to use them in their practices. Thus, they readily "switch" their own clients to a counterproductive preoccupation with transference phenomena. Preoccupied with how clients relate to them, analytic therapists respond more to the dogma of their theory than to the welfare of their clients.

IGNORING CLIENT NEEDS

A married woman in her late-thirties felt exceedingly conflicted about her marriage. Specifically, she was unsure as to whether she should divorce. As a result, she sought the services of an analytic therapist. The therapist explained that the client candidly discussed her marital problems.

> She talked freely about her marital difficulties. Her husband was an impossible man to live with. He forced her to have sexual relations with him regardless of her wishes. He accused her of being a harsh and demanding mother. She complained that he was niggardly. To avoid

arguments about her inability to manage the household on the meager allowance he provided, she supplemented it from her more modest earnings, approaching him only when her own funds were exhausted. They did not talk for days on end.

Seeking solace, she had indulged in brief erotic episodes with several professional acquaintances. These had proved disappointing, and a long-term relationship with another man had ended in a fiasco. Her husband also engaged in extramarital relationships, but steadfastly denied doing so when she confronted him with the evidence. In an emotionally explosive situation, she admitted to her affairs but he continued to deny his own. States of withdrawal and depression followed such confrontations.

The therapist went on:

She reported a dream in which someone was overpowering her and she was suffocating. In another version, the attacker was choking her. For many years she had dreamed of being in this terrifying situation. I attached great importance to this dream because of its frequent occurrence. She responded to my questions and interest in it by reporting many dreams.[3]

Clearly, this woman felt overwhelmed and overpowered; this conclusion was readily evident without examining her dreams. Nevertheless, this analytic therapist persistently pursued his interest in the client's dream reports. As the therapist responded to his interest in the client's dreams, he neglected to assist her with a seriously conflicted marriage causing her considerable distress. Though fascinated by the client's dreams, the therapist's symbolic interpretations could only belabor the obvious: This woman was caught in a marital nightmare.

For this woman, analytic therapy was a futile endeavor. Committed to a course of individual treatment, the therapist failed to resolve the marital conflicts ultimately responsible for the client's distress. Instead, he reduced himself and the client to merely talking about her marital conflicts.

DEFINING UNRESOLVABLE PROBLEMS

Analytic therapists often define the problems of their clients so that they remain unresolvable. Consider the hypothetical example of a thirty-year-old, married male who seeks treatment because of marital problems. Given the theoretical persuasion of an analytic therapist, our hypothetical client might be told: "Your marriage is failing because your mother was seductive and too close with you when you were a child. As a result, you are unconsciously motivated to not allow any female, especially your wife, to replace your mother in your life."

Even if legitimate concerns about the accuracy of this historical interpretation are temporarily suspended, the therapist has still created difficult problems for this client. In view of this interpretation, what is the client to do? The therapist's interpretation raises the question of how does the client change his own history? Obviously, neither client nor therapist can modify events that occurred between twenty and thirty years ago. By virtue of how he formulated his problems, the therapist has left the client trapped in his past.

Because of how long ago he was allegedly damaged, the client could assume that his situation is hopeless and his problems are unresolvable. The analytic therapist has not, and most assuredly will not, provide any course of constructive action for the client to undertake in the here and now. The therapist assumes that the client's insightful understanding will emancipate him from his pattern of marital conflicts. As emphasized previously, assumptions about the therapeutic value of insight are, at best, gratuitous. Clients need more than a better understanding of a bad situation.

The marital distress of our hypothetical client could have been handled more effectively. Focusing on contemporary events in his life would allow him to effectively resolve his conflicts. A contemporary focus would explain to the client: "Your marriage is failing because your mother seeks to keep you very close to her. She is very concerned about your welfare and she needs to know that you are happy and content. You and your wife will need to demonstrate to your mother that you are happy and content in this marriage. As you do this for your mother, she will not feel the need to pull you away from your wife."

This hypothetical example illustrates the differences between analytic therapy and psychotherapeutic intervention that is genuinely effective. Preoccupied with questions of *why* about a client's formative history, analytic therapists require clients to assume a role of passive, cerebral rumination. Rumination does not assist clients to change the life situations that are distressing them. An effective therapist emphasizes *what* a client can do to resolve his psychological distress.

ANALYTIC AUTHORITY

Not all clients docilely accept the ineffectiveness of analytic therapy. One client explained:

> **Patient:** I feel awful.
> **Therapist:** Um . . . why?
> **Patient:** Well, it seems like we're just not getting anywhere.
> **Therapist:** How so?
> **Patient:** How much longer am I going to lie there telling you my mother was an obsessional neurotic with neatness rituals? We know already how I suffered from the starch in my diapers. I just don't think we're making progress.
> **Therapist:** (With a kind, fatherly, and condescending smile) Not making progress? I wish you could hear a tape of yourself three years ago.[4]

If such a tape were available, any verdict of progress would likely stretch the imaginations of client and therapist. This client needed reassurance that he had realized some return on his investment of time and money. The therapist was more than happy to meet his needs. The unavailability of any objective evidence for this reassurance did not cause the therapist any distress. He was content to offer this client comfort and encouragement—and maintain the regularity of his appointments as he did so.

ANALYTIC THERAPY AND GEOGRAPHY

How does the client feel as analytic therapy ends? Our married attorney reached that goal after more than 189 sessions. In the 128th session, the therapist asked:

Analyst: What did you hope to achieve by being analyzed?

Patient: It's strange. I don't remember. It's gone. I have to think all the way back there. It's hard. To get rid of the guilt and not to feel inferior. I wanted to be more secure in myself. I wanted to have poise. I mean I had poise, but it was put on, forced. Most important of all, I wanted improvement with Tom [her son].[5]

At this point in the client's therapy, she had been thoroughly indoctrinated by the therapist's agenda; thus, she was unable to clearly remember her own agenda. This is the ultimate example of a "bait and switch" tactic in psychotherapy. Unable to clearly recall her own therapeutic goals, the client had been effectively switched to the therapist's goals. Client confusion of this sort makes the therapist's job profoundly easier. The therapist need not worry too much about servicing the client's welfare under these circumstances.

When the effectiveness of analytic therapy is weighed against the therapist's criteria—as opposed to those of the client—the therapist can appear moderately competent. Nevertheless, in assessing the quality of therapeutic services provided for this client, a brief review of the first session is rather illuminating. In the first session, the therapist inquired:

Analyst: What about the parental family?

Patient: A problem. Father and mother and my sister were no problem while we lived in San Francisco [the client had moved from San Francisco to Chicago and was residing in Chicago at the time of her therapy]. Therefore we loved it, but they are a problem here.[6]

Even though the client reported a period of time that she was free of family conflicts, the therapist ignored those relatively contemporary events. He also disregarded the family conflicts the client endured while residing in Chicago.

The therapist ignored the role of geography in this case. When the attorney lived in San Francisco, some distance from her parents, she encountered no difficulties. Her move to Chicago brought her closer to her parents and aroused previously dormant problems. In his summary of this case, the therapist did explain: "The patient, together with her husband and children, returned to San Francisco to live. She did very well except for a few brief episodes of conflict with her mother and sisters."[7]

It is tempting to conclude that a moving van serviced this client more effectively than her therapist. His theoretical assumptions left the client unable to resolve the interpersonal conflicts distressing her at the time she initiated therapy. Instead, she simply put substantial, geographical distance between herself and those conflicts.

CREDIT WHERE CREDIT IS DUE

There are circumstances in which analytic therapy might receive credit for positive outcomes when that credit is undeserved. Many of the problems that clients present at the start of therapy are time-limited in duration. The mere passage of time, and the inevitable changes that transpire in the life situations of clients over time, can facilitate relief from psychological distress. Nevertheless, a client attributes his progress to the insights of analytic therapy, the therapist immodestly concurs, and another satisfied customer goes forth to spread the good word about the good works of analytic therapists.

Or, a cold, distant, analytic therapist might help clients to more appreciate those people in their lives with whom they have been conflicted. Clients can view those people more positively in comparison to their sober, emotionally unresponsive therapist. Conflict resolution, with significant others in a client's life, may be selected as an option preferable to enduring additional therapy.

As Haley has emphasized, all psychotherapy is an ordeal to one degree or another, and analytic therapy is a particularly arduous ordeal. Most likely, the only sane response to the ordeals of analytic therapy is to flee from it as rapidly as possible. There are substantial numbers of clients who probably elect this option.

Unable to tolerate therapy any longer, some clients emphatically declare themselves cured. The therapist, knowing that such a client is not to be dissuaded, concurs with his decision as a means of saving face, and the client exits therapy. Surprisingly enough, some analytic therapists would describe such a case as a moderate success. They would attribute success to having "mobilized the ego resources" of the client. Such "mobilization," however, is merely a face-saving euphemism to which analytic therapists resort when they can find no other evidence of progress.

Analytic therapy fails because its theoretical convictions lead it into a futile quest for insight. It demands that clients understand issues that are often irrelevant to their psychological distress. Analytic preoccupations with insight, formative history, and dream symbolism betray clients who seek solutions to the anxiety-arousing dilemmas of everyday life. This therapy typically requires clients to sacrifice their needs in deference to its theoretical expectations.

When clients are distressed by problems in the here-and-now, they can wonder why they are discussing dreams about their childhood. Clients might also question how *their* insight can influence *other* important people in their lives. A client's esoteric insights often encourage others to understand that his therapist is a fool and therapy is a waste of time. This kind of outcome does not enhance any client's relationships with significant others. Instead, it usually contributes to further deterioration of those relationships.

While CC-H therapy responds to a vastly different theoretical orientation, it assists clients no more effectively than analytic therapy.

22

The world is a comedy to those that think, a tragedy to those that feel.

— HORACE WALPOLE

CLIENT CENTERED-HUMANISTIC GOALS: ENSHRINING THE PLACEBO

C C-H therapy has developed its own variation of the "bait and switch" procedure. It baits clients with expectations of problem resolution and corresponding hopes for psychological relief, and then it switches them to a potentially endless examination of their feelings. Rogers was emphatically clear on this issue when he indicated, "Therapy seems to mean a getting back to basic sensory and visceral experience."[1]

It is often difficult to understand how CC-H procedures are appropriate to the presenting problems of clients. CC-H therapists single-mindedly commit themselves to exploring their clients' immediate emotional experience in the here and now. Simultaneously, they overlook important background information about their clientele. Obsessed with emotional experiences, CC-H therapists also disregard presenting problems. It is almost as if they are telling clients, "I don't care what is happening in your life outside of therapy, just tell me how you feel right now."

PSYCHOTHERAPY AS ART

Because CC-H therapists disregard the technical skills of
therapists as inconsequential considerations, they define psychotherapy as an "art." They moreover assume that they practice the "art of relationships." Such assumptions serve as a
convenient rationale for the ineffectiveness of CC-H therapy.
Determined to express themselves as artists, CC-H therapists
ignore pragmatic concerns about the effectiveness of their endeavors. Attending to these practical issues apparently violates
their "artistic freedom."

For example, Rogers regularly neglected his responsibilities
to rapidly resolve the problems of his clientele. In discussing
the process of CC-H therapy, he emphasized: "The more I am
open to the realities in me and in the other person, the less do I
find myself wishing to rush in to 'fix things.' "²

When insulated from pragmatic considerations of "fixing
things," a therapist is free to pursue emotionally close relationships with his clientele. A CC-H therapist need not consider
what end is served by such relationships. Instead, he assumes
that clients desperately need the charismatic relationship he
supposedly affords them.

CC-H therapists like to think of themselves as facilitating
the "existential quests" of their clientele. These "quests"
often involve little more than clients meandering from one
topic to another, while lingering on whatever seems dramatically compelling. CC-H therapists are disinclined to focus
therapy on any specific goals. They disregard considerations
about the relevance of their work to the day-to-day problems
of their clients. Clients are not encouraged to ask themselves
if therapy is alleviating the distress that motivated them to
seek it.

Instead, therapy acquires the status as an end in its own
right. The value of therapy is determined exclusively by events
in the session. The "experiencing of experience" is considered a
valuable undertaking for all clients at any time. A therapist's
time and attention is consumed by a therapeutic relationship
that "transcends itself." CC-H therapists do not ask themselves
how these events, in the session, are relevant to resolving a
client's problems outside the session. A sobering question such
as this might diminish a therapist's "inner spirit."

CC-H THERAPY AND "PSYCHOBABBLE"

Rogers reported the case of Mrs. Oak, a housewife in her late thirties, who presented problems in her marital and family relationships. The following dialogue is taken from the fifth session:

> **Client:** It all comes pretty vague. But you know I keep, keep having the thought occur to me that this whole process [of therapy] for me is kinda like examining pieces of a jig-saw puzzle. It seems to me, I'm in the process now of examining the individual pieces which really don't have too much meaning. Probably handling them, not even beginning to think of a pattern. That keeps coming to me . . .
>
> **Therapist:** And that at the moment that, that's the process, just getting the feel and the shape and the configuration of the different pieces with a little bit of background feeling of, yeah they'll probably fit some-where, but most of the attention's focused right on, "what does this feel like? And what's its texture?"

The client later explained:

> **Client:** M-hm. And yet for the first time in months I am not thinking about my problems. I am not actually, I'm not working on them.
>
> **Therapist:** I get the impression you don't sort of sit down to work on "my problems." It isn't that feeling at all.
>
> **Client:** That's right. That's right. I suppose what I, I mean actually is that I'm not sitting down to put this puzzle together as, as something, I've got to see the picture. It, it may be that, it may be that I am actually enjoying this feeling process. Or I'm certainly learning something.
>
> **Therapist:** At least there's a sense of the immediate goal of getting that feel as being the thing, not that you're doing this in order to see a picture, but that it's a, a satisfaction of really getting acquainted with each piece.[3]

It might be appropriate to remind the reader that this client presented problems involving her marital and family relationships. The therapist somehow shifted the focus of therapy away from these presenting problems. He focused on the "shape and configuration" of the client's feeling while also determining its "texture." For the therapist, there was the " . . . immediate goal of getting that feel as being the thing."

The previous dialogue was little more than irrelevant "psychobabble." Distracted by this focus on feelings, the therapist neglected his responsibility to alleviate the client's marital and family problems. Because her therapist had so effectively indoctrinated her, the client enjoyed this "feeling focus." In fact, it was so enjoyable that client and therapist appeared to forget why she sought psychotherapy.

After thirty-nine sessions, Mrs. Oak's course of treatment was coming to an end. The following dialogue took place:

> **Client:** I wonder if I ought to clarify—it's clear to me, and perhaps that's all that matters really, here, my strong feeling about a hate-free kind of approach. Now that we have brought it up on a rational kind of plane, I know it sounds negative. And yet in my thinking, my—not really my thinking but my feeling, it—and my thinking, yes, my thinking, too,—it's a far more positive thing than this—than a love—and it seems to me a far easier kind of a thing—it's less confining. But it—I realize that it must sort of sound and almost seem like a complete rejection of so many things, of so many creeds and maybe it is. I don't know. But it just to me seems more positive.
>
> **Therapist:** You can see how it might sound more negative to someone but as far as the meaning that it has for you is concerned, it doesn't seem as binding, as possessive I take it, as love. It seems as though it actually is more expandable, more usable, than . . .
>
> **Client:** Yeah.

Toward the end of the session, the client commented on the pending termination of her therapy.

> **Client:** . . . I'm prepared for some breakdowns along the way.
>
> **Therapist:** You don't expect it will be smooth sailing?

Client: No.[4]

The absence of enthusiastic optimism on Mrs. Oak's part, despite the fact that her therapy was about to terminate, is not surprising. Her course of therapy was neither relevant nor responsive to the problems she presented at intake.

The client developed what she called "a hate-free kind of approach." She then brought this strategy to bear on her marital and familial relationships. It was unclear whether this strategy actually resolved some of her marital and familial problems? Or did it merely help her to endure those problems? Beyond the development of this "hate-free approach," her therapy disregarded her relationships with her parents, husband, and children.

The CC-H therapist made no inquiry regarding how the client employed her newly developed strategy. The therapist also could not know how his client's "hate-free approach" influenced other people in her family. Individual therapy, that excludes other family members, precludes the therapist from obtaining such information. Basically, this client's therapy merely encouraged her increasing introspection.

Introspection promotes exaggerated self-absorption; and self-absorption fails to assist clients in resolving interpersonal dilemmas such as familial or marital problems. Self-absorbed people ignore the interpersonal features of relationship problems; they do so because of their preoccupation with themselves.

LOOKING FOR CONNECTIONS

A fifty-three-year-old, married male client was contending with various, difficult dilemmas of middle age. He had already reached the maximum point of advancement in his career. His two children (ages eighteen and twenty-three) were moving into adulthood and gravitating out of the family home. He also felt estranged from his wife.

This client was not particularly pleased about his individual therapy with a CC-H therapist. In one session, he explained:

> Jim, I'll level with you. I don't like what's been happening here lately, and I don't think it's helping me. In fact, I think I may be getting worse. You are doing every-

thing you can, I know, but maybe I'm just not the kind who can do this stuff. I mean, maybe some people just aren't put together solidly enough to deal with all the junk that gets turned up by this process.

Later on in the same session, the therapist explained:

> **Therapist:** You want very much to have somebody know where you are and you want to read that knowing as meaning it will all come out all right, eh?
> **Client:** You know it!
> **Therapist:** Todd, I have a general notion of what's going on with you, but I need to be straight with you: Each person's journey into this place is unique, and it's up to you what you will make of it. I'm with you, but I can't promise you more than that. I can't promise happy endings or even solid guardrails on the curves.[5]

To a limited extent, this CC-H therapist was correct; the client did want to be understood. The therapist, however, was presumptuous enough to assume that his understanding would alleviate the client's distress. This assumption encouraged the therapist to appoint himself to a position of central significance in the client's life.

In fact, this client needed more than the understanding of his therapist. Dramatic metaphors about navigating the highways and byways of life were irrelevant to his welfare. Later in the same session, the client explained:

> Well, I think about my family, and then I think about being middle-aged, and then I wonder if I really do love them as much as I say I do. Am I just doing what I'm supposed to do by saying they're so important? Who are they? Sometimes when I think of them I can't remember who they are or what they're doing in my life. I mean, I know who they are all right, but I can't feel any connection to them.[6]

This client *and* his family had undergone substantial changes in their lives as a family unit. The passage of time created significant changes in the life cycle of this entire family. The client's children were now adults, he was losing the stamina of his youth, and his career no longer demonstrated its former promise. These changes influenced all the members of the client's family, not just the client himself.

The client spoke of an elusive sense of "connection" in relation to his family. As a result, he needed to share his concerns with his wife and children; and likely, his wife and children needed to share their concerns with him. The client and his family needed the reassurance of warmth and genuine understanding from each other. Therefore, effective therapy for this client should have involved his entire family.

Organized this way, therapy would have provided the opportunity for this client and his family to work together. By working together, the client and his family could have helped each other to reorganize their lives more effectively. In turn, they would have shared greater levels of trust and cohesiveness with each other.

Unfortunately, the presumptuousness of an excessively central therapist sabotaged this client's welfare. His therapy failed to promote warmth and genuine understanding with the most important people in his life—his wife and children. CC-H therapy confined those kinds of experiences to the therapist.

This therapist was also callous enough to foreclose future options for the client as a parent. In summarizing this case, the therapist commented that the client was forced to contend with the fact that he ". . . certainly would never be the parent to his children that he always intended to be (for they were already young adults)."[7]

Admittedly, this client could not regain lost parental opportunities from the past. Nevertheless, he would continue to be a parent in the future. An effective therapist would have assisted this client, and his children, to constructively reorganize their relationships with each other.

In retrospect, it must be concluded that CC-H therapy did little for this client. When his treatment terminated, he felt no greater "connection" to his wife and children than before therapy. This case demonstrates how deeply shared feelings, exchanged between a client and an excessively central therapist, are irrelevant to a client's life situation. However touching the therapist's offer of "I'm with you" may have been, his companionship was insufficient to meet this client's needs.

THE PLACEBO QUESTION

To the degree that CC-H therapy enjoys a respectable reputation in therapeutic circles, that reputation is firmly established upon placebo phenomena. While analytic therapy is the ultimate master of bait and switch tactics, CC-H therapy has elevated placebo phenomena to the status of a cure-all.

As outlined in Chapter Four, clients who trust a warm and genuinely understanding therapist may find some relief from their problems. Expecting that such a kind and benevolent individual can help them, they "experience" a cure. Thus, placebo cures transpire when the quality of the client-therapist relationship eases a client's psychological distress. In the case of analytic therapy, the quality of the client-therapist relationship reduces the likelihood of placebo cures to a remote possibility. In CC-H therapy, however, placebo cures are alive and well.

A placebo requires that an authority figure, recognized by the client as an expert, provides the explanation justifying its therapeutic value. Relationships with friends and family typically will not qualify; their familiarity usually precludes their designation as an expert. An expert might be defined as an individual who is unfamiliar enough to us; that we remain unaware of his foibles as a human being. A therapist who may have the prefix "doctor" before his name possesses more than enough credibility to qualify as an expert.

Many CC-H therapists are so gullible that they actually believe their placebos possess an inherent therapeutic value. Paradoxically enough, placebo effectiveness is enhanced by therapists who assume that placebos are inherently effective techniques. Such therapists do not understand that their therapeutic procedures are little more than placebos. Consequently, their naivete effectively protects the zeal they bring to their therapeutic work.

Zealous enthusiasm, and corresponding effusiveness, can elevate client expectations for therapeutic success. Clients who expect success at the start of therapy are more likely to regard it as successful at its termination. Clients who regard their therapy experience as successful, no matter how illusory that success may be, can certainly enhance the reputation of CC-H therapy.

Is It Enough?

Some researchers advocate that the field abandon its search for effectiveness in specific therapy techniques.[8] They suggest that the placebo effectiveness of conventional psychotherapy prevail as an acceptable status quo. Future research, they indicate, should focus on the characteristics of the client-therapist relationship that predict psychotherapeutic effectiveness.

In fact, such research endeavors would be tantamount to reinventing the wheel. Those relationship characteristics have already been well identified and extensively documented. Investing additional time and money into such research would be a waste of resources.

Still others have recommended that conventional psychotherapists take more pride in the power of their placebos.[9] Such therapists insist that they should not have to apologize for the placebo effectiveness of their work. Admittedly, conventional therapists may avoid a large number of malpractice suits as a result of their placebo procedures.

Because they are regarded as pleasant, cordial people, therapists are less apt to be harshly judged by their clientele. Consequently, they should probably acknowledge the potency of their placebo procedures with deep gratitude. Without such procedures, the cost of their malpractice insurance would likely soar.

Though placebo procedures can protect the reputations of therapists, one must ask how they serve the welfare of clients? These clients deservedly expect psychotherapy services that are legitimately effective. A respected researcher has emphasized that any client initiating psychotherapeutic treatment " . . . . has a right to know what he is buying . . . "[10] Are these clients to be told that they can expect no more than placebo treatment—some kind words and a sympathetic ear?

One critic of the contemporary therapy scene reported a case:

> At the end of the client-centered treatment he had undertaken several years earlier for severe depression, this young man thought it had been very helpful. Some of the reasons for his assessment were: "Therapy helped me think about what was going on . . . I felt that I was doing something about my problems and in that sense felt less stuck . . . The fact that my therapist didn't

dislike or reject me made me feel kinda good."

In retrospect, however, he realized that except for getting out of bed to keep his therapy appointments, "there was no specific way that I was doing better."[11] For this client, the placebo effectiveness of CC-H therapy did not stand the test of time too well.

Like analytic therapy, CC-H therapy fails because it rests on theoretical premises that are fundamentally flawed. The preoccupation with feelings and emotions leads therapists to neglect well-defined goals relevant to the client's everyday life. CC-H therapy also makes the client's relationship with his therapist virtually the only relationship of consequence. Even when clients cry out for stronger connections to family and friends, CC-H therapists make themselves excessively important to their clientele.

Behavior therapy avoids some of these problems; it addresses goals that are relevant to the client's real life. Unfortunately, it does not realize its goals consistently; and when it is effective, the results are often fortuitous—not planned.

. . . we have to remember that what we observe is not nature itself, but nature exposed to our method of questioning

— WERNER HEISENBERG

BEHAVIOR GOALS: NEGATIVE OUTCOMES AND FORTUITOUS RESULTS

A thirty-eight-year-old married male, diagnosed as neurotically depressed, was admitted to the psychiatric inpatient facility of a general hospital.[1] At the time of his admission, the client reported thoughts of suicide, increasing feelings of worthlessness, and generalized feelings of inadequacy. Moreover, the client's explosive anger often precipitated his serious losses of behavior control.

He was most likely to lose control of his behavior when interacting with his children. Though not an abusive parent, the client would resort to physical punitiveness and threats of force when enraged by his children. He was particularly apt to lose control when his children misbehaved in church. As a former seminarian, church attendance and family cohesiveness were especially important to this client.

Treatment for this client consisted of a behavioral procedure called stress inoculation. This procedure involved four separate steps. First, the client was trained to recognize situations that could arouse his anger

205

before he lost control. Second, he was taught to remain relaxed while exposed to an anger-arousing situation. Third, the client was taught to problem-solve effectively when confronted with circumstances that aroused his anger. Finally, he was trained to reflect on and learn from his experiences of success with the first three steps of this procedure.

The behavior therapist regarded the course of therapy for this client as successful. He described the client as exhibiting a remarkably good adjustment after completing the inoculation procedure and being discharged from the hospital. The therapist was particularly impressed by the client's self-control demonstrated under arduous circumstances.

After the client's discharge, he encountered situations where "Fistfights between the boys [the client's children] resulted in bleeding mouths, black eyes, and lumps on the head. In one instance, a weightlifting bar was used as a weapon."[2] While the therapist felt pleased with the client's apparent progress, the client's children still persisted in their pursuit of familial anarchy—and these circumstances did not bode well for the client.

The client clearly endured his psychological distress as a parent. Nevertheless, he was not treated as a *parent*; instead, he was treated as a *patient*. Appropriate therapy for this client as a parent would have included his wife and children. Such treatment could have reduced the escalating anarchy between the client and his children. Unfortunately, appropriate treatment was not forthcoming for this client.

Once the client was admitted to the hospital and designated as the *patient*, a counterproductive myth developed. His family, friends, and treatment personnel all assumed that the problems existed *within* the client. The reality of this situation, however, failed to support that assumption. Fundamentally, the problems existed *between* the client and his children.

The client's children were the significant stimuli provoking his episodes of uncontrolled anger. Individual behavioral treatment disregarded the controlling stimuli in this case. The client's behavioral therapy failed to stabilize a chaotically disorganized family. Therefore, the continuing chaos in his family jeopardized his psychological welfare.

Since his admission to the hospital and subsequent discharge, the frequency and intensity of chaos in this family appeared unchanged. Continued calm and tranquility for this client, in the face of such a disorganized family environment, could be regarded as less than well-adjusted on his part. Other therapists might define such behavior as maladjusted in its passivity. This consideration suggests that the client's course of therapy was even less than ineffective, and instead, it must be regarded as counterproductive.

The behavior therapist disregarded the stimulus conditions of the client's familial environment. His unresponsiveness neglected the welfare of the client and his family. A more effective therapist would have sought to determine who was influencing these children in their pursuit of familial anarchy.

Despite the assumptions of most traditional therapists, it is unlikely that these children were merely responding to conflicts within themselves. More likely, other people in their lives influenced their behavior. Indeed, one might ask who would benefit from the familial anarchy they created?

The ill-mannered antics of uncontrollable children certainly influence their parent's marriage. One might well wonder if the client, and/or his wife, felt relieved by the marital distance that must have ensued as a result of this family's chaos? Perhaps the client's wife did not share his values about church attendance and family cohesiveness. It is possible that when these children behaved outrageously in church, they were making a commentary for someone else about their father's values.

Admittedly, the issues raised in the previous paragraph are speculative. Nevertheless, this speculativeness does not excuse behavior therapists from the obligation to make fundamental changes in their procedures. It is imperative that this therapy respond more effectively to the family context of its clientele. Without such changes, behavior therapy will continue to neglect the needs of many clients.

FORTUITOUS OUTCOMES

As a result of her chronically elevated anxiety level, a middle-aged housewife was typically unable to leave home. Except for when her husband chauffeured her about in the family vehicle, she was practically housebound. The client's children were all mature adults who lived on their own. Her husband was a very busy, successful man; he left the responsibility for running the family home to the client and a full time, live-in maid.

The behavior therapist who undertook the treatment of this case employed desensitization techniques. She developed assignments requiring the client to contend with real life situations outside her home. The therapist explained:

> The first assignment involved a taxi ride alone to favorite restaurants; later ones included shopping trips to buy gifts for the family, going to the beauty parlor, gradually working up to a move closer to the city where Mrs. D could walk to all the shops, actively shop for groceries, take over many of the household management tasks, begin a sewing course, etc., and do volunteer work at a local hospital with children. All along reinforcements were provided by the family for active, independent behavior and withdrawn for the passive, dependent phobic behavior. The patient also received assertive training to help her express herself more directly. The relationship with the therapist was an additional source of reinforcement. While limited goals were set, a lot of improvement occurred, with the patient reporting increased vitality in life and feeling useful again. Furthermore, as she became more assertive, her relationship with her husband improved as well.[3]

Most behavior therapists would attribute the success of this case to the desensitization procedures. Nevertheless, various members of the client's family participated in her treatment. Their involvement allowed them to view the client as motivated to overcome her problems. The client's completed "assignments" could be shared as "victories" with her family. They no longer felt discouraged and resentful by the client's former patterns of clinging dependency. Instead, client and family could approach each new assignment with increasing confidence and optimism.

The members of the client's family probably felt a renewed respect for her. The client, in turn, surely appreciated her family more because of their demonstrated commitment to her welfare. Obviously, the patterns of family interaction that prevailed when she felt debilitated by anxiety no longer existed. The vicious cycles of the past, characterized by heightened family resentment and elevated client anxiety, were brought under control.

Consequently, it can be argued that any therapeutic procedure that gave the client a well-defined course of action, while strengthening family ties, would have resulted in success.

As a result of the family's supportiveness, the desensitization procedures employed by the therapist are best considered placebo techniques. These procedures merely provided the circumstances that allowed client and family to enhance their relationships. This was a fortuitous outcome that the therapist did not plan. Indeed, the client and her family deserved more credit for her recovery than the desensitization procedures.

Too often, behavior therapists ignore the total life situations of their clientele. Neglecting to consider an agoraphobic's status as wife and mother, and overlooking an angry patient's status as husband and father, are both examples of acontextual errors.

Therapists commit acontextual errors because they assume that psychological distress confines itself *within* clients. Behavior therapists who commit acontextual errors cannot accurately assess the full range of stimuli controlling a client's psychological distress. Consequently, their attempts at alleviating that distress are too often doomed to failure.

The Role Of Family

Other examples further underscore the significance of family support in traditional psychotherapy.

A group of British therapists developed a particularly ingenious program for the treatment of agoraphobia.[4] This program was a home-based procedure that systematically involved a client's spouse. Specifically, the program sought to increase the amount of time an agoraphobic could spend away from her home. It was designed so that client and spouse assumed the major responsibility for realizing the goals of treatment. The therapist's involvement was limited to consulting with clients and spouses about their course of treatment.

Detailed treatment manuals were developed for both the agoraphobic and her husband. These manuals spelled out specific practice procedures to assist clients in dealing with increasingly difficult situations. The husband's manual also summarized the reasons for needing his help, emphasized his role in rewarding his wife's progress, and outlined methods affording him an active role in the treatment program.

The results of this program were exceedingly impressive. The effectiveness of this home-based procedure, utilizing spousal involvement, compared favorably to more conventional behavioral programs after ten weeks of treatment. After a six month follow-up, the home-based procedure had facilitated additional progress that was not evident in other programs. The clients in this treatment program continued to exhibit progress; in contrast, the progress of clients in more conventional programs dissipated.

The home-based, spouse-assisted procedure enjoyed the success it did because the husbands were such a significant factor in the treatment program. The program created an atmosphere between client and husband that dramatically supported the client's progress. The husbands were not threatened by the progress of their wives. Instead, clients and husbands could celebrate their successes with each other.

Shared success in a mutual endeavor inevitably pulls people closer together while increasing their respect for each other's competence. Consequently, this program allowed both husbands and clients to redefine their relationships more constructively. The husbands did not feel excluded and reduced to a role of passivity. As a result, they were not threatened by some anonymous therapist creating changes in their marital relationships.

Admittedly, the effectiveness of the home-based procedure may have been a fortuitous outcome. The article reviewing this procedure was primarily concerned about its cost-effectiveness (the demands on the time of a therapist were minimal). It ignored the significance of the supportive atmosphere that this procedure created. This is an example of how behaviorists sometimes respond more effectively to their clients than they realize.

Obviously, however, effective psychotherapy should not be a gamble. Anxious, depressed, or troubled people deserve more than a therapeutic lottery. The effectiveness of psychotherapy should not be limited to those lucky circumstances when a therapist happens upon an appropriate procedure.

The fortuitous successes of behavior therapy point in the right direction: Not only must psychotherapy define goals relevant to the client's everyday life, it must also involve the important people with whom the client regularly interacts. And instead of talking about those people in their absence, effective therapy starts by including them so the therapist can talk with them. This first step allows the therapist to mobilize significant others to assist the client.

PART FIVE

CAN PSYCHOTHERAPY SURVIVE?

24

An error is more dangerous, the more truth it contains.*

—HENRI-FREDERICK AMIEL

TRADITIONAL PSYCHOTHERAPY AND EFFECTIVE ALTERNATIVES

There are elements of credibility within traditional systems of psychotherapy. The analytic therapist is correct: Psychologically distressed individuals do contend with complex, intrapsychic conflicts. The CC-H therapist is also correct: The emotional life of distressed individuals often reflects severe inhibition. Moreover, the behavior therapist is correct: Habitual patterns of thinking and behaving sabotage the efficiency with which distressed people live their lives.

Traditional therapists seek to resolve intrapsychic conflicts, or alleviate repressed feelings, or modify habitual patterns of thinking and behaving. In their attempts, however, they appoint themselves to an impossible task that practically guarantees their failure.

Without major changes in the life circumstances of their clients, individual therapists are at a loss to alter these characteristics of psychological distress. Nevertheless, they remain determined to effect changes in the internal experiences of their clientele. Simul-

215

taneously, they disregard the extent to which ambivalence is an enduring characteristic of psychologically distressed individuals.

The ambivalence of a client's interpersonal relationships creates ambivalence at an intrapsychic level, and in his feelings, and for his habitual patterns of thinking and behaving. Any therapist who attempts to focus on these internal experiences of a client is trying to hit a rapidly moving target with a poorly aimed rifle. He is responding to fluid processes as if they were static events.

For example, consider a client who resents her husband, but also loves him, and still seeks his love and affection. At an intrapsychic level, our hypothetical client both idealizes and rejects her husband at different points in time. Her feelings about her husband swing back and forth between affection and resentment. Her thinking about a satisfactory relationship with her husband ranges from optimism to pessimism.

The ever-shifting complexity of these internal experiences precludes their adequate definition at any one point in time. Our client's images, feelings, and thoughts about her husband fluctuate in response to changes in their marriage. Just when a therapist thinks he understands the internal experiences of this client, they can rapidly shift.

While focusing on the internal experiences of any client, a therapist is reduced to searching for a proverbial needle in a haystack. There is also nothing a therapist can say that alters these internal experiences. He can label them as ambivalence and discuss them as such with his client; but labeling them and discussing them does not change them.

The internal experiences of clients respond more to their life circumstances in general, and to their interpersonal relationships in particular, than to a therapist's words. Many therapists, however, attribute therapeutic powers to their vocabularies which they do not actually possess.

THERAPEUTIC VOCABULARIES

Traditional psychotherapy provides clients little more than the "wise words" of analytic therapists, the "kind words" of CC-H therapists, or the "encouraging words" of behavior therapists. Admittedly, these options create an interesting range of topics for therapeutic dialogue. Nevertheless, whether clients choose wise words, kind words, or encouraging words, they are still reduced to "talking about" their problems. Sadly enough, psychological distress is not effectively resolved by discussing it.

Given the futility and frequent counterproductiveness of individual therapy, the time is long overdue for traditional therapists to undertake a wholesale paradigm shift. Unfortunately, traditional therapists have locked themselves into their prevailing paradigm. They remain convinced that psychotherapy should focus on events which transpire within clients.

Whether their focus addresses itself to intrapsychic conflicts, repressed feelings, or maladjusted responses, a preoccupation with the internal experiences of clients flourishes as the prevailing paradigm for individual therapists. Locked into this paradigm, these therapists have lost their objectivity. Too often, they cannot see beyond their clientele as individuals.

PARADIGM SHIFTS

It is rare that psychological distress confines itself to any individual. The psychological distress of individuals profoundly affects their relationships with other people. Any change in the psychological distress of any individual affects his relationships with others important to him. As previously emphasized, psychotherapists can no longer focus their attention exclusively on events that transpire *within* clients. Instead, therapists need to address the relationships that exist *between* their clients and important others in their lives.

To the extent that therapists define psychological distress as an indication of problems between clients and significant others, their therapeutic endeavors are more likely to meet with success. This paradigm shift results in profound changes in psychotherapy's direction and goals. When therapy addresses itself to the relationships between clients and others important to them, the therapist assumes a more peripheral role.

Though often reassuring, a warm and understanding relationship with a therapist is a second-order priority compared to warmth and understanding between clients and significant others. The latter outcome allows therapeutic progress to maintain itself independent of the therapist's influence, and clients feel less dependent on their therapy.

Emphasizing what takes place between clients and others is incompatible with vague goals like insight and existential beingness. It is exceedingly difficult to directly observe insight or existential beingness—those are "private" events that transpire within people. Greater trust and increased understanding, however, are readily observable when exchanged between people—these are "public" events that both therapist and family can directly see and appreciate.

Finally, when psychotherapy responds effectively to a client's relationships with important others, the futility of individual therapy becomes strikingly evident. When people plan and coordinate courses of action together, they can move mountains. When people are reduced to isolated individuals who "think about" or "experience" their problems, hopelessness may prevail and molehills seem overwhelming.

The paradigm shift from *within* to *between* satisfies all three criteria for effective psychotherapy outlined in Part One. It obviously revises the nature of the client-therapist relationship. It surely emphasizes clearly defined goals and the need for action. And, it not only focuses on a client's relationships with significant others such as their family, it also enlists them in the effort.

Asking the traditional therapies—analytic, CC-H, or behavior—to meet these criteria is a futile request. They are looking in the wrong place with visual acuity so diminished they rarely see what clients really need.

FAMILY THERAPY

Some non-traditional therapy procedures exhibit remarkable effectiveness. At this point in time, the most effective methods of psychotherapy have been labeled "family therapy." One should not assume that family therapy is a homogeneous enterprise characterized by one, predominant set of procedures. Family therapy exhibits a range of techniques and practices that are very diversified. Indeed, the techniques of family therapy are almost as diversified as those of traditional, individual therapies.

Analytic therapy influenced Murray Bowen's "family of origin therapy."[1] CC-H procedures substantially influenced the late Virginia Satir's development of "experiential family therapy."[2] Jay Haley's "strategic family therapy"[3] and Salvadore Minuchin's "structural family therapy"[4] share their emphasis on a well-defined problem focus with behavior therapists. Family therapists vigorously debate among themselves about the merits of different family therapy procedures. This is not an endeavor whose development is stagnating because of oppressive conformity.

The term *family therapy* is probably an unfortunate misnomer. Effective psychotherapy addresses itself to the resolution of any interpersonal problems relevant to the psychological distress of a client. As a result, effective psychotherapy does not necessarily confine itself to a client's family.

For example, effective therapy for an adolescent who is exhibiting school problems would include his parents, one or more teachers, the school principal, and a school psychologist or social worker. Effective therapy for an alcoholic might include his spouse, his children, his parents, his siblings, his neighbors, his co-workers, his minister, and even his family physician.*

These kinds of therapeutic procedures are most appropriately designated as systemic therapy. This designation recognizes the complex, interlocking system of interpersonal relationships that prevail in the lives of all people.

FAMILY THERAPY RESEARCH

Family therapy also satisfies the most important condition for effective psychotherapy—the research evidence available to verify its effectiveness is impressive. The accumulated research clearly indicates that when children and adolescents present problems of conduct disorders, depression, anxiety, substance abuse, or school avoidance, family therapy involving the parents is the treatment of choice.[5]

When adult clients exhibit depressive symptoms, work avoid-

---

* In this writer's training, a "family therapy" session was observed which was structured in this manner. More than 30 people gathered in a large room to respond to the problems of a particular alcoholic. Because it was structured in this manner, this session was exceedingly powerful and very effective. The alcoholic could no longer cling to his massive denial about his condition. Instead, he acknowledged that he needed help and admitted himself into a detoxification program.

ance, sexual dysfunction, or psychosomatic disorders, family therapy and/or conjoint marital therapy (involving both spouses) is the treatment of choice.[6] Moreover, when clients undertake treatment because of marital problems, conjoint marital therapy is the treatment of choice.[7]

Duncan Stanton and his colleagues have reported the most impressive data substantiating the positive effects of family therapy. They developed family therapy techniques for treating heroin addicts and their families.[8] Stanton and his group assumed that heroin addicts are substantially influenced by unresolved conflicts within their families of origin (the family in which they grew up). The family therapy techniques of Stanton and his group were designed to resolve these conflicts, and ultimately to resolve the client's addiction.

Stanton and his colleagues undertook a research program to assess the impact of family therapy as a treatment method for heroin addicts. In their exceedingly well-designed and well-controlled study, they compared the effectiveness of family therapy with two control conditions: (1) Individual psychotherapy and methadone maintenance, and (2) A "family movie" condition. The individual psychotherapy condition employed standard, traditional techniques.

The "family movie" condition was designed so that the addict and his family viewed movies about various cultures. The addicts and their families were required to attend these movies together once a week for ten weeks. The "family movie" condition was actually controlling for placebo effects. Family therapy could exhibit illusory effectiveness because of complex placebo considerations. Such placebo considerations could evolve merely by bringing the addict together with his family in a therapeutic atmosphere.

The design of this study allowed Stanton to determine whether the techniques of family therapy were legitimately effective or whether they merely possess illusory effectiveness. If any apparent effectiveness of family therapy was merely the result of a placebo effect, then the effectiveness of family therapy could not exceed the "family movie" condition.

For purposes of research clarity, the family therapy treatment condition in this study was limited to only ten sessions. Thus, Stanton and his group imposed a very demanding task upon themselves. They were obligated to obtain significant results with heroin addicts in no more than ten sessions of family therapy. In this study, the effectiveness of all therapeutic conditions was determined by the number of days that the addict remained free of opiates over a one year follow-up.

The results of this study are very significant and exceedingly impressive. Slightly over sixty-six percent of the addicts in family therapy exhibited an outcome rated as "good." Only thirty-three percent of the addicts in the individual therapy and methadone maintenance program exhibited "good" outcomes. Interestingly enough, just under thirty-nine percent of the addicts in the placebo condition exhibited "good" outcomes. "Good" outcomes were defined as those cases in which the addict remained free of illegal opiates from eighty to one hundred percent of the time, during the one year follow-up.

The outcome of this study allows at least two major conclusions: (1) Family therapy is exceedingly impressive in treating heroin addicts. (2) Family therapy techniques, per se, are legitimately effective. Their effectiveness is not an illusion created by placebo factors.

Parenthetically, it is also interesting to note that a "family placebo" (the family movie condition) was slightly more effective than traditional therapy procedures. It seems that the placebo status of traditional psychotherapy has again reared its ugly head.

It should also be emphasized that the therapists in Stanton's project benefitted from live, moment-to-moment supervision. Experienced supervisors used one-way mirrors to observe the family therapy sessions. Their input was immediately available if the therapists found themselves floundering.

In monitoring the effectiveness of treatment for these families, therapists were not reduced to relying on their intuitive impressions. Additionally, the sessions were also recorded on videotape. As a result of reviewing these videotapes with their supervisor, the therapists enjoyed greater objectivity about themselves and their work. In this project, therapists and supervisors accomplished much more than merely "talking about" a course of treatment.

In 1980, the American Association of Marriage and Family Therapy honored Stanton for the outstanding significance of his research. The work of Stanton and his group has also been described as ". . . the finest example of the integration of theory, research, and practice in the family therapy research literature."[9] Nevertheless, Stanton's research has been limited in its impact on psychotherapy practice.

Generally, the influence of this research has been confined to the geographical area where it was conducted. The states of New York and Pennsylvania require that nonprofit clinics develop family therapy components for their substance abuse treatment programs. Otherwise, state funding is not available for those programs. Outside of the northeast portion of the United States, however, this research has not significantly influenced the psychotherapeutic treatment of substance abusers.

Despite the overwhelming significance of Stanton's work, it is business as usual for most substance abuse programs. They continue to focus on pharmacological palliatives, conventional psychotherapy, and group counseling.

There are some substance abuse treatment programs that boast about a "family focus." Nevertheless, it is common for such programs to hospitalize the substance abuser for two to four weeks, involve the family in a family therapy session with the substance abuser once a week (or at the most twice a week), and then discharge the substance abuser without providing for family therapy after-care. Post-discharge planning focuses on conventional therapy and/or group counseling.

Compelling as the evidence is for reforming these treatment programs, prevailing practices in this area remain deeply entrenched and exceedingly resistant to change. Nevertheless, Stanton's research serves as an excellent example of the fundamental paradigm shift that is needed in psychotherapy. His research moves psychotherapy into an entirely new dimension—the dimension of real interpersonal relationships as they actually exist.

For a therapist, there is a profound difference between "talking about" a client's interpersonal relationships in an abstract manner, and observing a client's interpersonal relationships as they spontaneously transpire. In the latter example, the therapist is in a position to assist a client, and his significant others, to resolve problems in their relationships with each other.*

---

* This difference is equivalent to the dissimilarities between the *in vivo* and *in vitro* techniques of the biological sciences. For too long, conventional therapists have embraced the artificiality of *in vitro* techniques. Nevertheless, the welfare of their clientele demands *in vivo* procedures.

Changes in significant interpersonal relationships, especially the resolution of interpersonal problems, enhance the psychological welfare of all people. Such changes can resolve intrapsychic conflicts, alleviate repressed feelings, and modify habitual patterns of thinking and behaving.

Clients are no longer conflicted by someone once they have resolved their problems with that person. As a result, they no longer need to repress former feelings of resentment because they feel better about that person. Moreover, future problems with that person are no longer anticipated as inevitable; consequently, habitual attitudes of discouragement no longer dominate a client's thinking and behavior.

When psychotherapy focuses on the resolution of problems *between* people, it also effectively alleviates the psychological distress *within* people.

25

*Nobody who has not been in the interior of
a family can say what the difficulties of
any individual of that family may be.*

— JANE AUSTEN

A ROLE FOR
THE FAMILY

An analytic therapist reported the
course of therapy for women who suffered perinatal loss.* This therapist
assumed that the problems associated with
perinatal loss involved unresolved, intrapsychic conflicts within the mother. Thus,
the mothers who experienced this loss were
treated via individual, analytic therapy.

The husbands of these women were systematically excluded from the therapy process. The therapist disregarded the impact of
perinatal loss on the clients' marital relationships. Presumably, the husbands encountered
no feelings of grief as a result of perinatal loss.

The therapist was eminently confident
that *his* empathy could alleviate his clients'
feelings of grief. He explained, "The sense of
feeling nurtured by an empathic therapist
who can help the bereaved mother better
understand and accept her grief may also
help to repair the maternal identification
damaged by having had a perinatal loss."[1] In
attempting to justify this course of treatment, the therapist proudly reported how a

*The death of a baby between the 20th week of
gestation and 28 days after delivery.

225

particular client terminated her therapy, " . . . feeling warm and appreciative toward her therapist."[2]

Fundamentally, this was a cruel and insensitive treatment procedure. It deprived the client and her husband of the opportunity to assist each other in resolving their mutual grief. An effective therapist would have structured therapy so that this woman and her husband could have benefitted from each other's nurturing empathy. It would have been more appropriate for them to have terminated therapy feeling "warm and appreciative" about each other.

Under different circumstances, the client and her husband could have felt this way as a result of therapy. If afforded the opportunity, they could have helped each other to resolve this tragic experience. An effective therapist would have recognized that both mothers *and* fathers share the grief of perinatal loss. These couples sometimes try to keep their grief to themselves as individuals. Because they are motivated to protect each other, both husband and wife may attempt to conceal how empty and disappointed they feel.

In response to these kinds of circumstances, effective therapy mobilizes the spouses to assist each other. A competent therapist would assess relevant dimensions of the couple's religious and ethnic background. In turn, he would find out how those religious and ethnic traditions could help them resolve their grief. When a therapist treats a couple this way, he creates a situation where they respond to each other with greater warmth and understanding. The couple's exchanges of support and appreciation evolve as the central focus of therapy, and the therapist progressively assumes a peripheral role.

An effective therapist assists families to solve their problems in ways that make sense to them. An effective therapist also understands and respects the psychological significance of a family's relatedness with each other. Even more importantly, therapy should never assault a family's dignity or divide its members with unfounded accusations. A competent therapist organizes the family around its strengths and assists it to function more effectively.

EFFECTIVENESS OF FAMILY THERAPY

The effectiveness of psychotherapy dramatically increases

when clients are seen with other people in their family. This does not imply that those people are malevolent figures who have caused the client's distress—or that they are "part of the problem." Rather, it is necessary to involve a client's family in therapy because of how effectively its members can help him. A competent therapist who has included a client's family in therapy can ask: "What strengths and resources do you enjoy as a family, and how can those strengths and resources be brought to bear on the client's problems?"

A therapist must also be prepared to bring a family's attention to strengths they may have ignored. Sometimes, families can feel so discouraged by a family member's distress that they overlook their strengths as a family unit. An effective therapist restores a family's confidence in itself, and then mobilizes it to aid the client. When families have been mobilized in this manner, they are substantially less inclined to sabotage a course of therapy. They can endorse a family member's treatment because they are in a position to approve a therapist's goals and methods.

Therapists who work *with* clients *and* their families increase the availability of social support in the lives of those clients. Social support refers to the encouragement, assistance, and reassurance available to individuals from their network of recurring relationships with other people. Previous research has demonstrated that high levels of social support protect people from the adverse effects of stressful life events and chronic life strains.[3] There is also evidence indicating that the unavailability of social support jeopardizes physical health to an even greater degree than cigarette smoking.[4]

Accumulating research has also distinguished between social support that is actually enacted and *perceived social support*—the latter concept referring to an individual's perceptions regarding the availability of social support.[5] Interestingly enough, perceived social support exerts a greater influence on psychological welfare than enacted support.[6] In other words, people who *think* they enjoy a network of supportive relationships —even if they may be mistaken—benefit from social support effects.

In view of the demonstrated impact of social support on the psychological welfare of all people, any reasonable standard of practice demands that psychotherapists address themselves to increasing the availability of perceived social support in the lives of their clients. A look at some case histories shows how such an approach could make dramatic differences in outcome.

UNDERSTANDING THE SITUATION

Joann, who is six years old, was referred for play therapy as a result of appearing nervous, tense, and withdrawn. Joann's father had been deceased for three years. She lived with her mother and her ten year old sister. In her fourth play therapy session, the play therapist described this scene:

> Joann comes into the playroom, sits down at the clay table, plays with the clay. She is usually very quiet and does very little talking. Every time she comes in she plays with the clay and makes the same thing—a figure of a man carrying a cane. Each time, after he is finished, awful things happen to him. He is punched full of holes, beaten with a stick, run over by the toy truck, buried under a pile of blocks.[7]

By the seventh session, Joann was disinclined to continue her assault on the clay man. Instead, she was content to make cats and dishes from the clay and to play with dolls. The therapist never determined the identity of the clay man during the therapy sessions. She thought it inadvisable to do so because ". . . it seemed important to Joann that she hide him behind anonymity."[8]

After Joann's therapy terminated, the play therapist met Joann's mother under coincidental circumstances. The mother informed the therapist that she was considering remarriage, and explained: "The only drawback . . . is the fact that he [the man in mother's life] is a cripple and carries a cane. Joann acts as if she is afraid of him."[9]

The play therapist was very pleased to have this information. For her, it explained why Joann had assaulted the clay man with such vigor. Pleased as the therapist was by this news, her pleasure did not increase the effectiveness of Joann's therapy.

At the time of her play therapy, Joann faced potentially distressing changes in her life. Her mother was contemplating remarriage; the mother's decision to remarry would create wholesale adjustments for Joann. Her mother would no longer be exclusively a mother, she would also be a wife. Joann would have a stepfather with whom she was forced to share her mother's attention. She would also no longer reside in an exclusively female domain. Instead, Joann would find herself interacting with an adult male on a regular basis.

Play therapy failed to assist Joann in adjusting to these potentially significant changes in her life. Despite the intensity with which she ventilated her feelings in therapy, her fears and conflicts remained unresolved. She felt no more prepared to accept her mother's fiance than before therapy. Unfortunately, the therapist only discovered the circumstances of the mother's fiance in a fortuitous manner.

This case dramatically demonstrates how individual therapists can reduce themselves to stumbling about in the dark. Without sufficient knowledge of a client's life situation outside of therapy, individual therapists cannot effectively aid their clients. Psychological distress often begins with significant changes in life circumstances that substantially alter a client's relationships with important others. If psychotherapy is to be effective, it must respond to those kinds of changes.

Effective therapy for this little girl should have included her mother, potential stepfather, and older sister. Organized in this way, therapy could have assisted Joann in adjusting to the possible changes in her family's life. A competent therapist would have helped her learn about the joy and happiness a "Daddy" shares with a little girl.

If used appropriately, play therapy could have encouraged affectionate bonding between Joann and her future stepfather. Consider the trust and security a child develops with an adult, as they giggle conspiratorially with each other, while discovering impromptu uses for wet clay. Unfortunately, the therapist failed to exploit these opportunities on Joann's behalf.

Determined to establish herself as the source of trust and security for Joann, the play therapist neglected this child's needs. Any therapist who attempts to substitute himself for the significant others in a client's life usually fails—and these attempts are often worse than naive, they can be exceedingly counterproductive.

A "POOR LITTLE RICH BOY"

An eleven-year-old boy was referred for individual psycho-therapy with a play-oriented therapist. The therapist provided the following intake narrative:

> Colin is a "poor little rich boy" who was referred for difficulties concentrating in school, self-derogatory state-ments ("I'm no good," "I'm dumb"), social withdrawal, and a marked difficulty in expressing feelings and ideas. He often appeared ready to burst yet could say nothing. His father was quite distant and preoccupied with him-self and his business affairs. He involved himself in at best a peripheral way with the family. Mother was involved and concerned, yet had great difficulty behav-ing toward Colin and his older brother in a consistent manner. She was unable effectively to set limits on the physical and verbal abuse Colin received from his brother. (Colin's brother was also in treatment and had been hospitalized twice.) Colin struggled with a pro-found sense of rage toward every member of his family.[9]

Establishing any kind of personal relationship with Colin, and obtaining his participation in the therapy process, chal-lenged this therapist's persistence. Card games, discussions of dreams, and conversations about TV shows, all failed to cap-ture this child's interest.*

Eventually, the therapist discovered that Colin seemed to enjoy drawing pictures. On occasion, he would even talk about his drawings with the therapist. The therapist attributed sub-stantial significance to Colin's drawings. He explained:

> About two months into the therapy a character emerged in his drawings who would remain a central focus in the next stage of therapy. This was Calator, an incredibly powerful and sadistic creature who controlled the uni-verse. Calator could live forever and could change his shape at will. He had slain his parents and had taken

---

*Given the irrelevance of play therapy for children, any child who regards this treatment as tedious and boring deserves credit for his perceptive judgment.

his father's magic sword and his mother's chin which gave him the power to control minds. Acquiring their magic powers made him invincible. Calator's rationale for this sadism was his parents' preferential treatment of his brother, Nocan. After destroying his parents, Calator relegated Nocan to eternal torture in jail. Calator had no remorse over his actions since, he said, "There is no good power in this universe." Colin had found a vehicle to express his rage.

The therapist also explained:

The case is still in process after one year. Recently his mother has reported that Colin has begun more effectively to stand up to his brother and avoid the provocative traps set by his brother. She also reports him to be much more direct in his statements to her at home. In school his concentration is better.[10]

While the therapist applauded Colin for ventilating his anger, he ignored the problems creating that anger. The therapist failed to resolve the conflicts between Colin and other members of his family.

Admittedly, Colin's mother reported some moderate gains on his part. Nevertheless, the therapist could not know how accurate those reports were. The therapist never took the opportunity to observe Colin's interactions with his brother, mother, and father. The mother's feedback may have been motivated by her desire to encourage a therapist who appeared committed to her son's welfare.

The therapist saw Colin twice a week, and he likely spent more time interacting with Colin than his own father did. By virtue of this therapist's treatment decisions, a compensatory relationship developed between himself and Colin. The therapist may have enjoyed the special significance he acquired in Colin's life. Ultimately, however, that significance was counterproductive. The therapist neglected to change the distant relationship that prevailed between Colin and his father. Instead, he merely compensated for it.

Preoccupied with the distress supposedly confined within Colin, the therapist disregarded the distress in Colin's family. For example, one must wonder how distressed Colin's mother felt with a husband who was so distant and aloof? One should also question how upset Colin could feel as a result of his mother's distress?

Clearly, Colin's mother felt overwhelmed by the burden of her parental responsibilities. Because of how her family was organized, the mother was forced to function as if she were a single parent. Colin's therapist ignored a family situation that demanded greater involvement from Colin's father.

Quite possibly, Colin's distressing symptoms were designed to increase his father's participation in the family. The readiness of children to engage in self-sacrificing behavior, while pursuing the welfare of their parents, should not be underestimated. If Colin was responding to concerns about his parents' marital happiness, and/or to his own needs for a closer relationship with his father, play therapy neglected his psychological welfare.

Instead of attempting to mobilize strengths that the father might have brought to bear on his son's problems, the therapist merely jumped to unsubstantiated conclusions about the father's supposed deficits. How did this therapist know that the father was "... preoccupied with himself and his business affairs?" Had the therapist ever met Colin's father, and if so, what had he done to obtain the father's assistance and cooperation? One would also want to know if the therapist even attempted to contact the father.

Likely preoccupied with dogmatic considerations of parental noninterference, the therapist probably never took the initiative to personally contact Colin's father. Even more disconcerting is the likelihood that the therapist let Colin see his disdain for the father. Subjecting this boy to the covert assassination of his father's character would not enhance his psychological welfare.

This case illustrates the damage that therapists do when they elevate themselves to the status of surrogate parent or surrogate spouse. Merely "filling in" for the important people in a client's life is not enough. Psychologically distressed people require relationships with significant others that are reorganized around experiences of mutual trust and understanding.

Disregarding the inappropriate sarcasm attendant to labeling Colin a "poor little rich boy," this statement allows one to assume that the father was financially successful. A competent therapist would want to know what personality strengths of the father contributed to his career success, and how could those strengths be activated on Colin's behalf?

Fathers who assume a distant role in relation to their children often do so because they doubt their own competence as a father. Self-doubting fathers do not need the callous indictments of a presumptuous therapist. Instead, they need a therapist's encouragement and assistance to increase their sense of paternal competence and self-confidence. Colin's welfare would have been more effectively served had the therapist established a supportive alliance with the father. With this kind of an alliance, a competent therapist could have increased the father's participation in the family.

The therapist could have asked the father and Colin to draw pictures together. Perhaps father and son could discover a plot that would allow "Calator" to develop into a better-adjusted, more compassionate figure. Dad and Colin might attend movies together to obtain ideas for a happier ending for Calator's drama. Working together as "script writers" would pull father and son into a closer alignment with each other.

The therapist could also have told Colin's parents that their son worried about their welfare. As a result, Colin needed to know that his parents were closely aligned with each other. The parents could be asked to reassure their son by demonstrations of mutual warmth and affection in front of him. This procedure would alter the parents' behavior without assaulting their dignity.

Once this goal was realized, Colin's mother would no longer feel burdened by the responsibilities of functioning as a single parent. In turn, Colin would no longer worry about his mother's distress. Moreover, Colin could enjoy a positive relationship with his real father. He would no longer need the presence of some intrusive figure who was paid to spend two hours a week with him.

After more than a year of therapy, however, Colin's therapist appeared to have only escalated the alienation between Colin and his father. One can only shudder at the thought of how much longer this therapeutic nonsense continued.

Therapists who treat youthful clients effectively are as sensitive to parental strengths as they are to parental deficits. A competent therapist assiduously addresses himself to identifying parental strengths. When a therapist includes parents in the course of their child's therapy, he can exhibit respect for a family's history of competence and success. Effective therapy also brings a family's attention to the bonds of loyalty and affection which exist between them.

Renewed awareness of past accomplishments and affectionate bonding creates collective feelings of confidence and optimism for a family. Confident, optimistic families are able to reorganize their relationships more appropriately with each other; and then, they can develop new and more effective methods for resolving their problems. Consequently, an effective therapist extricates clients *and* the other people important to them from persistent problem cycles; he does so by seeing them together as a family.

*One of the greatest pains to human nature
is the pain of a new idea.*

—WALTER BAGEHOT

EFFECTIVE PSYCHOTHERAPY

In our review of traditional therapies, we tested them against three criteria: an appropriate client-therapist relationship, focus on the client's everyday relationships, and the definition of clear and achievable goals. While it is logically valid to view these criteria separately, the reality of psychotherapy usually leaves them intertwined.

Individual therapists too often make themselves excessively important to their clients, as they pursue ill-defined goals while overlooking the significance of a client's relationships with important others. Interestingly enough, traditional therapists could learn a great deal from organizational psychologists.

Few organizational psychologists would attempt to influence an entire organization while limiting their attempts to one individual in that organization (no matter how important he may be). Organizational changes require the involvement of all of the key personnel in an organization. Correspondingly, change within a family system requires participation from all of its significant members.

For example, a father was severely frustrated by the defiant disobedience of his sixteen-year-old daughter. In the course of his individual treatment with a CC-H therapist, he explained:

> Dorothy, I think she's going to drive me right up the
> goddamn wall! She's ready to trust anybody who sweet
> talks her. But not me. Whenever I try to talk to her, try
> to be reasonable, she just shuts off. I want to woodshed
> her, but my wife says she'll report me for child abuse if
> I do. Christ! What am I supposed to do? Just stand by
> and see her ruin her life with pot and God knows what
> else?[1]

Encouraging this client to dwell on his feelings of frustration
would have been a futile endeavor. Given the situation, the
father's frustration was easy to understand and hardly in need
of "experiential clarification." Teaching the father how the "deal
with" his frustration would have been counterproductive. The
father's welfare necessitated that therapy address the problems existing *between* his wife, his daughter, and himself.

Above all else, the client and his wife needed to cooperate
with each other. Their daughter's welfare required that they
agree about expectations and limits for her behavior. Without
such expectations and limits, the chaos of this family would
deteriorate into anarchy, and the client's feelings of frustration
could only increase. In order to prevent such anarchy, a competent therapist would have seen this client and his wife together.

The client, his wife, and the therapist could have planned
how to set limits for the daughter's behavior. The mother could
have been directed to *appear* harsh and punitive with her
daughter. Simultaneously, the father would have been coached
to assume a clucking, overprotective role—but to understand
that his wife would have to win this staged disagreement.
When parents reverse their usual patterns in this manner,
their children are left confused and bewildered. Confused, bewildered adolescents find it difficult to resist parental influence; consequently, they more readily comply with it.

Without these changes in the client's family, he was resigned
to a cycle of escalating frustration. As long as his wife seemed
overprotective of their daughter, the client felt compelled to
compensate by responding punitively. But as long as the client
appeared punitive, the wife felt compelled to respond
overprotectively. This impasse between her parents led the
daughter to her own conclusion. She knew she was a belea-

guered victim requiring her mother's services as a savior to shield herself from her villainous father.

To the extent that this triangulated pattern perpetuated itself, the daughter was able to do what she wanted whenever she pleased. Locked into their conflict with each other, the parents could not effectively control her behavior. Their inability to work together encouraged her willful impulsiveness. The daughter was like an overgrown cookie-monster gleefully clutching her keys to the bakery.

In dealing with this situation, a competent therapist would understand it from everyone's point of view. As a result, no one in the family would find him or herself singled out for blame. Without the burden of defensiveness that traditional therapists too often create, this family could undertake necessary changes. An effective therapist would promote those changes in the manner previously outlined—by helping the parents respond to their daughter quite differently.

Traditional therapists, however, too often attempt to work around the influence of a client's family. Simultaneously, they overlook the necessity for changing those familial influences. When therapists employ flanking maneuvers to skirt around these issues, they are acting as if familial influence dissipates when ignored. Therapists who respond to a client's family in this manner are engaged in a futile endeavor, and this kind of futility neglects the welfare of their clientele.

OVERCOMING CONFLICT

Two analytic therapists reported how the mother of a twenty-year-old female client, who was treated for excessive weight and poor school grades, reacted to her daughter's analytic therapy. The mother protested that the therapist and her daughter " . . . have all the secrets."[2]

This mother felt distressed as a result of being excluded from the therapy process. She worried how her daughter's treatment would influence the future of their mother-daughter relationship. The mother also experienced "'misgivings about his [the therapist] being qualified enough to tamper with my child's feelings'."[3]

The mother's doubts were entirely justified. Since she could not participate in this therapy, how could she know whether the therapist was genuinely committed to the best interests of her daughter? Caring parents are understandably reluctant to surrender the psychological welfare of their children—in an act of blind faith—to some anonymous therapist.

The reaction of the therapist in this case was particularly callous. The mother was covertly castigated for her alleged worry that "... the therapist can help her [the daughter] where she [the mother] has failed."[4] Presumably, the mother's concerns merely concealed her maladjusted feelings of jealousy and possessiveness.

Whether traditional therapists like it or not, the overwhelming majority of clients do have families. Those families are almost always affected by the course of a family member's therapy. If a therapist wants to enjoy a reputation of credibility in the eyes of a client's family, he must earn it. Such credibility is lost by attempting to erect rigid barriers between the therapy process and a client's family.

Effective treatment for this client should have assisted the mother to help her daughter. If allowed to participate in her daughter's therapy, the mother could have helped her to lose weight and accomplish better grades. A competent therapist would have explained that one never learns material so effectively as when they have to teach it. Thus, the client would have been designated a "teacher," and the mother would have assumed the role of "student." This way, the mother would have known whether her daughter was progressing in school.

Additionally, if the mother needed to lose weight, an exercise and diet program could have been designed for both mother and daughter. As a result, they would have encouraged each other's weight loss. As a result of this symptomatic progress, this client and her mother could have shared an enormous sense of pride. In turn, that sense of pride could have facilitated additional successes, and ultimate conflict resolution between the client and her mother.

Admittedly, analytic therapists would probably dismiss the goals of this treatment strategy as superficial symptom removal. Nevertheless, disregarding the analytic penchant for bait and switch tactics would serve this client more effectively.

Unfortunately, the manner in which the therapist proceeded in this case precluded a positive outcome, and it also practically guaranteed deterioration of the client's psychological welfare.

An intense, three way conflict—between therapist, client, and mother—developed as a result of this therapy situation.

The client was caught in the middle between her mother and her therapist. Her movement in either direction would anger someone. If she established a "working alliance" with her therapist, she was in jeopardy of angering her mother. If she maintained her loyalty to her mother, she would endure untold numbers of resistance interpretations from her therapist. Immobilized in this manner, the likelihood of this client making any progress in her therapy was effectively sabotaged.

ENLISTING SUPPORT

Effective therapy addresses itself to resolving the interpersonal conflicts in a client's life, and most importantly, it avoids escalating those conflicts. For example, a high-school basketball player consulted this writer with a frustrating problem— he made free-throws about as often as he sighted dinosaurs.

The client's father also felt frustrated by his son's problem. He had played high-school basketball and this activity was an important father-son bond. Neither father nor son felt pleased that their mutual bond was rapidly deteriorating into mutual frustration.

The son's problem invited opponents to foul him with great regularity because the cost of their transgressions was minimal. At six feet, six inches tall, and with the strength of a football player, the son had attracted considerable attention from college recruiters. Now, however, their interest was starting to wane. This left the son discouraged, and the father was discouraged by the son's discouragement. They explained that they often expressed their mutual discouragement by yelling at each other.

Father and son wanted to use hypnosis to improve the son's accuracy from the free-throw line. They were told that their expectations were altogether appropriate, and that the father's participation would be necessary for success. The father readily volunteered to do anything that would help.

The therapist taught the father how to hypnotize his son. Once the son was in trance, the father was directed to tell him that one makes free throws with the legs—as the strongest part of the human body, the legs ultimately provide the impetus for successful free-throws.

This procedure was a placebo, but it was a carefully planned placebo. The level of muscle tension in his hands, arms, and shoulders guaranteed the son's failures at a free-throw line. Directing his attention to his legs effectively reduced this tension. Rather than think about the critical parts of his body when at a free-throw line, he thought about his legs as "pistons."* As a result, his hands, arms, and shoulders were free to do what they had done in the past—shoot free-throws with a high degree of accuracy.

If the client had just been told not to think about his hands, arms, and shoulders, that procedure would have failed. It would have been tantamount to telling him not to think about his left heel when he walked. People rarely consider this sensation while walking, but when *advised* to ignore it, the advice itself directs their attention to their heel so they are compelled to think about it.

The father was also told that brief hypnosis sessions of fifteen minute duration should be used at least four to five times weekly. This "homework" required that the father speak softly and reassuringly to his son as the latter relaxed in an easy chair. Other than these sessions, there was to be no discussion of free-throws, but they could discuss defensive skills as often as they wanted. (Heightened anxiety immeasurably improves a basketball player's defensive prowess.)

As the father understood how to talk to his son—because they were doing hypnosis—the therapist avoided humiliating him. The father discovered for himself that yelling at his son was counterproductive. Basically, this element of hypnosis was another placebo designed to change how the father interacted with his son.

Finally, the father was told that "side-line coaching" during his son's games was no longer necessary, and in fact, it was inadvisable. Such "coaching" risked breaking the son's concentration that the father would build during the hypnosis sessions. The father was told that during stoppages of play, he could catch his son's eye, nod knowingly about their conspiracy, and smile reassuringly. Even if this procedure had not yet

---

*A metaphor so appropriate for a Detroit area basketball player that it could not be resisted!

returned benefits, father and son knew they were a formidable team that would eventually succeed.

Within one week, the father phoned to report how very successful the hypnosis had been. He asked for another appointment as soon as possible, but the therapist politely declined. He explained that his involvement at this point might interfere with the father's work—and the father had surely demonstrated that he knew how to handle these matters! The father was reassured that if he still felt the need to consult the therapist in two more weeks, an appointment would be made.

After the father was congratulated on *his* success, the therapist spoke with "the free-throw shooter." The son was asked to purchase a personal gift for his father that would symbolize his appreciation for the father's wisdom. There was one condition: the gift had to be small enough so the father could take it to a basketball game inside a pocket.

This procedure was designed so that the father could attend all the son's basketball games with tangible evidence of how much his son appreciated his assistance. This symbol would also remind the father not to sabotage his own assistance by inappropriate "coaching." While father focused on this symbol, the therapist's contribution would fade into an afterthought—and that would be as it should.

The unusual circumstances of this case allowed the therapist to unobtrusively monitor the son's progress. The sports section of a suburban newspaper statistically summarized his performance after every game. His free-throw percentage rapidly increased, and his number of free-throws attempted progressively decreased. Opponents learned not to foul him because he was collecting an impressive toll at the foul line.

Interestingly enough, the father never found it necessary to call the therapist again. He and his son must be quite confident in their ability to handle any problems that confronted them.

Effective Individual Therapy

Family therapy, or the creation of a therapeutic system that can pursue a client's welfare, is not always possible. Our nation's population is so mobile that simple considerations of geographical distance can prevent a therapist from initiating family therapy.

In such circumstances, individual therapy can be effective. Its effectiveness necessitates that a therapist recognize that any client is much more than merely an individual. Even when someone is geographically separated from his family, the family can still exercise substantial influence in his life. When it is effective, individual therapy addresses itself to the interpersonal problems of a client.

Effective individual therapy also requires that therapist and client establish well-defined goals for therapy. Well-defined goals allow a client to determine whether he is making progress. Once the goals of therapy are designed in this manner, an effective therapist focuses on courses of action that a client can undertake to resolve his psychological distress.

Effective therapy is characterized by a therapist's forethought and planning. Therapy sessions that meander to whatever topic spontaneously captures the interest of therapist or client neglect a client's welfare.

As emphasized earlier, an effective therapist is also regarded by a client as warm and genuinely understanding. When such a therapist views a client as more than an individual, develops well defined goals, and outlines effective courses of action, a client develops a determined sense of optimism.

This kind of optimism is not merely the product of a placebo; instead, such optimism reflects the appropriateness of how therapy has been structured. Determined optimism substantially aids a client in resolving his psychological distress.

Effective individual therapists do acknowledge the significance of insight in therapy. Nevertheless, insight is meaningful when it evolves in response to changes in a client's behavior. When behavior change precedes insight, a client can understand himself in terms of: "Now that I am doing things differently, I can understand what was wrong before."

Meaningful insight is discovered by a client; it does not come from the interpretations or explanations of a therapist. Insights discovered by a client serve to maintain positive changes in his behavior. In such circumstances, a client understands: "Now that I am doing things differently, I know why it works."

27

We must learn to welcome and not to fear voices of dissent. We must dare to think about "unthinkable things" because when things become unthinkable, thinking stops and action becomes mindless.

— **J. WILLIAM FULBRIGHT**

TRUTH AND CONSEQUENCES

As the number of therapists grows exponentially, many therapists are faced with declining practices.* Profound changes in health care in general, and in the mental health community in particular, have left therapists preoccupied with marketing their services. They are so concerned with *who* to market, and *how* to market, they overlook *what* they are marketing.

Determined to position themselves effectively in the health care marketplace, traditional therapists neglect the compelling need for a profound shift in their paradigm. Instead, they cling tenaciously to an antiquated paradigm despite its increasing obsolescence. They remain bound and determined that psychotherapy must be a predominantly individual endeavor.

Paradigm shifts cannot occur in any profession unless a newer, viable paradigm is available to replace an antiquated, obsolete paradigm. Twenty-five years ago, even fifteen years ago, there were no alternatives

*The writer was tempted to describe these circumstances as "shrinking practices." Nevertheless, such an obvious pun might stretch the patience of a reader.

243

well enough developed to replace psychotherapy's prevailing paradigm. Moreover, most therapists were unaware that the effectiveness of therapy was more illusory than legitimate. The research leading to this sobering conclusion had not yet been published.

The decade of the 1980s, however, saw accumulating research to which all therapists must respond. That decade also saw the development of a family therapy paradigm which is now a well-developed alternative. The future status of psychotherapy depends on its collective willingness to accept this new paradigm.

THE DANGERS OF DELAY

If the majority of therapists refuse to make the paradigm shift necessitated by the present research, the future viability of psychotherapy will be sorely threatened. Psychotherapists could rapidly lose the respect and prestige they have enjoyed over the past thirty years. The public could become as reluctant to seek psychotherapeutic services as it was in the 1940s and 1950s.

The psychotherapy professions could also lose the influence they enjoy with lawmakers and policymakers. Psychotherapists have long sought to influence legislation and policy regarding health care, health insurance, and reimbursement procedures. As policymakers understand more about the illusory effectiveness of traditional therapy, they may be less inclined to respond to the influence attempts of psychotherapists.

If traditional therapists continue to resist the necessity of a paradigm shift, they could also encounter a malpractice crisis. The legal test of malpractice has traditionally been determined by three questions: (1) What is the prevailing standard of practice to which a therapist should adhere in providing services for a client? (2) Did the therapist in question violate that standard by virtue of the treatment he provided for a particular client? (3) Was the client substantially damaged as a result of the therapist's violation?

Unfortunately, there are too many situations where borderline incompetence, or worse, prevails as the usual standard of psychotherapy practice. In the past, this situation has discouraged malpractice suits against psychotherapists

There are legal precedents, however, that could suspend considerations of prevailing standards of practice in psychotherapy malpractice suits. Some courts have taken the position that they must assume the responsibility for defining appropriate standards of practice.[1] When courts have ruled in this manner, they have emphasized that the public's welfare demands a standard of practice greater than that which practitioners define for themselves. Consequently, a therapist could be judged by whether his techniques meet a test of reasonableness.

Because of recently developing legal precedents, clients may file more lawsuits against incompetent therapists. Moreover, the relatives of clients—who feel they have been damaged by a family member's therapy—could also begin to initiate legal action against therapists. When therapists intrusively and divisively disorganize family relationships, they are exceedingly vulnerable to malpractice suits.

Intramural debates between therapists will not resolve the question of an appropriate standard of care for psychotherapists. Ultimately, these questions, and the corresponding issues of psychotherapy malpractice, demand resolution in courts of law. Courts will likely deal with these issues more often in the future. As the public learns more about the ineffectiveness and counterproductiveness of traditional therapy practices, psychotherapy malpractice cases will probably appear in courts with increasing frequency.

HELP FROM THE PUBLIC

Despite the specter of litigation, traditional therapists remain entrenched in the esoteric nonsense of analytic therapy, the inspirational theatrics of CC-H therapy, and the pseudoscience of behavior therapy. Unless psychotherapists undertake the necessary paradigm shift, they will reduce themselves to the status of charlatans and faith-healers.

The American public deserves more than the illusory effectiveness of wise words, kind words, and encouraging words. Most likely, the impetus for a paradigm shift will come from an informed public demanding it. At this point in time, the public possesses greater potential for objectivity about psychotherapy than psychotherapists do. In their dogged determination to protect their obsolete paradigm, traditional therapists have sacrificed their objectivity.

The observation of Max Planck, a Nobel laureate in physics, unfortunately applies to the prevailing practices of psychotherapy. Planck emphasized that the necessity of a paradigm shift " . . . rarely makes its way by gradually winning over and converting its opponents . . . what happens is that its opponents gradually die out." Consequently, only an eternal optimist could expect the majority of traditional therapists to willingly make the necessary changes in their procedures.

This book has been an effort to inform public opinion so that it can assist in bringing about that change. It insists that psychotherapists must undertake wholesale changes in their theories, techniques, and training procedures. Superficial, cosmetic changes will not suffice. Psychotherapy finds itself in a catastrophic crisis that demands a profound shift in its collective thinking. In its effects, this shift is tantamount to rejecting the superstitious rituals of astrology while seeking the scientific respectability of astronomy.

Hopefully, this volume has taken at least one step in the direction of this desperately needed shift. In turn, it might serve to spare others, including tortured souls like Robert Andrews, from ineffective, even destructive therapy; and direct them to a more positive, truly helpful therapeutic experience.

Afterword

Hiring And Firing
A Therapist

C hoosing a therapist is a mind-boggling
endeavor. Neither a therapist's degree,
nor his professional identity, predict
his competence. Moreover, one cannot assume
that an older, experienced therapist possesses
greater competence than a younger, inexperienced therapist. Experienced therapists are
more inclined to cling tenaciously to an obsolete paradigm.

Above all else, training-supervisory experiences determine a therapist's competence.
Though they are relatively few in number,
there are therapists who have undertaken
training organized around live, moment-to-
moment supervision. These training-supervisory experiences enhance their ability to
develop well-defined courses of therapeutic
action.

Since live supervision usually involves a
group of supervisees, they also learn from
observing each other. Because they enjoy
greater objectivity as a result of their training, these therapists respond more effectively
to their clients' needs.

In contrast, a therapist who has never been
observed by a supervisor or a colleague is a

247

therapist who can conceal his incompetence behind closed doors. He understands very little about his weaknesses—and his strengths—as a therapist. Consequently, he does not know what he needs to do to increase his therapeutic competence. Training that emphasizes live supervision is the best standard for evaluating a therapist.

Prospective clients should not hesitate to ask a therapist about his training. Such questions are altogether necessary and appropriate. Any therapist who refuses to answer, or responds evasively, is a therapist to avoid.

There may be readers who are presently involved in psychotherapeutic treatment. Such a reader may confront the problem of evaluating the effectiveness of ongoing therapy. This is especially troublesome because firing a therapist is a more difficult decision than hiring one.

Any client who wonders whether his therapist is effectively aiding him contends with substantial frustration and self-doubt as he weighs what to do next. If a client terminates treatment with a therapist he regards as ineffective and/or incompetent, he is faced with the question of who he will find now to aid him.

The following forty questions are designed to help clients evaluate and make decisions about their ongoing therapy. Prospective clients can also use these questions to interview a potential therapist, and bring greater objectivity to their impressions of that therapist. Additionally, any client who has found it necessary to terminate an incompetent therapist, can use these questions to assess a potential replacement.

EVALUATING THERAPEUTIC EFFECTIVENESS

Directions: In taking this inventory, merely respond "yes" or "no," and count how many questions you answer "yes."

1. Has your therapy limited itself to giving you a better understanding of the difficult situations in your life?
2. Do you feel more worried and discouraged since you began therapy?
3. Is your therapist so preoccupied with your insight that he neglects to outline specific courses of action for you to undertake?
4. Is your therapist intensely interested in the minutiae of your

fantasies, feelings, and/or thoughts?

5. Does a great deal of your therapy seem to focus on issues that are trivial or obscure?

6. Is your therapist more curious about you than he seems committed to helping you (do you feel reduced to an object of study by your therapist)?

7. Despite a situation where you have felt ready to terminate therapy, has your therapist repeatedly advised you not to?

8. Does your therapist focus primarily on the events of your childhood and overlook the present-day issues of your life?

9. Does your therapist overemphasize your deficits and short-comings while ignoring your strengths and resources?

10. Does your therapist frequently tell you things about yourself which seem wildly speculative?

11. Does your therapist spend a good deal of time explaining how you supposedly feel about him?

12. When differences of opinion exist between you and your therapist, does he almost always insist that you are mistaken?

13. Does your therapist seem to see himself as intellectually superior?

14. Does your therapist appear to distrust you; is he quick to assume that you are merely victimizing yourself and sabotaging your therapy?

15. Does your therapist insist that he is a much more important figure in your life than he really is?

16. Does your therapist frequently talk about other people in your life, but refuse to include them in your therapy despite their availability?

17. Does your therapist attribute malevolent motivations to other people in your life, and indict them as a result?

18. Does your therapist insist that you postpone important decisions in your life (marriage, job change, educational plans), pending his permission for you to make those decisions?

19. Has your therapy created a situation where you feel pulled in one direction by your therapist, and pulled in another direction by someone else in your life?

20. Is your therapist a remote, aloof individual who exhibits all the human warmth of a computer?

21. Has your therapist insisted that you cannot discuss your therapy with anyone else in your family?

22. Has your therapist become a good friend with whom you spend most of your sessions chatting amiably?

23. Have you assumed that your therapist is competent merely because he seems to be a pleasant, personable individual?

24. Does your therapist act as if he provides you with a uniquely important relationship that is unavailable to you in other sectors of your life?

25. Does your therapist seem to assume that he is a charismatic figure?

26. Is your therapist committed to pursuing ill-defined goals such as "growth" and "existential quests?"

27. Does your therapist seem so bound and determined to be your friend that he disregards the resolution of your problems?

28. Is your therapist preoccupied with telling you about his own feelings?

29. Does your therapist seek to determine where some feeling or emotion is located in your body?

30. Is your therapist more concerned about how you experience your feelings, compared to what (or who) influences those feelings?

31. Does your therapist seem more interested by what transpires in a session, than by what transpires in your life outside of therapy?

32. Does your therapist expect that you should imitate him and adopt his values?

33. Does your therapist assume that his relationship with you will suffice to resolve your problems?

34. Does your therapist often seem as bewildered and confused by your problems as you are?

35. Does your therapist rely on sympathetic platitudes advising you to "trust yourself" and/or "be kind to yourself?"

36. Has your therapist subjected you to any kind of physical ordeal?

37. Instead of planning a therapy session, does your therapist merely react to whatever direction a session spontaneously takes?

38. Is your therapist unaware of who is included in your family and how they influence you?

39. Instead of planning how to influence the behavior of someone else in your life, does your therapist merely hope that those changes will transpire by themselves?

40. Is your therapist unresponsive to the idea of including other people in your therapy?

If you answered "yes" to only one or two questions, the chances are better than fifty-fifty that your therapist is competent. You and he will probably be able to resolve whatever doubts you have about your therapy.

If you answered "yes" to between three and five questions, it is imperative that you and your therapist resolve your concerns. Otherwise, therapy may deteriorate into a waste of your time, money, and energy.

If you answered "yes" to between six and nine questions, you need to seriously discuss the direction of your treatment with your therapist. Nevertheless, do not feel too optimistic about the outcome of such a dialogue. A therapist who provokes this many "yes" answers, is likely very entrenched in an antiquated paradigm. You may find it necessary to fire this therapist.

If you answered "yes" to ten or more questions, you need to carefully question your therapist about the relevance of your therapy. If the outcome of this discussion fails to reassure you, decisive action is warranted. Rather than walk away from this therapist, or even trot, consider sprinting from therapy as rapidly as you can. Any therapist who elicits this many "yes" responses is likely incompetent. He is probably doing you much more harm than good.

FOOTNOTES

CHAPTER ONE

1. DeLeon, P.H. & Borreliz, M. Malpractice: Professional liability and the law. *Professional Psychology*, 1978, 9, 467-477.

CHAPTER TWO

1. Hunt M. Navigating the therapy maze. *The New York Times Magazine.* August 30, 1987. p. 28-49
2. Hunt, M. Same as above.
3. Hunt, M. Same as above.
4. Hunt, M. Same as above.
5. Eysenck, H. J. The effects of psychotherapy: An evaluation. *Journal of Consulting Psychology.* 1952, 16, 319-324.
6. Truax, G. B. Effective ingredients in psychotherapy: An approach to unraveling the patient-therapist interaction. *Journal of Counseling Psychology.* 1963, 10, 256-263
7. Lambert, M.J. J Bergin, A.E., & Collins, J.L. Therapist induced deterioration in psychotherapy. In A.S. Gurman & M. Razin (Eds.). *Effective Psychotherapy: A Handbook of Research.* New York: Pergamon Press, 1977.
8. Haley, J. *Ordeal Therapy.* San Francisco: Jossey-Bass, 1984.
9. Cummings, N.A. Prolonged (ideal) versus short term (realistic) psychotherapy. *Professional Psychology,* 1977, 8, 491-501.
10. Chapman, C.R. Prior probability bias in information seeking and opinion revision. *American Journal of Psychology,* 1973, 86, 269-282.
11. Zilbergeld, B. *The Shrinking of America,* Boston: Little, Brown; 1983, p.190.
12. Lambert, M. J , Shapiro, D. A., & Bergin, A. E. The effectiveness of psychotherapy. In J. Garfield & A. E. Bergin (Eds.). *Handbook of Psychotherapy and Behavioral Change.* (Vol. 3). New York: Wiley, 1986.
13. Strupp, H.H. Psychotherapy: Gan practitioners learn from the researcher? *American Psychologist,* 1989, 44, 717-724.
14. Whiston, S.G. & Sexton, T.L. An overview of outcome research: Implications for practice. *Professional Psychology,* 1993, 24, 43-51.
15. Weisz, J.R., Weiss, B., & Donenberg, G.R. The lab versus the clinic: Effects of child and adolescent psychotherapy. *American Psychologist,* 1992, 47, 1578-1585.

CHAPTER THREE

1. Pekkanen, J. M.D. *Doctors Talk About Themselves.* New York: Delacorte, 1988. (Dell Edition, 1990, p. 16)
2. Xenakis, S.N., Hoyt, M.F., Marmar, G.R., & Horowitz, M.J. Reliability of self-reports by therapists using the therapist action scale. *Psychotherapy,*

1983, 20 t 314-320.

3. Barnat, M.R. Some characteristics of supervisory identification in psychotherapy. *Psychotherapy: Theory, Research & Practice.* 1974, 11, 189-192.

4. Barnat, M.R. Same as Above.

5. Kingsbury, S.J. Cognitive differences between clinical psychologists and psychiatrists. *American Psychologist,* 1987, 42, 152-156.

6. Shiffman, S. Clinical psychology training and psychotherapy interview performance. *Psychotherapy,* 1987, 24, 71-84.

7. Fix, A.J. & Haffke, E.A. Relationship between psychotherapy skillc and level of training in psychiatric residency prooram. *Social Science & Medicine,* 1975, 9, 489-481.

8. Howell, J. N. & Highlen, P.S. Effects of client effective self-disclosure and counselor experience on counselor verbal behavior and perceptions. *Journal of Counseling Psychology,* 1981, 28, 386-398.

9. Strupp, H.H. & Hadleyj S.W. Specific vs nonspecific factors in psychotherapy. *Archives of General Psychiatry;* 1979, 36, 1134-1140.

CHAPTER FOUR

1. Truax, G.B. & Garkhuff, R.R. *Toward Effective Counseling and Psychotherapy.* Chicago: Aldine, 1967.

2. Shapiro, A.K. & Morris, L.A. The placebo effect in medical and psychological therapies. In S.L.Garfield & A.E. Bergin (Eds.) *Handbook of Psychotherapy and Behavior Change: An empirical analysis.* 2nd Ed. New York: John Wiley, 1978.

3. Frank, J.D. Therapeutic components shared by all psychotherapies. In Harvey, J. H. & Parks, M. M. (Eds.) The master lecture series, Vol. 1. *Psychotherapy Research and Behavior Change.* Washington, D.C.: American Psychological Association, 1981.

4. Zilbergeld, B. *The Shrinking of America.* Boston: Little, Brown, 1983, p 164.

5. Watzlawick, P., Weakland, J., & Fisch, R. *Change: Problem Formation and Problem Resolution.* New York: WW. Norton, 1974.

CHAPTER FIVE

1. Zilbergeld, B. *The Shrinking of America.* Boston: Little, Brown, 1983, p.190.

2. Striano, J. *Can Psychotherapists Hurt You?* Santa Barbara, Cal.: Professional Press, 1988, p.103.

3. Bugental, J .F. *The Art of the Psychotherapist.* New York: Norton & Co., 1987, p. 60-61.

4. Maeder, T. Row, 1989. *Children of Psychiatrists.* New York: Harper & Row, 1989.

5. Williams, M.H. The bait-and-switch tactic in psychotherapy. *Psychotherapy,* 1986, 22, 110-113.

6. Williams, M.H, Same as Above.

7. Todd, T.C. & Stanton, M.D. Research on marital and family therapy: Answers, issues, and recommendations for the future. In B.B. Wolman & G. Stricker (Eds.) *Handbook of Family and Marital Therapy.* New York: Plenum, 1983.

CHAPTER SIX

1. Sarason, S.B. An asocial psychology and a misdirected clinical psychology. *American Psychologist,* 1981, 827-836.

2. O'Donohue, W., Fisher, J.E., Ploud, J.J., & Curtis, S.D. Treatment decisions: Their nature and their justification. *Psychotherapy,* 1990, 27, 421-427.

3. Norris, E.L. & Larson, J.K. Critical issues in mental health service: What are the priorities? *Hospital and Community Psychiatry;* 1976, 27, 561-566.

4. O'Donohue, W.T., Curtis, S.D., & Fisher, J.E. Use of research in the practice of community mental health: A case study. *Professional Psychology,* 1985, 16, 710-718.
5. Gohen, L.H., Sargent, M.M., L Sechrest, L.B. Use of psychotherapy research by professional psychologists. *American Psychologist,* 1986, 41, 198-206.
6. Kuhn, T.S. *The Structure of Scientific Revolutions.* 2nd Ed. Chicago: University of Chicago Press, 1970.
7. Zilbergeld, B. *The Shrinking of America.* Boston: Little, Brown, 1983, p. 156.
8. Maeder, T. *Children of Psychiatrists.* New York: Harper & Row, 1989.
9. Stanton, M.D. Who should credit for change which occurs in therapy? In A.S. Gurman (Ed.) *Questions and Answers in the Practice of Family Therapy.* New York: Brunner-Mazel, 1981.
10. Szasz, T. *The Myth of Mental Illness: Foundations of Theory of Conduct.* Rev. Ed. New York: Harper & Row, 1974.
11. Peele, S. *Diseasing of America: Addiction Treatment Out Of Control.* Lexington, Mass.: Lexington Books, 1989.

CHAPTER SEVEN

1. McIntyre, J.S. & Romano. J. Is there a stethoscope in the house (and is it used?). *Archives of General Psychiatry,* 1977t 34, 1147-1151.
2. Buie, J. Medicare win looms after hearing. *The APA Monitor.* April, 1989, p. 17.
3. Hollander, E.P. *Principles and Methods of Social Psychology.* 3rd Ed. New York: Oxford, 1976.

CHAPTER EIGHT

1. Haley, J. *Strategies of Psychotherapy.* New York: Grune Stratton, 1963.
2. Shepard, M. & Lee, M. *Games Analysts Play.* New York: Berkley, Medallion, 1972, p. 54-55.
3. Shepard, M. & Lee, M. Same as above, p. 70-71.
4. Prochoska, J.O. & Norcross, J.G. Contemporary psychotherapists: A national survey of characteristics, practices, orientations, and attitudes. *Psychotherapy: Theory, Research & Practice,* 1983, 20, 161-173.
5. Greenson, R.R. *The Technique and Practice of Psychoanalysis.* New York: International Universities Press, 1967.
6. Haley, J. Response to Masterson. In J. Zeig (Ed.) *The Evolution of Psychotherapy.* New York: Bruner-Mazel, 1987, p. 244

CHAPTER NINE

1. Zilbergeld, B. *The Shrinking of America,* Boston: Little, Brown, 1983, p. 154.
2. Shepard, M. & Lee, M. *Games Analysts Play,* New York: Berkley, Medallion, 1972, p. 56.
3. Shepard, M. & Lee, M. Same as above, p. 56.
4. Zilbergeld, B. *The Shrinking of America,* Boston: Little, Brown, 1983, p. 157.
5. Shepard, M. & Lee, M. *Games Analysts Play.* New York: Berkley, Medallion, 1972, p. 12.
6. Dall, Q.B. & Claiborn, W. An evaluation of Aetna pilot peer review project. *Psychotherapy: Theory, Research & Practice,* 1982, 19, 3-8.
7. Saul, L. *Psychodynamically Based Psychotherapy.* New York: Science House, p. 555.
8. Bonanno, G.A. Remembering and psychotherapy. *Psychotherapy,* 1990, 27, 175-186.
9. Spence, D.P. Narrative Truth and Historical Truth. New York: Norton, 1984.
10. Saul, L. Same as above, p. 581.
11. Saul, L. Same as above, p. 586.

12. Saul, L. Same as above, p. 589.
13. Saul, L. Same as above, p. 603.
14. Saul, L. Same as above, p. 737.

CHAPTER TEN

1. Rogers, C.R. Some directions and end points in therapy. In O.H. Mower (Ed.). *Psychotherapy: Theory and Research.* New York: Ronald Press, 1953.
2. Rogers, G.R. *On Becoming a Person.* Boston: Noughton-Mifflin, 1961, p. 22.
3. Rogers, G.R. Same as No.1.
4. Orlinsky, D.E. & Howard, K.I. The relation of process to outcome in psychotherapy. In S.L. Garfield & A.E. Bergin (Eds.). *Handbook of Psychotherapy and Behavior Change* (2nd ed.). New York: Wiley, 1978, p. 283-330.
5. Philipst L.k. & Kantner, C.N. Mutuality in psychotherapy supervision. *Psychotherapy,* 1984, 21, 178-183.
6. Perls, F.S. *Gestalt Therapy Verbatim.* Lafayette, Cal: Real People Press, 1969.
7. Rogers, C.R. Client-centered therapy. In B. Kutsab & A. Wolf (Eds.). *Psychotherapist's Casebook: Theory and Technique in Practice.* San Francisco: Jossey-Bass, 1986.

CHAPTER 11

1. Larsont, V.A. An exploration of psychotherapeutic resonance.*Psychotherapy,* 1987, 24, 321-324.
2. Neuhas, M. Primal analysis in the 45 minute hour. *Psychotherapy: Theory, Research & Practice,* 1974, 11, 199-201. 3.
3. Neuhas, M. Same as above.
4. Neuhas, M. Same as above.
5. Dosamantes-Alperson, E. The interaction between movement and imagery in experiential movement psychotherapy. *Psychotherapy, Theory, Research, & Practice,* 1981, 18, 266

CHAPTER 12

1. Fodor, I.E. Sex role conflict and symptom formation inwomen: Can behavior therapy help? *Psychotherapy: Theory, Research & Practice,* 1974, 11, 22-29.

CHAPTER 13

1. Hafner, R.J. The marital repercussions of behavior therapy for agoraphobia. *Psychotherapy,* 1984, 21, 530-542.
2. Hafner, R.J. Same as above.
3. Haley, J. *Reflections on Therapy.* Chevy Chase, Md.: Family Therapy Institute of Washington, DG, 1981, p. 197.
4. Fodor, I.E. Sex role conflict and symptom formation in women: Can behavior therapy help? *Psychotherapy: Theory, Research & Practice,* 1974, 11, 22-29.
5. Roberts, A.H. Biofeedback: Research, training, and clinical roles. *American Psychologist,* 1985, 40, 938-941.
6. Roberts, A.H. Same as above.
7. Skinner, B.F. The origins of cognitive thought. *American Psychologist,* 1989, 44, 13-18.

CHAPTER 14

1. Lazarus, A.A. If this be research... *American Psychologist,* 1990, 45, 670-671.
2. Henry W.P., Strupp, H.H., Butler, S.F., Schact, T.E., & Bender, J.k. (1993). Effects of training in time-limited dynamic psychotherapy: Changes in therapist behavior. *Journal of Consulting and Clinical Psychology,* 61, 434-440.
3. Wogan, M. & Norcross, J.G. Dimensions of psychotherapist's activity: A

replication and extension of earlier findings. *Psychotherapy: Theory, Research & Practice,* 1983, 20, 67-74.
4. Kernberg, O. Notes on countertransference. *Journal of the American Psychoanalytic Association,* 1965, 13, 38-56.
5. Wile, D.B. Kohut, Kernberg, and accusatory interpretations. *Psychotherapy,* 1984, 21, 353-365.
6. Strupp, H.H. *Three Approaches to Psychotherapy III.* Gorona Del Mar, Cal.: Psychological & Educational Films, 1986.
7. Strupp, H.H. Same as Above.
8. Strupp, H.H. Same as above.
9. Greenson, R.R. *The Technique and Practice of Psychoanalysis.* New York: International Universities Press, 1967.
10. Langs, R. *Resistance and Interventions.* New York: James Aronson, 1981, p. 568.
11. Larson, V.A. An exploration of psychotherapeutic resonance. *Psychotherapy,* 1987, 24, 321-324.

CHAPTER 15

1. Haley, J. *Strategies of Psychotherapy.* New York: Grune & Stratton, 1963.
2. Minsky, T. Prisoners of psychotherapy. *New York Magazine,* August 31, 1987, p. 34.
3. Wachtel, P. Behavior therapy and the facilitation of psychoanalytic explorations. *Psychotherapy: Theory, Research & Practice,* 1975, 12, 68-72. Wachtel was not the therapist in this case. He reported the case in this article because of his familiarity with it.
4. Wachtel, P. Same as above.
5. Rogers, C. F. *On Becoming a Person.* Boston: Houghton-Mifflin, 1961, p. 283.
6. Truax, C.B. Reinforcement and non-reinforcement in Rogerian psychotherapy. *Journal of Abnormal Psychology,* 1966, 71, 1-9.
7. Dublin, J.E. A bio-existential therapy. *Psychotherapy: Theory, Research & Practice,* 1981, 18, 3-10.
8. Dublin, J.E. Same as above.

CHAPTER 16

1. Brody, E.M., & Farber, B.A. Effects of psychotherapy on significant others. *Professional Psychology,* 1989, 20, 116-122
2. Hatcher, S.L. & Hatcher, R.L. Set a place for Elijah: Problems of the spouses and parents of psychotherapy patients. *Psychotherapy: Theory, Research & Practice,* 1983, 20, 75-80.
3. Hatcher, S.L. & Hatcher, R.L. Same as above.
4. Hatcher, S.L. & Hatcher, R.L. Same as above.
5. Hatcher, S.L. & Hatcher, R.L. Same as above.
6. Hatcher, S.L. & Hatcher, R.L. Same as above.
7. Campbell, T.W. Therapeutic relationships and iatrogenic outcomes: The blame-and-change maneuver in psychotherapy. *Psychotherapy,* 1992, 29, 474-481.
8. Minuchin, S., Rossman, B., & Baker, L. *Psychosomatic Families.* Cambridge: Harvard Press, 1978, p. 26.
9. Sorotzkin, B. The quest for perfection: Avoiding guilt or avoiding shame? *Psychotherapy,* 1985, 22, 665-571.
10. Sorotzkin, B. Same as above.
11. Sorotzkin, B. Same as above.
12. Lazarus, A.A. *Behavior Therapy and Beyond.* New York: McGraw-Hill, 1971, p. 118.
13. Lazarus, A.A. Same as above.
14. Durkheim, E. *Suicide* (1897) translated by J. Spaulding & G. Simpson.

New York: Free Press, 1958.

CHAPTER 17

1. Baruch, D.W. *One Little Boy.* New York: Laurel, 1952, p. 15.
2. Gorin, S.S. The prediction of child psychotherapy outcome: Factors specific to treatment. *Psychotherapy,* 1993, 30, 162158.
3. Axline, V.M. *Play Therapy.* New York: Ballentine, 1969, P. 9.
4. Axline, V.M. Same as Above, p. 17.
5. Axline, V.M. Same as Above, p. 17.
6. Baruch, D.W. *One Little Boy.* New York: Laurel, 1952, p. 14.
7. Phillips, R.D. Whistling in the Dark?: A review of play therapy research. *Psychotherapy,* 1985, 22, 752-76Q.
8. West, M. Building a relationship with the unmotivated client. *Psychotherapy: Theory, Research & Practice,* 1975, 12, 48-51.
9. West, M. Same as above.
10. Buie, J. Wedico leads kids out of the woods. *The APA Monitor,* Oct. 1988, p. 19.
11. Buie, J. Same as above.
12. Buie, J. Same as above.

CHAPTER 18

1. Greenspan, M. & Kulish, N.M. Factors in premature termination in long term psychotherapy. *Psychotherapy,* 1985, 22, 75-82.
2. Luborsky, L. Research can now affect clinical practice--a happy turnaround. *The Clinical Psychologist,* 1987, 40, 56-60.
3. Goldfried, M.R. & Davidson, G.C. *Clinical Behavior Therapy.* New York: Holt, Rinehart & Winston, 1976, p. 246.
4. Goldfried, M.R. & Davidson, G.C. Same as above; p. 249.
5. Goldfried, M.R. & Davidson, G.C. Same as above, p. 254.
6. Goldfried, M.R. & Davidson, G.C. Same as above, p. 255.
7. Goldfried, M.R. & Davidson, G.G. Same as above, p. 259.
8. Goldfried, M.R. & Davidson, G.C. Same as above, p. 265.
9. Leon, I.G. Short term psychotherapy for perinatal loss. *Psychotherapy,* 1987, 24, 186-190.

CHAPTER 19

1. Madanes, C. *Strategic Family Therapy.* San Francisco: Jossey-Bass, 1984.

CHAPTER 20

1. Freud, S. The aetiology of hysteria. In J. Strachey (Ed.). *The Standard Edition of The Complete Psychological Works of Sigmund Freud* (Vol. 3). London: Hogarth, 1896/1962.
2. Masson, J.M. *The Assault on Truth: Freud's Suppression of The Seduction Theory.* New York: Farrar, Strauss, & Giroux, 1984.
3. Deighton, J. & McPeek, P. Group treatment: Adult victims of childhood sexual abuse. *Social Casework,* 1985, 66, 403-410.
4. Gelinas, D.J. The persisting negative effects of incest. *Psychiatry,* 1983, 46, 312-322.
5. Reickerl P.P. & Carmen, E.H. The victim-to-patient process: The disconfirmation of abuse. *American Journal of Orthopsychiatry,* 1986, 56, 360-370.
6. Okami, P. Socio-political biases in the contemporary scientific literature on adult human sexual behavior with children and adolescents. In J.R. Feierman (Ed.). *Pedophiliia: Biosocial Dimensions.* New York: Springer-Verlag, 1990.
7. Russell, D.E. *The Secret Trauma: Incest In The Lives of Girls and Women.* New York: Basic Books, 1986.
8. Herman, J.L. *Trauma and Recovery.* New York: Basic Books, 1992.

9. Gil, E. *Treatment of Adult Survivors of Childhood Sexual Abuse.* Walnut Creek, CA: Launch Press, 1988.
10. Suffridge, D.R. Survivors of child maltreatment: Diagnostic formulation and therapeutic process. *Psychotherapy,* 1991, 28, 67-75.
11. Holmes, D.S. Investigations of repression: Differential recall of material experimentally or naturally associated with ego threat. *Psychological Bulletin,* 1974, 81, 632-653.
12. Holmes, D.S. Holmes, D.S. The evidence for repression. In J.L. Singer (Ed.). *Repression and Dissociation.* Chicago, U. of Chicago Press, 1990. (p. 96).
13. Malmquist, C.P. Children who witness parental murder: Post-traumatic aspects. *Journal of the American Academy of Child Psychiatry,* 1986, 25, 320-325.
14. Jones, D.P. & Krugman, R.D. Can a three-year-old child bear witness to her sexual assault and attempted murder? In J. Krivackska & J. Money (Eds.). *Handbook of Sexology,* Vol. 8: *Sexology and the Law.* Amsterdam: Elsevier Science, 1986.
15. Briere, J. & Gonte, J. Self-reported amnesia for abuse in adults molested as children. (In press). *Journal of Trauamtic Stress.*
16. Summit, R. Misplaced attention to delayed memory. *The Advisor,* 1992, 5, 21-25. (p. 22).
17. Herman J.L., & Schatzhow, E. Recovery and verification of memories of childhood sexual trauma. *Psychoanalytic Psychology,* 1987, 4, 1-14.
18. Williams, L.M. Adult memories of childhood abuse. Preliminary findings from a longitudinal study. *The Advisor,* 1992, 5, 19-20.
19. Loftus, E.F. The reality of repressed memories. *American Psychologist,* 1993, 48, 518-637.
20. Loftus, E.F. Same as above.
21. Kihlstrom, J.F. & Harckiwicz, A. The earliest recollection: A new survey. *Journal of Personality,* 1982, 50, 134-148.
22. Pillemer, D.B. & White, S.H. Childhood events recalled by children and adults. *Advances in Child Development and Behavior,* Volume 21. New York: Academic Press, 1989.
23. Winograd, E. & Killinger, W.A. Relating age at encoding early childhood to adult recall: Development of flashbulb memories. *Journal of Experimental Psychology: General,* 1983, 112, 413-422.
24. Campbell, T.W. Diagnosing incest: The problem of false positives and their consequences. *Issues in Child Abuse Accusations,* 1992, 4, 161-168.
25. Loftus, E.F. & Goan, D. The construction of childhood memories. In D. Peters (Ed.). *The Child Witness in Context: Cognitive, Social and Legal Perspectives.* New York: Kluwer, (In press).
26. Miller, T. Opinion-Letters: Child abuse assumptions. *The APA Monitor,* Nov. 1991, 22 (11), p. 4.
27. Lewinsohn, P.M. & Rosenbaum, M. Recall of parental behavior by acutre depressives, remitted depressives, and nondepressives. *Journal of Personality and Social Psychology,* 1987, 52, 611-620.
28. Goodwin, A.H. & Sher, K.J. Effects of induced mood on diagnostic interviewing: Evidence for a mood and memory effect. *Psychological Assessment,* 1993, 5, 197-202.
29. Dolan, B. My own story. Time, 1991 Qct 7, 138 (No. 14), p. 47.
30. Lendabaker, M.A. Letters to the Editor, *Time,* 1991 Oct 28, 138 (No. 17), p. 11.
31. Dolan, B. & Horowitz, J.M. Incest comes out of the dark. *Time,* 1991 Oct 7, 138 (No. 14), p. 47
32. Haaken, J. & Schlaps, A. Incest resolution therapy and the objectification of sexual abuse. *Psychotherapy,* 1991, 28, 39-47.
33. Miller, A. *Thou Shall Not Be Aware.* New York: Farrar, Strauss & Giroux, 1985. (p. 59).

34. Katz, S.J. & Liu, A.E. *The Co-Dependency Conspiracy.* New York: Warner, 1991, (p. 38).
35. O'Hanlon, W.H. & Weiner-Davis, M. *In Search of Solutions: A New Direction in Psychotherapy.* New York: W.W. Norton, 1989.
36. Brooks, G.R. Therapy pitfalls with Vietnam veteran families: Linearity, contextual naivete, and gender role blindness. *Journal of Family Psychology,* 1991, 4, 446-461.
37. Beutler, L.E. & Hill, C.E. Process and outcome research in the treatment of adult victims of childhood sexual abuse: Methodological issues. *Journal of Consulting and Clinical Psychology,* 1992, 60, 204-212.
38. Dickson, J.Z. In the interest of H.R.K. and due process: Can a juvenile court terminate parental rights without an adjudication? *Issues in Child Abuse Accusations,* 1991, 3, 204-214.

CHAPTER 21

1. Saul, L. *Psychodymanically Based Psychotherapy.* New York: Science House, 1972, p. 610-611.
2. Maquire, T.V. & Miller, J.R. The professional culture of the mental health center as a defense against confronting organizational dysfunction: A case study. *Psychotherapy: Theory, Research & Practice,* 1982, 19, 18-25.
3. Spotnitz, H. Psychoanalytic technique with the borderline patient. In J. LeBoit & A. Capponi (Eds.). *Advances in Psychotherapy of the Borderline Patient.* New York: Aronson, 197q, p. 212-213.
4. Shepard, M. & Lee, M. *Games Analysts Play.* New York: Berkley, Medallion, 1972, p. 62.
5. Saul, L. Same as above, p. 716.
6. Saul, L. Same as above, p. 560.
7. Saul, L. Same as above, p. 780.

CHAPTER 22

1. Rogers, C.R. Some directions and end points in therapy. In O.H. Mower, (Ed.). *Psychotherapy: Theory and Research.* New York: Ronald Press, 1953.
2. Rogers, C.R. *On Becoming a Person.* Boston: Houghton-Mifflin, 1961, p. 22.
3. Rogers, C.R. in O.H. Mower. Same as above.
4. Rogers, C.R. in O.H. Mower. Same as above.
5. Bugental, J.F. & Bugental, E.K. A fate worse than death: The fear of changing. *Psychotherapy,* 1984, 21, 543- 549.
6. Bugental, J.F. & Bugental, E.K. Same as above.
7. Bugental, J.F. & Bugental, E.K. Same as above.
8. Butler, S.F. & Strupp, H.H. Specific and nonspecific factors in psychotherapy: A problematic paradigm for psychotherapy research. *Psychotherapy,* 1986, 23, 30-40.
9. Hynan, M.T. On the advantages of assuming that the techniques of psychotherapy are ineffective. *Psychotherapy: Theory, Research & Practice,* 1981, 18, 11-13.
10. Strupp, H.H. On failing one's patient. *Psychotherapy: Theory, Research & Practice,* 1975, 12, 39-41.
11. Zilbergeld, B. *The Shrinking of America.* Boston: Little, Brown, 1983, p. 157.

CHAPTER 23

1. Novaco, R.W. Stress Inoculation: A cognitive therapy for anger and its application to a case of depression. *Journal of Consulting and Clinical Psychology,* 1977, 45, 600-608.
2. Novaco, R.W. Same as above.
3. Fodor, I.E. Sex role conflict and symptom formation in women: Can behavior therapy help? *Psychotherapy: Theory, Research & Practice,* 1974, 11, 22-29.

4. Mathews, A. et.al. A home-based treatment program for agoraphobia. *Behavior Therapy,* 1977, 8, 915-924.

CHAPTER 24

1. Bowen, M. Family Therapy and Clinical Practice. New York: Jason Aronson, 1978.
2. Satir, V. Family communication and conjoint family therapy. In B.N. Ard & C.C. Ard (Eds.) *Handbook of Marriage Counseling.* Palo Alto, Gal: Science and Behavior Books, 1976.
3. Haley, J. Bass, 1976. *Problem Solving Therapy.* San Francisco: Jossey-Bass, 1976.
4. Minuchin, S. *Families and Family Therapy.* Cambridge, Mass: Harvard Press, 1974.
5. Olson, D.H., Russell, C.S., & Sprenkle, D.H. Marital and family therapy: A decade review. *Journal of Marriage and the Family,* 1980, 42, 973-993.
6. Todd, T.C. & Stanton, M.D. Research on marital and family therapy: Answers, issues, and recommendations for the future. In B.B. Wolman & G. Stricker (Eds.). *Handbook of Family and Marital Therapy.* New York: Plenum, 1983.
7. Gurman, A.S. & Kniskern, D.P. Research on marital and family therapy: Progress, perspectives, and prospect. In S. Garfield & A. Bergin (Eds.). *Handbook of Pschotherapy and Behavior Change* (2nd Ed.) New York: Wiley, 1978.
8. Stanton, M.D. & Todd, T.C. *The family Therapy of Drug Abuse and Addiction.* New York: Guilford, 1982.
9. Piercy, F.P. & Sprenkle, D.H. *Family Therapy Sourcebook.* New York: Guilford, 1986, p. 334.

CHAPTER 25

1. Leon, I. G. Short term psychotherapy for perinatal loss. *Psychotherapy,* 1987, 24, 186-190.
2. Leon, I.G. Same as above.
3. Cohen, S. & Hoberman, H. Positive events and social supports as buffers of life change stress. *Journal of Applied Social Psychology,* 1983, 13, 99-125.
4. House, J.S., Landis, K.R. & Umberson, Social relationships and health. *Science,* 1988, 241, 540-545.
5. Barrera, M. Distinctions between social support concepts, measures, and models. *American Journal of Community Psychology,* 1986, 14, 413-445.
6. Heller, K., Swindle, R.W. & Dusenberry, L. Component social support processes: Comments and integration. Journal of Consulting and Clincial Psychology, 1986, 54, 466-470.
7. Axline, V.M. *Play Therapy.* New York: Ballentine, 1969, p. 179.
8. Axline, V.M. Same as above, p. 180.
9. Axline, V.M. Same as above, p. 180.
10. Last, J.M. Transitional relatedness and psychotherapeutic growth. *Psychotherapy,* 1988, 25, 185-190.
11. Last, J.M. Same as above.

CHAPTER 26

1. Bugental, J.F. *The Art of the Psychotherapist.* New York: Norton & Co., 1987, p. 101.
2. Hatcher, S.L. & Hatcher, R.L. Set a place for Elijah: Problems of the spouses and parents of psychotherapy patients. *Psychotherapy: Theory, Research & Practice,* 1983, 20, 75-80. 3.
3. Hatcher, S.L. & Hatcher, R.L. Same as above.
4. Hatcher, S.L. & Hatcher, R.L. Same as above.

CHAPTER 27

1. Deleon, P.H. & Borreliz, M. Malpractice: Professional liability and the law. *Professional Psychology,* 1978, 9, 467-477.

INDEX